The French Slave Trade
in the Eighteenth Century

THE
FRENCH SLAVE TRADE
IN THE
EIGHTEENTH CENTURY
An Old Regime Business

ROBERT LOUIS STEIN

The University of Wisconsin Press

Published 1979

The University of Wisconsin Press
114 North Murray Street
Madison, Wisconsin 53715

The University of Wisconsin Press, Ltd.
1 Gower St., London WC1E 6HA, England

First printing 1979

Printed in the United States of America

For LC and CIP information, see the colophon

ISBN 0-299-07910-4

For Mom and Dad

Contents

III The Traders and Their Business

Maps

Acknowledgements

This book could not have been written without the help I received in France and North America. Archivists in the major French ports were generous with their time and knowledge, and I thank them for all the trouble they put up with on my behalf. On this side of the Atlantic, I am most indebted to John Bosher, who suggested the topic, helped guide my research, and patiently suggested numerous improvements in the manuscript. I am grateful as well to Jean-François Brière, Martin Klein, Tim LeGoff, Paul Lovejoy, Graeme Mount, and Brinsley Samaroo for reading and criticizing the manuscript.

I would also like to thank the French Department for Foreign Affairs and the Canada Council for grants which enabled me to do research in France, and the *Journal of Economic History* for permission to reprint excerpts from my 1975 article "The Profitability of the Nantes Slave Trade, 1783–1792."

And finally, I want to express my gratitude to my wife Mindy for all her help and support. She made writing this book a pleasant experience.

Introduction

The slave trade is one of our principal branches of commerce.
Vicomte de Mirabeau

During the eighteenth century, French merchants sent out more than three thousand ships to the African coast in search of slaves. From Cape Verde to Angola and from Mozambique to Cape Delgado, French captains exchanged European or Asian textiles, jewelry, and hardware for African slaves. The French purchased over a million men, women, and children for transport to the New World; but one to two hundred thousand of these people died before reaching their new homes, many not surviving even until Africa had faded from view. The slave trade was a mighty killer of humanity, and more than ten thousand French sailors also lost their lives to it.

Thousands of Frenchmen participated in the slave trade, building the ships and manufacturing the cargoes, as well as actually sailing to Africa. Other men were responsible for organizing the trade: some six hundred merchants planned the expeditions and handled all financial matters. These men provided most of the capital needed to finance the trade and solicited investments for the rest. Hundreds, if not thousands, of other men throughout France purchased shares in slaving ships, people from all walks of life, including industrialists like Jean de Dietrich, writers like Beaumarchais, and officials like Baudard de Saint-James, *trésorier général de la marine*. Although the slave trade was fundamentally a local affair undertaken by residents of the major ports, it had a certain influence throughout the kingdom. Even abroad, the French slave trade had repercussions: commerce between France and Holland or Germany was largely dependent on colonial commodities and articles for the trade.

The production of tropical commodities provided the *raison d'être* for the French slave trade. During the second quarter of the seventeenth century, France established a tropical empire, with important colonies on Saint Domingue (Haiti), Martinique, and Guadeloupe. Although France later colonized other lands in the Caribbean and even in the Indian Ocean, the three original colonies were the heart of the French empire. At first this empire was a military one: France formed colonies to balance Spanish and English growth in the West Indies. Soon, however, the empire became commercial. Colbert, principal minister of Louis XIV during the 1660s and 1670s, believed that the strength of a nation was as much economic as military, and he worked hard to increase the economic value of the colonies. Most important, Colbert developed what has become known as the "colonial system." Under this system, the colonies were treated as economic units whose interests were clearly subordinated to the motherland. France expected the colonies to concentrate exclusively on producing vast quantities of tropical goods, particularly sugar, and later, coffee. Since the French did not have to worry about creating autonomous or even semi-autonomous economies in the colonies, the islands were burdened with plantation economies. These demanded a large labor supply, and it was believed that only black slaves could meet the demand. Free labor was out of the question: it was costly, and the natural desire of the free peasant to cultivate his own land went counter to the plantation system. Indentured or semi-free labor was also inappropriate: it too was costly, and there were not enough men willing to leave France to work like slaves in the Antilles. There remained only the system of slavery used with such success in the Iberian colonies. Amerindians and then black slaves proved to be the cheapest possible source of labor. Both groups had the added "advantage" of being non-white and therefore, according to the French, more appropriate to the peculiar climate of the tropics. Undoubtedly, the skin color of the Amerindians and the Africans also enabled the French to overcome any moral qualms about slavery. By the end of the seventeenth century, the transformation of the French islands was virtually complete: they were no longer crude military outposts, but highly developed producers of sugar and coffee.

French merchants began irregular deliveries of slaves to the French colonies almost immediately after their foundation, and a regular slave trade soon followed. This was necessary for two reasons: living standards in the colonies were so bad that slaves died before reproducing, and the cultivated area on the islands was always expanding and required new workers. At first, the slave trade was considered a necessary service and was reserved for large companies having monopolies over commerce with the islands. As the trade grew, however, it became an autonomous branch of commerce, closely related to trade in tropical commodities but still largely independent of it. In 1716 the government opened the French trade to independent merchants, and it remained so, except for one brief period, until the end of the old regime. The slave trade thus became a separate business with the sole purpose of making profits.

The French slave trade in the eighteenth century was a sophisticated enterprise with operations on three continents. Because of the route taken by the slave ships, the slaving circuit has become known as the slaving triangle. The first vertex of the triangle was in France, at any of a dozen ports where merchants organized expeditions by fitting out ships and finding investors. Fitting out a slave ship was a lengthy process which could take a considerable amount of time and money. In fact, expenses were so great that few *armateurs** could afford to finance their expeditions without help. The traders therefore asked their colleagues for investments, and in order to diversify their own risk capital, they reciprocated by investing in their friends' expeditions. This financial interdependence led to the creation of slaving communities in the major ports.

Once ready, the ship sailed to the African coast, where it began to search for a good site to trade slaves. The most popular sites for French slavers were along the Bight of Benin and the Angolan coast; so popular was the former that the French maintained their only permanent sub-Saharan outpost there, at Ouidah. Upon arriving, the captain paid his respects to the local rulers, built a small store, and commenced his trade. The normal practice was for black traders to purchase slaves being held in the interior and offer them to the Frenchmen on the coast. After carefully examining each captive, the captain made his choice, bargained for a price, and paid. These procedures were slow, and several months passed before a cargo of three to four hundred slaves was completed. When it was, the captain once again paid his respects to the ruler and set sail for the New World.

It normally took about two months to sail from Africa to the Caribbean, but some voyages took almost half a year. The duration of the voyage directly influenced the death rate among slaves and crew members alike: the slower the voyage, the greater the likelihood of scurvy and amebic dysentery and the higher the death rate. Usually 10 to 15 percent of the slaves and crew died, but exceptionally difficult crossings could claim close to 50 or even 75 percent. Most French slavers went to Saint Domingue, the rest going to Martinique, Guadeloupe, and Guiana. Upon arriving, the captain met the colonial agent of the armateur and arranged for the sale to take place as soon as possible. Slaves were sold, either singly or in groups, to well-to-do whites from all walks of life. Although the captain preferred payment in cash, he had to offer generous credit terms to the colonists, who were chronically short of money. Whatever the captain could get immediately was converted into sugar and coffee and taken back to France aboard the returning slave ship. It could take several more years before all the debts were repaid, a circumstance which sharply limited profits.

Historians have paid relatively little attention to the French slave trade.

---

*Armateur is here used to mean the merchant who organized and usually financed a large part of the slaving expedition.

The British slave trade, for example, has been the subject of much more historical research. There are two major reasons for this: the British trade was larger, and it ended in dramatic fashion. During the eighteenth century, the British were the world's leading slavers, trading some two and one-half million slaves or more than twice as many as the French. The very magnitude of the British operation combined with the influential role played by West Indian planters in British political life to draw public attention to the trade. For generations, slavery and the slave trade were major political issues in Britain, and the abolition of the slave trade was the goal of one of the largest popular movements in the country's history. This movement had a singular impact on British historians. Even in nineteenth-century Britain, the trade was a well-known topic complete with its own historical interpretation. Put bluntly by Eric Williams, "The British historians wrote almost as if Britain had introduced Negro slavery solely for the satisfaction of abolishing it."[1] The central issue in British histories of the slave trade was abolition, and a debate is still in progress between the "humanitarians," who believe that goodwill ended the trade, and the "materialists," who argue that economics dictated the trade's abolition.[2]

French historians have been much more circumspect in their treatment of the slave trade. This, too, has stemmed largely from the peculiar circumstances surrounding the abolition of the French slave trade. With the exception of Montesquieu, Turgot, and a few other voices in the wilderness, there was no significant abolitionist activity in France before 1788. By the time that abolitionists began to organize seriously, France was caught up in the Revolution, and the plight of the blacks was reduced to secondary importance. As the Revolution became more radical, the trade was threatened, and in 1794 the Convention abolished it along with slavery. Both the trade and slavery itself, however, had already ceased to exist, the former falling victim to the British naval blockade, the latter outlawed on Saint Domingue by the Convention's local representative. Thus the trade was abolished in France as part of a much larger revolution and not as the result of specific public pressure. The story, however, did not end in 1794. Eight years later Napoleon legalized the trade and re-imposed slavery. It was only strong British insistence that forced the French to abolish the trade in 1814-15, much against the wishes of the French government,[3] and the slaves had to wait for the Revolution of 1848 to achieve their emancipation.

The rather shameful history of French abolition prevented the French trade from having the same intrinsic interest as the British. There was little drama and less moral glory in the French actions, and during the nineteenth century, French historians almost completely ignored the trade. Only in the second quarter of the twentieth century did they begin to consider it seriously, but in a manner quite different from the British: instead of focusing on the abolition question, they concentrated on the trade itself. Since 1930 there have been three major historians of the French slave trade: Gaston Martin, Dieudonné Rinchon, and Jean Meyer. Martin was interested in the structure of the trade and tended to treat slaving as an isolated phenomenon.[4] Although he succeeded in calculating the annual volume of the Nantes slave trade and in describing the structure of the triangle, he did little to explain why Frenchmen engaged in such an activity. He had no interest in the profitability of the trade, in the sources of investment capital, in the relationship between the trade and colonial commerce, or in the role of the traders in French society.

Rinchon and Meyer studied the trade in the wider perspective of colonial commerce in general. Rinchon concentrated on the activities of a few men associated with slaving. In *Trafic négrier*[5] he traced the life of a certain ship's captain from his early years in Ghent to his career based in Nantes. In *Armements négriers*[6] he examined the commercial books of two firms, directly comparing the slave and colonial commodities' trades as practiced by these merchants. And in *Pierre-Ignace van Alstein*[7] he concluded the story of the Belgian captain begun in *Trafic*. The results of Rinchon's works formed one part of the documentation of Meyer's *Armement nantais*,[8] a work which sought to evaluate as many of the Nantes shipping enterprises as possible. It was Meyer who most clearly showed the relationship between the slave and colonial trades, at least in general terms. Meyer also stood alone in attempting to understand the complex financial arrangements behind the business.[9] It was the merit of Meyer's book to raise as many questions as it answered. With the publication of *Armement nantais* it became impossible to repeat the old clichés about the profitability of the slave trade or the wealth of the traders; it now seems clear that the slave trade was a business carried on for the sake of profits from the sale of slaves.

The trade was part and parcel of the old regime. It depended, for example, on a morality lacking a sense of common humanity: people believed that the enslavement of Africans was neither immoral nor criminal.[10] Eighteenth-century technology also influenced the trade: the existence of slavery itself, at least on such a vast scale, was the result of a pre-industrial plantation system, while the structure of the triangle was largely determined by the technical possibilities of the day. And the slave trade reflected the economic and social conditions prevailing in the ports. The traders organized their businesses along traditional lines and steadfastly maintained the old family companies. Beyond the family circle, there was little trust or confidence, and traders rarely created impersonal joint-stock companies; they did not even like to form partnerships with non-relatives. Certain modern traits notwithstanding, the slave traders, like the trade itself, belonged to an economic and social world long since past.

PART I
Growth of the Trade

1
Origins

A regular French slave trade developed in the seventeenth century to supply the French Caribbean colonies with slaves. Slaves at first had not been vital to the colonies; military considerations took precedence in Richelieu's mind over commercial ones. Indeed, French settlement in the Antilles was characterized by an increase in government interest and by a shift in emphasis from military to commercial considerations. The earliest French settlements were military or paramilitary. French pirates (illegal) and privateers (legal) operated off the Brazilian coast as early as 1504,[1] and soon established rudimentary colonies at strategic points in the West Indies. The most important of these colonies was on Tortuga Island off the northwest coast of Hispanola. In 1630, a group of English and French adventurers from Saint Barthelemy overcame the small Spanish garrison on Tortuga and created what Pierre Chaunu has called "an international association for crime."[2] They turned Tortuga into an outlaws' paradise inhabited by pirates preying on passing Spanish ships and by hunters (*boucaniers*) who supplied the pirates with food in exchange for arms.[3] Within a short time, the French had expelled the English from Tortuga and had begun to occupy Hispanola proper. Before the end of the century, Spain recognized French claims to the western third of Hispanola, known as Saint Domingue. Thus what was to become the most valuable colony in the French empire was settled by adventurers acting without the approbation of the French government.

Other French colonies were established in a more orderly fashion, but still for military reasons. The man responsible for this was Cardinal Richelieu, who believed that Caribbean bases were necessary in the fight against Spain. He therefore encouraged the creation of colonizing companies, the most important of which, the Compagnie des Isles de l'Amérique, undertook to settle and defend various islands in the Lesser Antilles, a region largely ignored by the Spanish. Accordingly, on June 28, 1635, colonists sent by the company landed near Sainte Rose on the island of Guadeloupe. A few weeks later, other company employees landed on Martinique. The company had fulfilled its mandate, and the cornerstones of the French Caribbean empire were in place. The company itself was not successful financially and in 1649, 1650, and 1651 sold its possessions. Guadeloupe and its dependencies (Marie-Galante, Désirade, and the Saintes) went to Sieur du Houel; Martinique, Saint Lucia, Grenada, and the Grenadines (not necessarily under the company's control) to Sieur du Parquet; and Saint Kitts to the Knights of Malta.[4] The new owners were unable to develop the islands, and the colonies stagnated.

A generation later, Colbert reorganized the French empire. According to the Edict of April 17, 1664, the crown, disturbed by the sale of the islands and by their slow growth, repossessed the French islands in the Lesser Antilles and placed them, as well as Saint Domingue, under the aegis of a new company, the Compagnie des Indes Occidentales. The emphasis was now on their commercial growth, and until the Revolution, France considered the colonies almost exclusively in terms of commerce. In spite of the quick demise of the Compagnie des Indes Occidentales and in spite of the ever-changing legal status of the various islands, Colbert's basic principle still applied: the colonies had one purpose, to make the motherland wealthier. After the advent of Colbert, interested Frenchmen said little of the islands' military value or of the importance of attacking Spanish shipping; they did, however, expound at great length on the economics of imperialism.

Colbert was the creator of the colonial system which regulated the relations between the colonies and the mother country. In theory, the system was relatively simple, relying on the subordination of the islands to French commercial interests. As one eighteenth-century merchant observed, "Colonies are made for the motherland. This maxim, so true and so general, is particularly valid for the French colonies. Since their foundation, they have belonged to France. . . . It is therefore correct to say that our colonies must be considered in the light of the particular interest of France."[5] The government saw in the promotion of commerce a way to increase national power by increasing revenues. As long as exports exceeded imports, France would grow richer at the expense of its enemies and competitors. Hence, to ensure a favorable balance of trade became an important goal for the government, and it designed colonial policy to help realize that goal. As Rinchon noted, "colonization under the old regime was only a vast enterprise of exotic plantations in the exclusive interest of French commerce.''[6]

Much as modern industrialized states rely on underdeveloped lands for natural resources, so the government in the old regime tried to exploit its colonies. The Antilles were expected to produce tropical commodities which would be taken to French ports aboard French ships for eventual distribution throughout France and Europe. Since the government's objective was to build up the wealth of France, and since wealth was equated with holdings of precious metals, the government prohibited the export of specie from France to the colonies; this meant that the planters had to barter their tropical produce for those items not made or grown in the colonies. As the Antilles were encouraged to produce little besides exotic commodities, the colonists were left dependent upon French merchants for everything from manufactured goods of all description to food. Indeed, interruptions in traditional shipping patterns, particularly severe and frequent during periods of war, could lead to famine on the islands.[7]

The cornerstone of the colonial system was the principle of the *exclusif:* French colonies were allowed to trade only with France and only via French ships. At first, exclusif went hand in hand with monopoly as the government reserved trade with the colonies for a royally chartered company; but although many such companies were formed, most disintegrated within a few years. Forming companies supposedly enabled the government to encourage, control, and profit from colonial commerce,[8] but in practice the companies were never strong enough to dominate the colonial trade. Although the government finally ended the company monopolies, it continued to believe in the exclusif, and colonial trade remained restricted to French merchants. Not only were the colonies forbidden to trade with European nations, they were restricted from dealing with neighboring colonies under foreign, and sometimes even under French, rule. Furthermore, all goods travelling between the Antilles and France had to be carried on French ships. According to the theory of the colonial system, the subordination of the colonies was total and uncompromising.

For the most part, the interests of the French merchants coincided with those of the government, but there were some differences, arising mainly from the granting of special rights or *privilèges.* The government desired a maximum of control over the colonial trade, and this frequently implied the creation of various limited monopolies. Just as Spain had tried to regulate its colonial trade by channeling it through one great port, so did France ordain that only certain companies or residents of certain ports should be allowed to engage in colonial commerce. Naturally, the merchants in the chosen ports fought to protect their privileged positions, but other businessmen fought for "free trade." Free trade in this context meant simply the right of all French merchants to participate in colonial commerce without having to pay special taxes to a company monopoly. No merchants wanted the free entry of foreigners into this lucrative field; neither did they especially want the colonists to have the right to engage in the shipping and selling of tropical commodities in Europe.

Although the colonial system largely satisfied the interests of the government and the French merchants, the colonists never tired of attacking the system and trying to upset it. Unlike their British counterparts, the wealthy French plantation owners had little political power, and their demands usually went unheeded by Versailles. Basically, they wanted an end to the exclusif and the introduction of free trade in the modern sense. When the government ignored these requests, the colonists attempted to circumvent the prevailing system by encouraging smuggling. Of course, there are no precise statistics on this illegal activity, but indications are that it was widespread and caused considerable concern to government administrators.[9] A second weapon in the hands of the colonists was financial; plantation owners could be slow in paying their debts. Whether they did this consciously to protest against the entire colonial system is uncertain, but it is clear that the lack of specie in the colonies—brought on largely by the restrictions imposed by the colonial system—rendered payment difficult. By the end of the eighteenth century, the shortage of cash had powerful repercussions in the mother country, as delays in payment became a factor in the ruin of French merchants along the Atlantic coast.[10]

How did the colonial system work in practice? In order to maximize profits from their colonies, the French copied current practices in the Spanish and Portuguese empires. At first, this meant looting the natives and carrying off any available gold and silver. But the French islands lacked easily accessible precious metals, and the colonists soon realized that agriculture was likely to be more profitable.[11] Only the production of tropical commodities for export could make investments in the French colonies pay high dividends. Hence the colonists gradually changed from adventurers to farmers and began to grow plants typical of tropical areas. The first export crop raised on the French islands was tobacco. As early as 1635, the year of its settlement, Guadeloupe produced tobacco,[12] and all the colonies enjoyed the tobacco boom of the mid-seventeenth century.[13] Other crops raised during these early days included cotton, indigo, and ginger, and most of them, like tobacco, had the advantage of being relatively easy for small farmers to produce. These first crops, however, were minor in comparison to the crops of sugar cane and coffee which came later. With the introduction of sugar cane, in particular, to the French islands, colonial society and economy underwent a radical transformation. No longer were the Antilles the home of a community of prosperous small farmers roughly equal in wealth and social status; instead, they became the preserve of a few great landowners who reduced their white compatriots to poverty and who imported thousands of black slaves. The introduction of sugar cane to the French West Indies was the most significant single event to occur there during the old regime.

Sugar cane's conquest of the French Antilles was but one step in a journey of thousands of miles over thousands of years. The exact geographical origins of sugar cane are uncertain; the plant came from somewhere in Asia and gradually worked its way westward towards Europe.[14] By the late Middle Ages, cane was growing in the south of Spain and was ready to follow the Spanish flag around the globe. After introducing the plant to the Canary Islands, the Spanish brought it to the Americas at the beginning of the sixteenth century; they planted it on Hispanola, where it was originally used for feeding cattle or producing rum.[15] The Portuguese were also familiar with sugar cane. They introduced it to their colony of Brazil in the sixteenth century, using sophisticated methods of treatment so that sugar could be shipped profitably on the long voyage to Europe. This technology led to the creation of a plantation economy in Brazil and ultimately transformed the West Indies. In 1654, the Portuguese expelled the Dutch and Jewish settlers from Brazil, an event of capital importance for the Antilles. Many of the exiles arrived in the French islands, bringing with them the secrets of successful sugar cane treatment.[16] Within a few years, the economies and societies of the French islands were changed beyond recognition, as the French colonists followed the example of the new arrivals and established large plantations devoted to farming cane and producing sugar. The "sugar revolution" had begun.[17]

What the exiles taught the French was how to transform the cane into an acceptable sugar.[18] This was basically a simple operation, made complicated only by the enormous needs for capital and labor to make it succeed profitably. Workers first prepared a carefully chosen plot of fertile and well-irrigated land by burning or clearing all grass and scrub. They then dug thousands of shallow holes, into each of which they placed a few pieces of stalk from mature sugar canes. The holes were then covered lightly with earth. After some fifteen to eighteen months, the new canes were mature and ready for harvest. It took only twelve to fifteen months for a second harvest of the same cane (known as ratoons), but this could be done only three or four times before exhausting the soil. Workers cut the grown cane with machetes and carried it by hand, or on larger plantations by ox-cart, to the mill. In the mill, driven by animals, water, or wind, giant iron rollers in the form of vertically mounted cylinders crushed the cane and liberated the sweet juice inside; the drained stems could be used as fuel in the boilers.

The next step in the operation took place in the boiling house and was devoted to purifying the sugar. Juice from the cane flowed through gutters into the first of a series of *chaudières* or boilers, where it was heated with a small quantity of lime to lose its impurities, and finally, its liquid state. This heating operation was repeated three or four times in progressively smaller and hotter moulds until there emerged a thick syrup, which was then poured into hogsheads to crystallize. The hogsheads were left unsealed along the bottom for three or four weeks so that impurities could drip out; the impurities—known as molasses—were used, usually, to feed the animals. Most of the hogsheads were then sealed and shipped off to France for further refinement; sugar thus dispatched was known as *sucre brut,* and suffered further spoilage on the ocean voyage. Frequently the sugar went through one more purifying operation before being shipped, and became *sucre terré.* Only rarely was sugar refined in the islands after 1700.[19]

Cultivating and processing sugar cane required much capital and labor, since the entire operation was most efficient when performed on a large scale. As opposed to tobacco production, for example, which would be handled by a small farmer with only minimal help and expense,[20] sugar cane production was arranged like a factory, necessitating the construction of several buildings and the employment of numerous workers. It was the cultivation of sugar cane which rendered the old system of land ownership obsolete and which led to the creation of the plantation system in the French West Indies. Hitherto, island administrators had encouraged the equitable division of good lands among the settlers. This satisfied the government, which wanted to populate the islands with enough peasants to defend them; it also satisfied the farmers who nourished dreams of independence. In the face of sugar cane's rise, this primitive egalitarianism could not survive; differences between rich and poor became more marked, with the rich increasing their holdings and the poor retreating to subsistence farming in the backwoods. Certainly by the end of the eighteenth century the day of the smallholder was over, except perhaps on the more remote parts of Saint Domingue.[21]

According to Labat, the ideal plantation was beside a river and contained about 750 acres divided into several sections.[22] At the front and back of the estate were uncultivated areas which could be used for further expansion. Towards the front of the plantation proper, on a rise if possible, came the master's house, usually fairly modest in spite of legends of its opulence.[23] Surrounding this *maison principale* were gardens with offices and stores where the plantation was managed. Also in this central area, but sufficiently removed so as not to disturb the owner, were the buildings for processing the cane—the mill, boiling house, and curing house, among others. Near these buildings came one or two rows of slaves' quarters, or *cases*, small, almost makeshift shelters; a small enclosure for cattle and other farm animals was usually close at hand. All of this built-up area was surrounded by fields of sugar cane, some 150 acres in all. Behind one of the fields came the slaves' gardens, where the slaves grew some of their own food, working the land on Saturdays or Sundays or even during their two-hour lunch break.[24] Finally, there was usually a rear woodland, where it was quite common to plant a secondary crop such as cocoa. A plantation like this typically counted 120 slaves, 4 ox-carts, 38 oxen, 20 cows with their young, 12 horses, and small flocks of sheep and goats.

The success of the plantations implied major changes in colonial society. A new elite of plantation owners arose, together with two lowly classes, one white and one black. The lower-class whites were free men who could not stand the competition from the plantations and either left the islands or engaged in subsistence farming, selling any surpluses to the estates. More important than the creation of a small class of indigent whites was the formation of a large class of black slaves. Although there had been a few African slaves in the French Antilles before the advent of sugar cane, it was only the success of the sugar plantation system which made slavery an integral feature of French colonial life. On Guadeloupe, for example, there were 12,000 Frenchmen and 3,000 slaves in 1656; in 1770, there were still 12,000 Frenchmen, but 80,000 slaves.[25] No longer were blacks merely domestics or supplementary laborers; after the conquest of cane, they formed the backbone of the islands' economies. The French believed that slave labor was the cheapest possible source of manpower: with luck, a plantation owner could receive several generations of toil for a reasonable initial investment plus a modest upkeep.

Black slaves were not the only laborers to be exploited in the West Indies; there were also native Amerindians and indentured servants. When the Europeans landed in the Caribbean, they found most of the islands inhabited by "barbarians" of questionable military potential. As the whites claimed the newly discovered lands, the Amerindians were all but eradicated. Those who did not fall victim to European diseases or European arms were enslaved and worked to death. On the French islands, the Amerindians virtually disappeared within a generation or two of the whites' occupation. Once it became obvious that native labor supplies were inadequate, it was necessary to import workers. Again there was a choice, for either Europe or Africa could furnish the needed manpower. Although the Spanish seemed to prefer African labor from the first,[26] the French experimented seriously with indentured servants or *engagés* from France.[27] Engagés were either criminals forced to work in the colonies or poor Frenchmen who wanted to try their luck in the New World. In return for three years of labor on a plantation, the engagé received a wage considerably higher than normally paid in France. While in the Antilles, the engagés lived like slaves, and few of them ever rose above the poor white class. These discouraging facts militated against the popularity of the institution, and in spite of much legislation to the contrary, *engagement* gradually faded away during the eighteenth century. The failure of the indentured servants to fulfill the manpower needs of the plantations did have one important consequence: it helped propagate the cruel myth that only blacks could work well in the tropical West Indian climate.[28] By the end of the seventeenth century, slavery was the base of the islands' economies.

When the French introduced slavery into their colonies, they were not innovating. During medieval times, slavery was widespread in Europe, but by the end of the Middle Ages, it was common only in those areas of the Iberian peninsula which had been recently won from the Moslems.[29] As it became unacceptable to own other Christians, Europeans could only enslave non-Christians, that is, Arabs or black Africans. This persistence of slavery in Iberia had disastrous consequences: when Spain and Portugal developed American empires, they introduced the institution into their new colonies. In the fifteenth century, the Spaniards transferred black slaves from Spain to the newly colonized Canary Islands. Then, scarcely a decade after Columbus's first voyage, Spain introduced African slaves into Hispanola; other Spanish and Portuguese colonies received slaves shortly afterwards.[30] More than a century later, France borrowed the idea of black slavery from the Iberians. The first African slaves arrived in Guadeloupe a year after the French did,[31] and this was no doubt true of the other French colonies.[32] Although the French required few slaves at first, plantation owners needed massive numbers of African workers after the introduction of sugar cane. To fulfill the needs of an expanding economy and to overcome the losses resulting from an appalling death rate, the French slave trade developed.

When the French established their slave trade, they were again following the examples set by other European nations. Even before the discovery of America, Spain had been importing slaves from Africa to work on the great estates of Andalusia, and when Spain's American empire began to grow, the Spanish imported blacks directly from Africa to America. Around 1520, the first licenses were granted to supply the colonies with slaves, while in 1538, the first permit of this nature was sold to a merchant.[33] By the end of the sixteenth century, furnishing the Spanish colonies with African slaves had become a big business, with merchants from many nations participating. Because of their strong position in Africa, the Portuguese dominated the trade at this time, but some French merchants still managed to engage in it. Thus the French developed a small, irregular slave trade even before the founding of the various French colonies in the West Indies. This trade, although almost trivial in itself, familiarized French merchants and sailors with the slaving triangle and facilitated the development of the more regular seventeenth-century trade.

There were in reality two French slave trades in the seventeenth century, one supplying the French colonies, the other the Spanish colonies. Neither was very large. At most, French traders delivered some one to two thousand slaves annually to the French West Indies late in the seventeenth century;[34] the number rose to some three thousand before the Treaty of Utrecht in 1713 marked the end of the seventeenth century, insofar as the French slave trade was concerned.[35] Until 1700 the French sold only a few slaves to the Spanish, but after 1700 the situation changed. In 1701, Spain conceded to France the *asiento,* or contract, to supply the Spanish colonies with slaves, and France agreed to deliver some four thousand slaves annually for a fifteen-year period.[36] But the size of the obligation, the demands already being made on French shipping by the French colonies, and the eruption of hostilities in Europe combined to keep France from fulfilling the contract. A victorious Britain gained the asiento in 1713.

The organization of the seventeenth-century trade was confusing and seemingly inconsistent. More so than in the eighteenth century, French administrators seemed to be unable to strike a balance between their preference for chartered companies and the demands of the colonies for more slaves. In 1664, Colbert granted the newly formed Compagnie des Indes Occidentales the monopoly over the French slave trade, but the company was simply incapable of delivering enough slaves to the Antilles. To supplement and ultimately to supplant the Compagnie des Indes Occidentales, the government encouraged the creation of other large companies, the most important of which were the Compagnie du Sénégal and the Compagnie de Guinée. According to the decree of January 6, 1685, the Compagnie du Sénégal (originally founded in 1672) received exclusive trading rights to the area between Cape Blanc and the Sierra Leone River.[37] Dominated by Parisian capitalists until 1709, when it was taken over by a group of Rouen businessmen, the Compagnie du Sénégal finally merged with the Compagnie d'Occident (Law's company) in 1718.[38] The Compagnie de Guinée was founded in 1685 with a mandate for trading slaves. In July 1701 it was reorganized, with the direction going to eight men, all of them financiers close to the government.[39] Then the company received the asiento and became the Compagnie de l'Asiente and later took over almost all the privileges that had been granted the moribund Compagnie des Indes Occidentales.[40] When France lost the asiento in 1713, the Compagnie de l'Asiente began its lengthy liquidation, a process which lasted until 1771.

The seventeenth century was thus a formative period for the French slave trade. To begin with, the French created their Caribbean empire, and only minor changes in its composition were to occur after 1700 or even after 1650. France established solid claims to Guadeloupe, Martinique, and Saint Domingue, and was prepared to defend these islands. Next, France developed a philosophy, or at least a plan, to govern the relationship between the colonies and the motherland. This was the colonial system which decreed that the islands should serve France alone as producers of tropical commodities and as consumers of French agricultural and manufactured products.[41] Although the colonial system in part confirmed the direction in which the colonies were already developing, it also encouraged the growth of the islands along certain lines; after Colbert, France considered the colonies almost exclusively in commercial terms. Finally, the French organized a regular slave trade in the seventeenth century primarily in response to the islands' ever-increasing demands for labor. Although small in scale, this trade displayed all the major characteristics of its eighteenth-century successor. When peace returned to Europe in 1713, the French merchants were ready to participate heavily in the slave trade.

2
1713 to 1744

With the signing of the Treaty of Utrecht in 1713, the French slave trade blossomed. The colonies began to expand production rapidly, and their increased labor demands more than compensated for the loss of the asiento. Furthermore, the chartered companies faded from view, leaving the trade open to individual merchants, at least in practice if not in theory. Before 1713, the Compagnie du Sénégal and the Compagnie de Guinée/Asiente had dominated the trade and had not allowed independent merchants to organize slaving expeditions; now, the independents had complete freedom to attempt to meet the obvious demands of a colonial market deprived by war. The trade, which had hitherto been primarily a service provided to colonial planters by chartered companies, was becoming a business run by merchants seeking profits. French merchants clearly thought highly of the trade, for they fitted out an average of seventeen ships per year in the three years following the treaty's signing; this was far more per year than the companies had achieved before 1713.[1]

Although the great companies were largely inactive after the war, they still retained the legal monopoly over large areas of the slave and colonial trades, and it was from a desire to reconcile theory with practice that the government reconsidered the administration of transatlantic commerce. The government published the new regulations in two series of *lettres patentes*, dated 1716 and 1717. The lettres patentes of January 1716 dealt with the slave trade,[2] a move made necessary by the apparent failure of the previous regime to keep the colonies well stocked with slaves. According to the preamble, the crown wanted to assure the delivery of "the number of Negroes necessary to maintain and to augment the culture of their lands [in the colonies]." In order to realize this

13

goal, the crown preferred to "assure the liberty of this commerce" by ending the old system of trading monopolies. The move represented a fundamental break with the past, and signified a victory for the business communities in the Atlantic ports: no longer would individual armateurs be prohibited from engaging in the slave trade because of a company monopoly. This principle was enunciated in the first article, which stated that "all merchants [might] participate freely in the slave trade . . . from the Sierra Leone River to the Cape of Good Hope" if their ships were fitted out at Rouen, La Rochelle, Bordeaux, or Nantes. Thus, the government opened all of black Africa except Senegal to individual merchants; the restriction on Senegal, imposed primarily because of the special gum trade in that country,[3] remained intact almost the whole of the eighteenth century. Merchants from the privileged ports had to pay a 20-livre tax for each slave imported into the colonies, money to be used for the construction and maintenance of French forts and trading posts in Africa.

Besides opening the trade to the merchants of five ports—article nine extended the privileges to residents of Saint Malo—the lettres patentes of January 1716 encouraged the trade with important fiscal concessions. Article six proclaimed that all manufactured French goods to be used for trading slaves were exempt from export duties. Article seven extended this exemption to cover most foreign items, in particular the cotton goods imported from the East Indies; foreign goods destined for the slave trade were to be deposited in bonded warehouses to await shipment to Africa. The final and perhaps most important fiscal advantage awarded the trade concerned imports from the colonies: "sugars and other types of merchandise from the islands purchased from the sale of slaves" received 50 percent reductions on entry duties to France, and were not taxed at all if reexported to Europe. The government allowed for the transfer of these duty-saving rights, and soon a brisk commerce arose in the so-called *acquits de Guinée*. Slave traders sold their unused exemptions to merchants with sugar that had not been purchased with money originating from the sale of slaves. When used by a particularly skillful trader, the acquits de Guinée could be most lucrative; and the fraud which they eventually engendered finally led the government to abolish them in 1784, in spite of bitter resistance by the slave traders. In fact, it took the government over thirty years to overcome merchant pressures and end the system of exemptions.[4]

Although modified in almost every particular, the lettres patentes of 1716 served as the legal charter for the eighteenth-century French slave trade. With the brief exception of the 1722-25 period, the trade remained open to individual merchants in an ever-increasing number of ports. Before the end of 1716 itself, Le Havre and Honfleur enjoyed much the same rights as Rouen,[5] and other ports received similar privileges soon after. Finally, in 1741, virtually all French ports were allowed to engage in the trade, thereby ending most traces of the old monopoly system. Of equal significance was the government's maintenance of the subsidy principle: until 1793, the French government encouraged the trade either with special duty rights or with outright grants for slave shipping. In so doing, the government recognized the importance of the slave trade as a necessary service for the islands.

What the laws of 1716 did for the slave trade the lettres patentes of 1717 did for colonial commerce in general, giving it a "fixed and certain law."[6] This lengthy proclamation determined who could deal with the colonies and under what conditions. Most significantly, the government prohibited direct commerce in either direction between the colonies and foreign nations, and thereby guaranteed the French merchants their exclusive rights in the islands. Since colonial commerce in general was a much more widespread activity than the slave trade, it was opened to merchants from thirteen ports: Calais, Dieppe, Le Havre, Rouen, Honfleur, Saint Malo, Morlaix, Brest, Nantes, La Rochelle, Bordeaux, Bayonne, and Sète. All merchants in these ports could participate in colonial commerce, providing they paid certain impositions and providing each ship returned to its port of departure. Besides having to pay some relatively small port taxes, merchants had to pay duties on the colonial commodities they imported into the kingdom: sucre brut, for example, was taxed at 2.5 livres per hundred pounds, sucre terré at 8 livres per hundred pounds, and coffee at 1 livre per hundred pounds. Because of the lack of a national customs union in old regime France, merchants in the Breton ports of Saint Malo, Morlaix, Brest, and Nantes received somewhat extraordinary treatment. Tropical produce entering Brittany—a so-called foreign province—had to pay the same minor taxes as in the rest of France, but was exempted from the larger duties mentioned above; re-exports from Brittany to France proper, however, were subject to these duties. This unique customs arrangement gave the Breton ports an advantage over their French counterparts, although a further provision of the lettres patentes reduced this advantage significantly. Merchandise in the nine non-Breton ports could be placed in bonded warehouses and re-exported to foreign destinations without paying the heavy import duties. This clause encouraged the re-export trade of the French ports, and Bordeaux and Le Havre in particular seemed to benefit from it.[7]

As with the lettres patentes of 1716, the government soon extended the privileges accorded by the decrees of April 1717 to cover other ports.[8] The first to be added officially was Marseilles, in February 1719, although it appears that the Marseillais were already trading with the islands long before then.[9] In 1721 came Dunkerque, the last of the important commercial ports; the major military ports of Toulon and Rochefort had to wait until the second half of the century. Gradually the minor ports also received permission, and by 1776 even a port like Saint Brieuc could participate. In 1784, all ports capable of handling ships of 150 tons were made eligible. It should be noted that most extensions of the privileges met with a certain resistance on the part of the already favored merchants, and even the inclusion of an insignificant port like Saint Valéry was not allowed to go without criticism.[10]

If the lettres patentes of 1716 and 1717 put the slave and colonial trades on a firmer legal footing, they did not have an immediate impact on the volume of traffic to the Antilles via Africa. Merchants may have been anxious to obtain the right to trade slaves, and they may have been concerned with preventing other ports from having the same privileges, but they still did not rush to fit out ships for Africa. In fact, 1716 and 1717 were among the slowest peacetime years of the eighteenth century as far as the slave trade was concerned, with only eleven departures each year. This increased to an average of twenty-five ships per year from 1718 to 1721. The ships at this time were small, but they still managed to deliver an average of 219 slaves each to the Antilles, for a total of about 30,000 Africans in six and one-half years (see appendix). Saint Domingue was the preferred destination of the ships, although Martinique was a close second; together, these islands claimed over 95 percent of the French ships, with Cayenne and Guadeloupe splitting the meager remains.

Nantes was the great slaving port at this time, and indeed, throughout the eighteenth century. Between 1716 and 1722, over two-thirds of all French slavers departed from Nantes, placing it far ahead of Saint Malo and Lorient, its two nearest rivals. This concentration on slaving was a recent phenomenon at Nantes, a port which had a medieval economy until late in the seventeenth century.[11] Nantes merchants traditionally limited their shipping to coastal waters, exporting local goods like salt and wine, although there was an early interest in fishing off of Newfoundland.[12] Towards the end of the seventeenth century, Nantes merchants developed an important commercial relationship with the French Antilles, sending out as many as seventy-three ships in one year to the islands;[13] at the same time, Nantes merchants learned the mechanisms of the slave trade from the Compagnie du Sénégal, which frequently used the port for its shipping. The emphasis, however, was clearly on direct commerce with the Antilles, and Nantes became the leading supplier of European goods to the colonies. Other ports had other specialities (such as fishing at Saint Malo) or lacked the incentives prompted by Brittany's privileged customs position, and Nantes retained its leadership in colonial trade until 1730. By the time

Nantes lost this position in relation to Bordeaux, the Nantais had begun to specialize in trading slaves. They did this for both positive and negative reasons. On the one hand, the selection of Nantes as the main site for the sales of merchandise imported by the Indies Company meant that the port was always well stocked with the materials which were the mainstay of slaving cargoes.[14] On the other hand, Bordeaux' emergence as the leading colonial port—made possible by the decrees of 1717 which equalized re-export duties—meant that Nantes could no longer prosper by shipping its inferior local commodities to the Antilles; Nantes merchants had to turn to Africa to find salable merchandise. By transporting slaves to the Antilles, Nantes was able to continue to participate in the rich colonial commerce and thereby enjoy an almost exclusively maritime, commercial economy. Although producing little itself, Nantes managed to realize profits by buying, shipping, and selling exotic commodities around half the globe.[15]

This extreme international, commercial bias made Nantes largely independent of internal French developments. Not having to rely heavily on French agricultural or industrial production, the Nantais needed from France only economic stability and the legal right to trade in slaves. The lettres patentes of 1716 and 1717 provided a legal basis for individual merchants to engage in the trade. The decrees also had the indirect effect of making the slave trade more attractive for Nantes merchants: by encouraging Bordeaux and other non-Breton ports to participate in colonial commerce, the decrees in effect reaffirmed Nantes' predilection for the slave trade, and for the next fifty years Nantes merchants sent out more than half of France's slaving ships.

The legal right to trade in slaves would have been moot without favorable economic conditions in France. Fortunately for interested merchants, the French economy received strong stimulation under the regency, and the period from 1716 to 1722 was generally a good one for speculative investments. In 1716 the Scottish banker John Law began to dominate French financial life, and he believed that disposable credit and not hoards of precious metals provided the key to greater national wealth. He proceeded to encourage the extension of credit, primarily through the creation of paper money and the establishment of a national bank. Although this is hardly the place to evaluate all of Law's measures, it appears that maritime commerce benefited, or at least did not suffer, from his manipulations. Reliable figures are lacking, but using the number of slaving departures as a measure, it seems that the "system," as Law's maneuvers were called, had only positive results. After the slow years of 1716 and 1717, slaving departures were up sharply in 1718 and 1719, and again in 1720 and 1721. If the loosening of credit had a positive effect on the slave trade, the collapse of the whole experiment in 1720 did not have a devastating effect.

Thus Law helped create a favorable environment for the trade to grow in, but did not have a decisive influence.

One lasting effect of the system was the creation of a new company, the Compagnie d'Occident or John Law's company. Founded by Law in 1717, the Compagnie d'Occident was from its inception intimately related to the system and soon became the financial guarantee behind the entire operation. Theoretically, Law's company was designed to exploit the supposedly inexhaustible riches of Louisiana; in reality, it was merely a toy in the hands of Parisian financiers, the men who ran the government's finances as their personal business.[16] At first the object of intense speculation, the company settled down to a more normal existence after the collapse of the system, and actually survived until 1769.

For the first few years, the company exercised real control over the slave trade, but after 1725 it was less and less active, content to collect impositions from independent traders. On December 12, 1718, the Compagnie d'Occident took over the Compagnie du Sénégal and the exclusive trading rights to the Senegal region, and proceeded the following year to merge with the Compagnie des Indes Orientales to become the Compagnie Perpetuelle des Indes.[17] During 1718 and 1719, the company commissioned merchants in Saint Malo and La Rochelle to fit out a total of three slavers, but did little shipping itself. Only in 1720 did the Compagnie des Indes begin to show a keen interest in the slave trade, sending out four ships to Africa from its home port of Lorient. Towards the end of that year, it received the exclusive right to the slave trade along the African coast south of the Sierra Leone River, which, added to its monopoly over French trade with Senegal, meant that only the Compagnie des Indes had the legal right to trade in slaves.[18] The company soon went into receivership and did not exercise its prerogatives immediately; but although it was content to sell trading permits to individual merchants, the writing was already on the wall. Restrictions placed on the trade by the Compagnie des Indes made slaving an uninteresting proposition for all but the merchants from Nantes, "the favorite city of the system,"[19] and businessmen from Bordeaux, for example, complained about these limiting practices:

> Thank you for the permission . . . accorded the merchants of the kingdom to engage in commerce along the Guinea Coast, including the slave trade, for which the exclusive privilege had been granted in perpetuity to the Compagnie des Indes, and for the conditions under which the merchants can obtain this permission . . . but . . . we feel that most probably none of our merchants will ask for this. The time allotted for the departure of ships for this voyage is too short, because the merchants who do participate in such enterprises are obliged to import most of their merchandise from abroad.[20]

In mid-1722, the company finally began to enforce its monopoly by refusing to issue trading licenses to independent businessmen. The last privately owned slaving ship left France (Nantes) on May 7, and for the next three and one-half years, the Compagnie des Indes was virtually the sole outfitter of slaving ships in France.[21] The results of the three and one-half year monopoly were somewhat better than those usually achieved by the chartered companies, as the Compagnie des Indes came close to performing its assigned task of supplying the French colonies with adequate numbers of black slaves. During the first half of 1722, the company dispatched five slave ships, of which three departed from Lorient and two from Le Havre, the preferred port of the old Compagnie du Sénégal.[22] The following year was less auspicious, with only seven company slavers leaving from France, six from Lorient and one from Nantes. However, just when it seemed that the Compagnie des Indes—now out of receivership—was beginning to lapse into the torpor which had characterized the earlier chartered companies, it aroused itself in 1724 and 1725 and sent out no fewer than twenty-nine slave ships, of which twenty-three left from Lorient. Although this was still a far cry from the pre-monopoly average of twenty-two departures annually, the company's larger ships were introducing almost as many slaves as the independents had delivered before 1722. But the company had apparently overextended itself, and at the end of 1725 it reversed its policy and began to sell licenses again. The French slave trade remained "open" until the Revolution.

Economic factors were almost certainly behind the decision of the Compagnie des Indes to renounce the exercise of its monopoly. The company suffered from a shortage of working capital and from a cash-flow problem; it was spending large sums on its slaving operations and was probably not receiving commensurate returns. In order to conduct what should have been the most profitable trade, it used exceptionally large vessels, averaging 301 tons as opposed to 130 tons for the typical private slaver. Although there was a tendency for larger ships to cost more to fit out, later experience showed that this was by no means necessary; therefore, the company began well. Where it went wrong was in failing to control outfitting expenses, and more important, in failing to trade enough slaves. The company spent an average of 205,000 livres to fit out each ship it sent to Africa, an extravagant figure.[23] Although exactly contemporary data is lacking for private traders, figures from slightly later periods are significantly lower, in spite of the generally inflationary trend of the eighteenth century. In 1729 and again in 1731, for example, Jean Marchais' 65-ton *Union* set sail from Bordeaux to Africa; the first time, the ship cost 44,000 livres to fit out, the second time 42,000 livres.[24] The same armateur's *Africain,* a 175-ton slaver departing in 1735, cost 124,000 livres. The

150-ton *Amiral* belonging to Elie Thomas cost 132,000 livres in 1743,[25] while Patric Archer purchased the 65-ton *Saint Edouard,* already on its way to Africa from Nantes in 1741, for 84,000 livres.[26]

Even granting the questionable assertion that the company's larger ships necessitated astronomical outfitting costs, company captains were clearly inefficient along the coast. Although the average company ship traded 367 slaves at this time, fully 40 percent more than the average independent trader, the company ship was 2.3 times larger than the private one. The company was loading only 1.1 slaves per ton as opposed to 2.0—in other words, its operation in Africa was only half as efficient. The one area where the company excelled was in the middle passage, and this was probably due not to the low slave-per-ton ratio on company ships but to the system of grants given to captains with low death rates during the crossing:[27] company ships lost only 13 percent of their human cargo as opposed to 16 percent for the independents. The net result of the company's inefficiency became clear when the slaves were finally sold in the Antilles. Given the average outfitting costs of 205,000 livres, plus the average added costs of 40,000 livres, each of the 320 slaves delivered live to the colonies had to be sold at 765 livres just for the expedition to break even. Again, contemporary figures are lacking, but unless an artificially starved market had forced prices to rise exorbitantly, the company stood no real chance of turning a profit. As late as the early 1740s, slaves were selling for around 600 livres.[28]

Given the unlikelihood of a profitable trade, the company's decision to slow down its slaving operations and renounce its monopoly was logical. It therefore began to grant licenses to all interested merchants upon payment of a tax of 10 livres per slave traded in Africa. At the same time, it continued to fit out slave ships at Lorient on a much-reduced scale; from 1726 to 1743, some seventy-seven company ships left Lorient for Africa, an average of four per year. These ships continued in the company tradition of large size, carrying an average of 299 tons. The interesting feature of this post-monopoly-era trade of the Compagnie des Indes was the choice of destinations, both in Africa and in the Antilles. While the company was exercising its exclusive rights, it traded in the most popular places in Africa, namely in Guinea and Angola; but as soon as the company allowed independents to compete, it fell back on the traditional preserve of the chartered companies, Senegal. Between 1726 and 1743, no fewer than fifty-four (70 percent) of the company's ships traded in Senegal, where it retained its monopoly and had no French competition. The case was similar with colonial destinations. During the 1722-25 period, the company sent about 55 percent of its ships to Martinique and 40 percent to Saint Domingue; but once it had to compete with private traders, the picture changed noticeably. From 1726 to 1730, the company sent a total of only six ships to the highly competitive markets of Martinique and Saint Domingue, but ordered eighteen ships to sail to the guaranteed markets of Louisiana and the Mascarenes, in the Indian Ocean. After the loss of Louisiana, however, the company acted like every other slaver and dealt almost exclusively with Saint Domingue. This lasted until 1744, when it ceased all slaving operations, with the exception of the infrequent expedition to the Mascarenes. When the company finally disappeared in 1769, its passing was scarcely noticed by slave traders long grown accustomed to its inactivity.

Throughout its existence, the Compagnie des Indes used the port of Lorient for its major maritime operations, and more than any other port in France, Lorient was associated with the exotic worlds beyond the seas. In fact, Lorient owed its very existence to international commerce: Colbert established the city in 1666 to serve as a base for the two Compagnie des Indes. The very name Lorient (originally, L'Orient) was chosen to celebrate the ties between the new town and the Far East, for the Compagnie des Indes Orientales had a monopoly of trade with the East Indies. With the creation of Law's company, Lorient came of age and became the site of intense commercial activity; this was particularly so after 1733, when the directors of the company decided to hold their sales of exotic merchandise there instead of at Nantes. As the company retired from most of its commercial ventures, military activity replaced mercantile, and Lorient became an important naval base. It remains so to this day.

With the end of the Compagnie des Indes' monopoly, the French slave trade began a long period of relative administrative stability, and the trade was open to all merchants who could fit out ships in certain ports and pay the company 10 livres per slave traded. Theoretically, the company used this revenue to build and maintain establishments along the African coast, but in fact they built very few.[29] In any event, the company's decline opened the way for individual traders, who seemed little concerned with the shortage of French facilities on the coast. What mattered was the legal right to engage in the trade, and as soon as the company began to issue permits again on demand, there was a modest rush to fit out slavers. The government dispelled any lingering doubts about the organization of the colonial trade in October 1727 when it issued lettres patentes reaffirming the prohibition on commerce between the colonies and foreign nations. Specifically, these lettres patentes reserved for French merchants the right to ship slaves to the French Antilles, a guarantee the traders welcomed.

The period extending from 1726 to 1736 was for all practical purposes a resumption of the decade preceding the company monopoly. Some 250 slave ships left France during the eleven years following the renunciation of the monopoly, for an average of 23 annually; between 1713 and 1722, an average of 22 slavers had departed from France each year. Nantes continued its domination of the slave trade at this time, sending out 50 percent of all French slaving ships. This was a critical time for Nantes merchants, as they were in the midst of losing their preeminent position in direct colonial commerce. Even in the slave trade, Nantes faced some competition, although the port was never seriously challenged for leadership; in fact, more slaving ships left Nantes than any other French port in each and every peacetime year until the Revolution. But the trade did begin to have a greater appeal for merchants in other ports, and especially in those ports with only a small share of colonial commerce in general. Throughout the century, the slave trade served as a means for merchants in secondary ports to participate in commerce with the colonies: such was the case in La Rochelle and Saint Malo.

The slave trade reached unprecedented heights after 1736: from 1737 to 1743, an average of 53 expeditions departed from France each year, more than double the 1726 to 1736 average. This growth occurred against the background of impressive gains registered by colonial commerce, as colonial production, world and French demand, and prices rose together. In 1738, for example, Bordeaux and Nantes imported a total of about 47,000,000 pounds of sugar from the French West Indies;[30] five years later, the same two ports took in almost 59,000,000 pounds, an increase of 26 percent.[31] Re-exports from these ports rose almost as rapidly, from 36,000,000 pounds in 1738 to 42,000,000 pounds in 1743, an increase of 17 percent. In terms of value, the sales soared, from 8,000,000 livres to over 12,000,000, as the price of sucre brut rose from 17.5 livres per hundredweight to 23 livres, and sucre terré from 25 to 36 livres per hundredweight.[32] These figures suggest that demand for sugar was all but insatiable, whether in France or in the rest of Europe, and that the French colonies expanded production to accommodate that demand. Other commodities fared somewhat differently, often even better than sugar; indigo re-export values increased by over 200 percent, from about 1,000,000 livres to 3,500,000 livres,[33] while coffee re-exports went from 500,000 livres in 1733 to well over 2,000,000 livres in 1743.[34]

The French colonies shared the prosperity reigning in Europe at this time. Years of decline, stagnation, and uncertainty in Europe finally yielded to a new era of growth which began in the 1730s and lasted, in spite of periodic declines, until the nineteenth century. One effect of this growth was a more widespread consumption of colonial commodities; although not every peasant now purchased sugar and coffee regularly, in good years such luxury items could be afforded by members of less-privileged classes. This meant that the re-export trade was worth more than ever before, and the French government was careful to facilitate the growth of this important commerce. One step the government took was framing the edict of September 30, 1741, which opened the slave trade to all those ports allowed to deal directly with the colonies.[35] Although the immediate effects of this edict were quite limited—few of the newly admitted ports were capable of participating in the trade in any but the most modest of ways—the edict did display the government's interpretation of the trade. Slaving was part of a colonial system which dictated the subordination of the colonies to France; at the same time, colonial needs had to be considered and the valuable service of slaving encouraged.

If general prosperity prompted the growth of the international demand for tropical commodities, it was the expansion of cultivation on Saint Domingue which won the European market for France. The 1730s marked the beginning of Saint Domingue's "golden age"[36] which made it the most valuable colony in the world. Indicative of Saint Domingue's increased importance was the number of French slavers arriving in the colony: of the 153 slaving ships leaving Nantes between 1737 and 1743 with a known colonial destination, 122 or 80 percent went to Saint Domingue; most landed at Cap Français (60 percent) and Léogane (30 percent).[37] This expansion of Saint Domingue enabled France to become a leading exporter of tropical goods; it also made France a dangerous commercial rival for Britain.

To supply Saint Domingue with sufficient numbers of slaves, French merchants had to mount a vast operation, sending out no fewer than 374 slaving ships in seven years, with as many as 69 in a single year (1740). As usual, the Nantais led the way with 188 ships, or just over 50 percent; then came the Rochellais (96 ships, 26 percent), the Bordelais (35 ships, 9 percent), and the Compagnie des Indes at Lorient (28 ships, 7 percent). The ships dispatched by independent traders during these seven years were almost the exact same size as in 1726-36, carrying an average of 142 tons as opposed to 145 tons; they loaded a similar number of slaves (averaging 335 instead of 333), displayed similar mortality rates along the coast and during the middle passage (15 percent), and delivered similar numbers of captives (286 rather than 282). Thus, it was only the sheer volume of ships sent out from France that made growth possible: since more than twice as many ships sailed the triangle as before, more than double the number of slaves arrived in the Antilles each year. All told, French slavers delivered about 110,000 slaves to the French Antilles from 1737 to 1743, or almost 16,000 annually.

Faced with the threat and then the reality of war, the trade slowed down and all but stopped early in 1744. This marked the end of the French slave trade's formative period, at least in the eighteen century. For thirty-one years, France had enjoyed peace and had been able to develop its colonies as it wished. Against the background of an ever-improving international economic situation, the French islands finally outgrew their role as strategically located military bases and emerged as major suppliers of sugar and coffee to Europe. But in order to increase production, the colonies required thousands of new slaves; and in order to provide these slaves, the government had had to end the company monopolies and open the slave trade to all Frenchmen. The trade now operated according to the law of the marketplace, with supply and demand dictating its development. For a while, both colonial planter and French merchant were satisfied: as long as production and prices increased, the colonists could afford to buy all the slaves they needed without incurring massive debts, and French slavers could sell their slaves profitably without fearing non-payment. In short, excellent economic conditions made possible a balance between colonial and metropolitan demands.

3
1744 to 1778

For forty years following 1743, the French slave trade stagnated, and the annual number of departures remained relatively constant until the War of American Independence. French merchants dispatched around 55 slavers during each year of peace from 1737 to 1783, when they suddenly doubled their efforts and sent out an average of 110 per year until the end of the monarchy. This long period of apparent stability in slaving actually represented a rather severe decline, because colonial commerce in general continued to grow steadily in volume and value. Quantities of sugar shipped from the colonies to French ports rose about 15 percent from the early 1740s to the 1750s, and then rose another 20 percent by the early 1770s; as sugar prices also climbed, the value of sugar imports nearly doubled in thirty years.[1] More outstanding was the performance of coffee: as cultivation of this plant became popular on Saint Domingue, production soared, with imports into French ports increasing tenfold between 1740 and 1770.[2] Thus the colonies were more and more productive during the third quarter of the eighteenth century, making the slave trade's failure to grow even more remarkable.

The increase in colonial production meant that either productivity was rising or the work force was expanding. Since the first explanation seems most unlikely—no techological breakthroughs occurred in the sugar industry during the eighteenth century—the labor force must have grown during the third quarter of the century. This, however, did not necessarily imply a growing slave trade, since natural increases could conceivably have explained the increase. They were also improbable, however, for according to the demographic estimates made by Philip Curtin, the black population of the French colonies always had a much higher death rate than birth rate.[3] Thus only an expanding slave trade could explain the rapidly increasing black population of the French islands and their growing production. But if the French slave trade did not grow perceptibly from 1740 to 1780, the colonists were obviously relying on alternate trades, in other words on smuggling. Further statistics compiled by Curtin support this conclusion. According to Curtin, France exported 197,000 Africans between 1721 and 1740, while the French colonists imported 191,000 from all sources.[4] Assuming a 15 percent mortality rate, France supplied 87 percent of the slaves required in the colonies. From 1740 to 1760, France furnished only 45 percent (134,000 of 298,000) of the slaves imported.[5] The colonists no longer depended almost exclusively on the French slave trade and turned instead to foreign sources.

The planters had several reasons for resorting to an illicit trade, the most important of which was the inability of French merchants to deliver captives during wartime. This weakness first became apparent during the War of the Austrian Succession, fought in the New World between France and Britain from 1744 until 1748. Until the end of 1743, French slavers had come close to supplying all the colonial labor needed, but in 1744, French slave deliveries declined by over 75 percent from 1737-43 levels. The next year, only one slave ship left France, followed by two in 1746 and three in 1747. At the most, French vessels managed to deliver some 750 slaves annually to the Antilles during the war, thereby satisfying scarcely 10 percent of the demand. The colonists had to resort to illegal foreign imports.

In this context, "foreign" meant British, for British merchants alone filled the vacuum left by the disappearance of the French traders; and since Britain exported far more slaves from Africa than the British colonies needed, British merchants had the slaves on hand to sell to the French planters.[6] This they did in three ways, of which only the first was of even a dubious legality.[7] It involved disguising the British ship as a neutral vessel and receiving the encouragement of French colonial officials. If conditions in the colonies were desperate enough or the bribes large enough, local administrators could be persuaded to ignore the rules and allow the import of foreign slaves. Similarly, a British ship in peacetime or a "neutral" ship in time of war might be "forced" to anchor in a French colonial port because of inclement weather. While thus detained, the ship might sell its living cargo more or less clandestinely. And lastly, there was the true smuggling of romantic imagery, complete with landings in obscure inlets on moonless nights. This was particularly common in the south of Saint Domingue, where French official presence was weakest and the English colony of Jamaica most accessible.[8]

The War of the Austrian Succession marked a turning point in the development of the French slave trade. Far from being a mere dress rehearsal for the "real" war of 1756-63, the War of the Austrian Succession had a significant effect on commerce in the West Indies. British naval might crippled French commercial shipping and forced the French colonies to deal with British slavers.[9] This ended the practice if not the theory of the exclusif: the French were now just one—and not necessarily the most important—supplier of slaves to the French colonies, and France was no longer the sole market for French colonial exports.

With the return of peace in 1748, the French slave trade quickly surpassed its pre-war levels (see appendix). A reaction soon set in, however: French traders had saturated the market and had overestimated colonial demands by not appreciating the scale of foreign slave imports during the war years. The traders, too, may well have overextended their own resources and therefore have needed time to reorganize; but while the French regrouped, the illicit trade continued to supply the rest of the needed slaves. Foreign slaves were notoriously cheaper than French ones,[10] and the fact of low prices, when added to the already intense competition caused by the sudden arrival of 77 French ships in one year (1749), probably rendered profits difficult to obtain. Still, the inter-war period was relatively active, and from 1749 to 1754 French merchants dispatched some 327 slave ships for an annual average of 55. Although these ships were slightly larger than their pre-war counterparts, they carried fewer slaves, as increased competition from French, British, and Portuguese traders made African slaves considerably scarcer. All told, French merchants imported about 14,700 slaves annually.

As always, Nantes was the leading port for the trade, and local merchants, in many cases backed by Parisian investors, sent out an average of 31 ships per year from 1749 to 1754. Nantes now accounted for 57 percent of the entire French slave trade, and no other port even approached it. La Rochelle was second, with an average of 7 ships annually, while Bordeaux followed with 6, Saint Malo with 5, and Le Havre with 4. Together, these five ports accounted for more than 95 percent of the French total from 1749 to 1754, an achievement made possible in part by the almost total disappearance of the Compagnie des Indes from the slaving scene. Only 3 slaving expeditions left the company's home port of Lorient, as the company abandoned what remained of its slaving operations to private merchants.

The company was involved in a curious affair in which independent merchants, backed by prominent Parisian financiers and bankers, attempted to acquire exclusive privileges along the African coast.[11] The origins of this affair can be traced to Nantes, where in 1742 an important slaving merchant, Gabriel Michel, agreed to buy slaves from the company post in Senegal in exchange for merchandise required by the outpost. The company had been thinking of suspending operations in Senegal since at least 1740, so Michel's offer was welcome. War, however, soon intervened, and when peace returned, two large Nantes companies appeared to succeed Michel and establish a certain hegemony along the African coast. Antoine Walsh was the guiding light of the first company, the Société d'Angole, created on September 7, 1748. This second-generation Irish immigrant was born in Saint Malo in 1703 but moved to Nantes at an early age; in 1728 and again in 1730 he served as captain on two slavers fitted out by Pierre Esturmy, the *Saint Jean Baptiste* and the *Saint Domingue*.[12] Walsh then turned to fitting out ships, sending out his first slaver in 1734 and fitting out more than a dozen others before the war. After the war, Walsh decided to enlarge his field of operations by organizing the Société d'Angole, the first privately established joint-stock company devoted to the French slave trade. With the generous backing of the Parisian bankers Tourton and Baur and the financier Pâris de Montmartel, Walsh managed to raise a capital of 2,000,000 livres, of which he furnished 250,000 livres. The company survived for the five years foreseen by the original contract, with Walsh directing operations in Nantes and Tourton and Baur controlling the Paris financing. During its existence, the company dispatched some 26 slave ships, but enjoyed only a limited success and was disbanded in 1753.

Two months after the founding of the Société d'Angole, Gabriel Michel organized a rival firm, the Société de Guinée, capitalized at 2,400,000 livres and placed under the patronage of Dupleix de Bacquencourt, a powerful Parisian financier. Shipping for this company was handled in Nantes by the partnership of (François Augustin) Michel and Grou, which sent out 32 slavers before the Seven Years' War. The Société de Guinée represented the more firmly established "French" group of Nantes merchants, and it appealed to the old Compagnie du Sénégal faction, which had remained intact within the directorship of the Compagnie des Indes. The goal of both new companies was the control of the French slave trade, a goal to be realized by discouraging individual slaving merchants from participating in the trade. Since freedom from competition was important to both companies, each believed that it was vital to secure control over the last great legal monopoly still obtaining in the French slave trade, the one held by the Compagnie des Indes over trade with Senegal. After a year and a half of rivalry, the two companies agreed on September 25, 1750, to work together to acquire the monopoly. The following day, in a rigged auction, the Compagnie des Indes—many of whose directors invested in one or other of the Nantes companies—sold to the two firms, for 1,600,000 livres, its exclusive rights. After the disappearance of the Société d'Angole in 1753, the Société de Guinée retained the privilege until the end of the Seven Years' War.

In one sense, the attempt of the two Nantes companies to dominate the trade represented a throwback to the chartered companies. As Lüthy observed, many of the investors in the two firms were directors of the Compagnie des Indes and conceived of business mainly in terms of monopolies and exclusive rights.[13] What was novel about the new companies was the fact that the initiative for their creation seemed to come from the ports instead of the government. If the creation of the Compagnie des Indes by John Law signalled the highwater mark in direct governmental control over the slave trade, the challenge mounted by the Nantes companies showed just how ineffective that control had become. True, the greater part of the capital raised by Walsh and Michel came from Paris financial circles, but the fact that these moneymen could be persuaded by provincial ship outfitters to join in an attempt to wrest a monopoly from a royally chartered company showed that the balance had shifted. Businessmen in the ports were signing the death warrant of the great slaving companies.

In addition to reflecting the growing strength of individual merchants in the ports, the Compagnie des Indes' relations with the slave trade after 1748 signified a basic doubt about the trade's worth. Not only did the company sell its exclusive rights over Senegal, which was never a great slaving region, but it also abandoned the slave trade almost completely following the War of the Austrian Succession. Although it had sent out as many as seven slavers a year just before the war (1740), it dispatched a total of three from 1748 to 1755, all of which departed during a nine-month period beginning in April 1749; and two of these three ships went to Mauritius, where the company had yet another of its commercial monopolies.[14] The company's abandonment of slaving was a further indication that the period between the Austrian and Seven Years' wars was a difficult one and that the days of growth on all fronts were over. During the entire second half of the eighteenth century, the French slave trade was to be troubled in one way or another. In this sense, the 1749-54 period was less an apogee than a transition,[15] leading from a generation of expansion to one of stability during which the French share of the African and colonial slave markets remained fairly constant in absolute terms but declined relatively. Only war could break or change the pattern.

The Seven Years' War interrupted the trade. Ever sensitive to international tension, the French slave trade began to decline a full year before the formal declaration of war in 1756. Almost as if they could foretell the gravity of the approaching conflict, French merchants cut their slaving operations sharply, from 59 departures in 1754 to only 38 the following year. Slave ships were particularly vulnerable to attack, given their small size, the nature of their cargo when travelling between Africa and the Caribbean, and their extended sailing times. Since slave ships carried exceptionally valuable cargoes until they arrived in the colonies some eleven months after leaving France, many merchants were careful not to take undue risks, and ceased slaving operations at the first sign of danger. Even with this cautious attitude, French armateurs suffered considerable loss of slaving ships, especially before war was declared,[16] and the mention *pris par les anglais* was quite common for slave ships at this time. Typical were two slavers belonging to members of the Rasteau family, the *Gentille* and the *Venus*.[17] Both left La Rochelle in late 1754 but were captured by the British before completing the triangular voyage: the *Gentille* was seized on December 14, 1755, with 169 captives aboard, while the *Venus* was taken thirty-two days later, with 357. Both ships were lost more than a year after leaving France, and only the most perceptive observer of international relations or the most cautious of businessmen could have foreseen the danger and acted accordingly.

After declaring war, the British were successful on all fronts, and especially in the Caribbean.[18] When national navies replaced privateers in 1759, the war in the West Indies became one of territorial conquest instead of simple plunder. In May of that year, the British formally took possession of Guadeloupe, an event which was not at all unwelcome to the French planters, who had grown disenchanted with French colonial policy. Guadeloupe had suffered as a part of the French empire, because of its administrative and economic subordination to Martinique, and the new regime promised to be open to local development. The British soon transported large numbers of slaves to the island and provoked a revival of the colony's sagging economy. Three years after the conquest of Guadeloupe, the British launched another Caribbean campaign, which also yielded impressive results: on February 16, 1762, Martinique capitulated, followed in nine days by Saint Lucia, and on March 4 by Grenada; only Saint Domingue and Guiana remained French. One reason for the rapidity and ease of the British successes was the attitude of the French planters. Although they may not have been as pro-British as the Guadeloupeans, the plantation owners on the threatened French islands certainly did not want to fight the British, at least not on land; they valued their estates much too highly to allow themselves to be swept away by a wave of potentially damaging patriotic fervor. The planters had no qualms about protecting their own economic interests instead of defending French military or political policies, a fact which served to add to the French merchants' complaints about colonial narrow-mindedness.

The provisions of the peace treaty of 1763 reflected the military results and were nearly as disastrous for France. New France disappeared, along with the entire French empire in North America, as France ceded Canada to Britain and most of the Louisiana territory to Spain; the only North

American possessions left to France besides the western part of Louisiana were the tiny islands of Saint Pierre and Miquelon off the Newfoundland coast. In Africa, France lost most of Senegal, while in Asia, the French had to abandon most of their outposts in India; even in the Mediterranean, France had to return Minorca. The only area where France managed to retain its former position was in the Caribbean, and this was of course because of the important concessions made elsewhere in the world. Guadeloupe, Martinique, and Saint Lucia reverted to France, which also was confirmed in its possession of Saint Domingue; only Grenada was lost. The British received the right to colonize Tobago, Dominica, and Saint Vincent, islands reserved for the Carib Indians by the terms of the Treaty of Aix-la-Chapelle (1748). That France managed to regain possession of its Caribbean colonies showed the importance attached to those islands by Versailles: almost the whole of the rest of the French empire was sacrificed, in part just to guarantee the return of Martinique and Guadeloupe. Mercantile considerations clearly held sway over strictly political ones, and the commercially important colonies were preferred to the colonies of settlement.[19]

Like the Austrian War, the Seven Years' War affected the slave trade both during and following the period of hostilities. During the war, the slave trade simply stopped: no more than two slaving ships left France from 1757 to 1761.[20] This was a more complete breakdown than during the previous war, and it reflected the more desperate military situation on the Atlantic front. The British navy had complete control of the seas and made commercial shipping extremely dangerous for France; since only the use of convoys could safeguard shipments to the Antilles, slaving was clearly out of the question. Some slave traders, however, did find alternative investment possibilities, usually in privateering. The high-risk *guerre de course* appealed to merchants used to the uncertainties of slaving, especially since privateering offered the possibility of enormous profits. Some traders may have resorted to more traditional commercial ventures; at Nantes, for example, there is evidence of a return to the ancient commerce in salt after 1755.[21] Many traders did very little at all during the war, content to invest in real estate or to wait until peacetime before resuming their international commerce.

The longer-term consequences of the war are harder to measure, but they were not positive. The planters' treason or benevolent neutrality reinforced the position of the British in the French colonies. During the British occupation of Martinique and Guadeloupe, it was legal for foreigners to ship slaves to the French islands, and so many commercial ties were established between British merchants and French planters that the latter began immediately after the war to lobby for the right to continue to trade with

Britain. Planters openly attacked the restrictive trade laws, saying that the French commercial monopoly over the Antilles hindered growth.[22] More important, the same demands were being expressed on Saint Domingue, where the nearly total absence of French shipping for seven years greatly encouraged the formation of ties with Britain and New England.[23] Thus the Seven Years' War gave an important impetus to colonial independence and reaffirmed the trend begun in 1744. At the same time, the war affected the French ports, although to what extent is debatable. The losses suffered by French shippers at the beginning of the war had a discouraging effect on the trade, as did the length of the war, but there is no clear evidence that the Seven Years' War was the decisive turning point in the trade's development.[24] Even in Nantes, the port which was probably most affected by the war, changes were subtle. The major slave traders were no longer as conspicuous as before, but they nonetheless were present as investors if not as outfitters. Local industry continued to develop largely in response to the slave trade's demands, and Nantes industrialists invested heavily in the trade. At most, the war forced a certain regrouping in Nantes to overcome the capital losses already suffered and to deal more securely with future risks.[25]

The end of the Seven Years' War inaugurated a new period of relative stability for the French slave trade. As in 1749-54, the trade from 1763 to 1777 registered only the most modest growth over pre-war levels in spite of significant advances in colonial commerce. Some 843 ships left France for Africa between the Seven Years' War and French participation in the American Revolution. This meant an average of 56 departures annually, an increase of only one over the previous yearly average. The ships, however, were finally more productive than they had been earlier. Although tonnages remained constant, the ships of the 1760s and 1770s were more fully used, loading an average of 364 slaves along the African coast, an increase of almost 15 percent. With slave mortality falling a fifth to less than 12 percent, each average ship now delivered about 320 living slaves to the French Antilles. Thus the French removed about 20,000 Africans each year from 1763 to 1777 and delivered about 18,000 to the West Indies, figures about 20 percent higher than in 1749-54.[26] This increase in productivity helped regain more of the colonial slave market for the French merchants, although they were still unable to realize in practice the monopoly they held in theory. According to Curtin, the French slave trade accounted for less than 60 percent of the slaves imported into the French West Indies at this time.[27] Revising Curtin's low estimates for French exports from Africa, the French share of the colonial market was around 80 percent, an important increase due primarily to the relatively long period of peace and to the lack of surplus British slaves. Even though the French colonists wanted to trade with Britain, it seemed that the British had few slaves to spare and had to reserve almost their entire trade for their own colonies.[28] French merchants were regaining the colonial slave market almost by default.

The traders also won an important victory in France at this time. In an effort to limit fraudulent practices in the ports, the government decided to abolish the acquits de guinée, the special duty exemptions on sugar purchased with money earned through the sale of slaves. Resistance from the ports prevented the government from substituting premiums based on shipping tonnage for the acquits, although the merchants were unsuccessful in their bids to have the exemptions extended to cover coffee as well as sugar.[29] The government, however, was still interested in promoting the expansion of the slave trade, and therefore officially ended the monopoly held by the Compagnie des Indes in Africa. In the decree of July 31, 1767,[30] the government criticized the company for not trading slaves and for merely selling licenses to all interested merchants for 10 livres per slave traded. The government relieved the company of its exclusive rights and appropriated for itself the 10-livre imposition; this money was to be used to build and maintain outposts and forts in Africa.

Besides trying to satisfy the slave traders, the government wanted to placate the colonists who had railed against the exclusif.[31] The colonial planters had enjoyed their freedom during the long periods of war and were in no mood to return docilely to the fold and restrict themselves to dealing with French merchants. To appease colonial demands and to restore at least the appearance of order, the French government—in this case represented by Jean Baptiste Dubuc, a Martinique planter appointed chief colonial administrator by Choiseul in 1764—decided to allow foreign ships to land and trade in the French West Indies under certain well-defined conditions. Further proclamations in 1767 opened the door to the French Antilles a bit wider to foreign merchants, but foreigners were still prohibited from selling slaves in the French colonies. In fact, the stated purpose of the legislation was to aid in feeding the islands, and only *tafia* and *sirop,* largely unwanted alcoholic by-products of sugar, were allowed to be sold to foreigners in exchange for cattle, mules, and wood. Nonetheless, even this limited modification of the French colonial system provoked outrage among French merchants, who claimed that this was but the first step down the path to colonial autonomy. The merchants feared that foreigners would next be authorized to import slaves and export sugar, fears which soon proved justified. They were also worried that the permission to trade with foreigners under any conditions was merely an invitation to fraud which the planters would eagerly accept; in this, too, the merchants were largely correct. Colonial and metropolitan commercial interests no longer coincided, and the government was more a mediator than a leader.

The slave traders reacted to the changing political climate with loud complaints but with few actions. The trade remained quite steady in volume through 1769, that is, through the period of administrative changes and acrimonious debate. In 1770, however, there was a marked decline, as only forty-two slavers left France. The trade remained sluggish until the American Revolution, with an average of fifty-three departures annually instead of the sixty recorded from 1763 to 1769. The decrease was provoked by the worsening state of the French economy: although the long-term trend continued upward until the nineteenth century, a shorter period of recession began in 1770. The effects of this decline—mostly coterminus with the reign of Louis XVI—were the most severe in the agricultural sphere, but industry and commerce may well have been hurt by the general decrease in the consumption of manufactured goods and by the lack of risk capital available. With cash or credit harder to find, slave traders had to scale down their operations, and the result was a 10 percent cut in slaving expeditions.

With the coming of the American Revolution, the long period of apparent stability in the French slave trade drew to a close. For forty years, French merchants had maintained a constant level of participation in the trade, sending out about one Africa-bound ship per week during each peaceful year from 1737 to 1777. This stability did not however imply strength, and the French slave trade was in a troubled position on the eve of the American Revolution. Wars had disrupted the old commercial patterns in the French Antilles and brought an end to the monopoly enjoyed by French merchants over the islands. The British challenged the French traders, and thanks to the Royal Navy, were successful in capturing a significant portion of the French colonial market. Since British merchants sold slaves more cheaply than did the French, British slaves were welcomed by planters on Martinique, Guadeloupe, and even Saint Domingue. Colonists were less willing to tolerate a restrictive mercantile regime which no longer served their immediate interests, and they began to clamor for change. The government finally replied by opening some colonial doors to foreigners, a step which infuriated the French slave traders. Thus as war clouds began yet again to appear on the horizon, the French traders had to face an important challenge. They had either to expand their operations to fulfill colonial needs or to watch the government intervene on behalf of the colonists and allow foreigners to trade slaves legally in the French West Indies. Nothing could be taken for granted by the traders who had long enjoyed—and according to the planters, abused—a legal monopoly in the Antilles, but their reaction would be largely dictated by the results of the War for American Independence.

4
After 1778

Although decisive in determining the relationship between the French and British empires in the New World, the Seven Years' War had only brought to the fore another conflict, that between Americans and British, and the resolution of that conflict had important effects on the Caribbean. France viewed the struggle between the Americans and British with interest, anxious not so much to win territory for itself as to defeat the traditional enemy. French volunteers under Lafayette joined the Americans, but only after the American victory at Saratoga in October 1777 did France enter the war formally. On February 6, 1778, France and the United States formed an alliance, with France promising to help the Americans gain recognition from Britain. To allay American fears of any imperial designs, France promised not to try to regain Canada; the French did, however, receive certain commercial privileges from the new nation. Similar treaties were signed by the United States with Spain and Holland, thereby isolating Britain and temporarily ending British naval supremacy in the North Atlantic. French troops were able to land in the United States, and a French army under Rochambeau won an impressive series of victories beginning in 1780. Finally, in October, 1781, the British general Cornwallis surrendered at Yorktown to the American army and the French navy, and the fighting was virtually over. A year later, the United States and Britain agreed to peace preliminaries, and the Versailles Treaty of 1783 officially ended the war between France and Britain.

French victories on the North American mainland were matched with French success at sea. In the Atlantic and the Caribbean, the Royal Navy was frequently on the defensive, and although France did not replace Britain as the world's foremost naval power, the French were equal for most of the war. The French-led coalition disrupted British troop movements across the Atlantic and played a vital role at Yorktown. The war in the West Indies was less important, as both nations focused their attentions on North America. In 1778, each nation made minor conquests, the French taking Dominica, the British Saint Lucia; but afterwards, the French usually had the advantage, gaining Tobago in 1781 and Saint Kitts and Nevis in 1782. The British, however, managed to win the biggest battle of the West Indian war when on April 8, 1782, Rodney beat de Grasse at the Battle of the Saintes and saved Jamaica from the threat of invasion. On the other side of the Atlantic, the two nations were also balanced, trading victories along the African coast in 1779. The 1783 treaty reflected this equality, and few territories actually changed hands, although several were returned to their former owners. France returned Saint Kitts, Nevis, Dominica, and some smaller islands in exchange for Saint Lucia. Britain did have to make some concessions and gave up Tobago and most of Senegal, both occupied under the terms of the 1763 peace treaty. The acquisition of Senegal was particularly welcomed by the French, who had dealt in the natural resources of that country for most of the century.

Besides ensuring favorable treaty provisions, French naval success also had the more immediate effect of allowing an appreciable wartime commerce to flourish between France and the Antilles. The situation during the American Revolution was quite unlike that during the Seven Years' War, and merchants no longer feared to fit out ships for the West Indies. The constrast between the two wars was sharp: Malvezin estimated the total French trade with the colonies to be just under 28,000,000 livres per year from 1756 to 1763, but over 150,000,000 from 1777 to 1783.[1] However imprecise these figures may be, they give a vivid impression of the improved state of commerce during the American War. Other figures confirm this conclusion. Meyer, for example, counted an average of eleven departures annually from Nantes for the Antilles between 1757 and 1762; he found an average of fifty-three from 1779 to 1782.[2] There were still losses, of course, but more efficient use of convoys protected by an improved navy kept losses at tolerable levels. French merchants no longer suffered from a paralyzing fear of the British, and given respectable official encouragement, they were willing to take once-unacceptable risks. This new-found confidence rubbed off on the slave trade, although the risks there were still great and militated against any large-scale operations. A few slave ships did manage to leave France during the American Revolution: at least thirteen between 1779 and 1782, and fourteen more in 1778.[3] Modest as these efforts were, they still far exceeded the performance during the Seven Years' War, when eight slavers left between 1756 and 1762. That

slaving expeditions were organized at all displayed a fundamental difference between the two wars.

If the navy made commercial shipping feasible during the American Revolution, government largesse made it attractive. In short, there was money to
be made by sending ships to the colonies at this time. To guarantee the
provisioning of the islands and to ensure colonial loyalty, the government
organized large convoys of royal and private ships. Although the government
had used this system before, it was successful only during the American War
because of the strength displayed by the navy. During the Seven Years' War,
for example, the government was willing to subsidize shipping to Canada in
particular, but merchants were afraid to confront the unquestioned British
supremacy at sea, especially after the fall of Louisbourg.[4] Only after the
debacle of the Seven Years' War had led to the successful reorganization of
the French navy were French merchants ready to consider the possibility of
shipping during wartime, especially when government offers made it lucrative. The government bought space on privately owned ships and paid hand-
somely for it. This *fret royal* consisted of troops or goods for the colonies, and
it was always paid at attractive rates. One example of this practice came from
the Chaurand Brothers, prominent Nantes merchants who were just beginning
to fit out ships themselves, after having invested in them for years.[5] On
August 6, 1778, the Chaurands dispatched the *Saint Honoré* to the Lesser
Antilles with a cargo including goods for the government; when the ship
returned to Nantes on March 14, 1780, the Chaurands sent their bill to the
government, asking some 90,000 livres for the royal freight. Since the
Chaurands had spent only 35,000 livres to fit out the vessel, the importance of
royal shipping was evident. For the government, the practice was yet another
expenditure in the prohibitively expensive war which ultimately bankrupted
the state.

The most significant consequence of the French naval resurgence was
the apparent elimination of British traders from French colonial markets.
Having temporarily lost their supremacy at sea, the British could no longer
continue to trade in slaves as freely as before, and there was a marked
decline in British slaving activity. Curtin estimated that Britain exported
some 272,000 slaves from Africa between 1761 and 1770 but only 196,000
from 1771 to 1780, a drop of 28 percent and a clear indication that the
British trade was in trouble.[6] Not since the decade from 1721 to 1730 had
the British trade been so modest. Thus the British were scarcely meeting
their own demands, let alone shipping surpluses to the French Antilles—a
task rendered more difficult, in any event, by the increased efficiency of
the French navy. The war also interrupted trading relationships between
New England and the French West Indies, another factor which helped
return the French colonies to France and leave them once again at the

mercy of the French merchants. These latter did well from 1778 to 1782; as the Chaurands said about a colleague, "Although he constantly cries poverty, he made a good business out of this war."[7]

When peace returned in 1783, the French slave traders were in a strong position. They had ample capital to invest, and they had a sound market for their product. Government subsidies, the high prices commanded by colonial commodities during the war, and privateering combined to give the most adventurous French merchants an important reserve of risk capital which they were willing to use after the war to finance slaving expeditions. During the war, the rough balance of power on the high seas had meant that neither France nor Britain could supply the French colonies with enough slaves. Conscious of the problem, the Minister of the Marine, the Marechal de Castries, tried to encourage neutrals to deliver slaves to the French islands.[8] These desperate maneuvers reflected the critical state of colonial needs, and when the war finally ended, there was an unprecedented demand for slaves which the French traders were in a position to meet. For the first time since 1740 there was a balance between French supply and colonial demand, and the final decade of the old regime witnessed the climax of the French slave trade in terms of numbers traded. French merchants regained control of the colonial slave market and overcame the war-caused shortages by dispatching more ships than ever before to Africa in every year from 1783 to 1792. More than 1,100 French ships sailed the triangular route during the decade, and they delivered about 370,000 slaves to the French West Indies, or 37,000 per year. This was double the previous annual rate, and it reduced the British to a trivial position in the French colonies.[9]

Ironically, the practical realization of the French monopoly over the colonial slave market came just when the government officially and radically modified the exclusif. For years, French traders had enjoyed a theoretical monopoly over the slave trade in the colonies, but only after the American War did the monopoly become a reality. Although this delighted the merchants, the colonists were not at all pleased, and they tried to convince the government to modify the exclusif in the interests of a more equitable colonial development. The planters accused the traders of plundering the colonies ruthlessly, now that the moderating influences of the chartered companies and foreign slavers were largely removed; they complained that French slaves were too expensive and always in short supply. The traders countered these charges, first by asserting that foreign slaves were cheaper only because inferior, and then by denying that there was any shortage of slaves in the French Antilles. It was up to the government to mediate the differences, and the results were embodied in a series of decrees proclaimed after the American Revolution. On June 28, 1783, the government declared the Lesser Antilles open to foreign slave traders under certain conditions. A foreign ship of more than 120 tons sailing directly from Africa to the principal ports in Martinique, Guadeloupe, Saint Lucia, and Tobago, could sell a minimum of 180 slaves if the captain paid a tax of 100 livres per slave sold; the imposition went to French traders. This edict was repeated and modified twice, on September 10, 1786, and on August 19, 1789. The renewals allowed all foreign ships of more than 60 tons to enter the Lesser Antilles, regardless of the number of slaves transported or their origin; the tax was lowered to 30 livres per slave, except on Saint Lucia and Tobago, where it was reduced to only 6 livres. French merchants now received 160 livres for each African delivered to the Lesser Antilles and 200 livres for each one delivered to the south of Saint Domingue. Thus the government encouraged the importation of slaves into the less-favored regions of the empire by reviving the old notion of the trade as a necessary service; the traders, however, viewed their commerce as a business and refused to engage in any endeavor that might hinder profits.

The problem of supplying slaves to economically questionable areas led to the creation of yet another privileged company, the Compagnie de la Guyane.[10] Founded in 1772, this company received the exclusive right to trade slaves at Gorée for fifteen years, a moot concession on the eve of French participation in the American War. According to the terms of the August 14, 1777, decree, the company had to send all the slaves it purchased at Gorée to Guiana, but was to receive 15 livres for each slave delivered alive. The outbreak of a protracted war almost ruined the company, and only the financial backing of a group of Le Havre merchants saved it from ruin. Investors in the company hoped to obtain the exclusive right to trade slaves and gomme in Senegal, a goal realized late in 1786 in spite of complaints from merchants in other ports. By this time, the company had changed its name to the Compagnie du Sénégal and had begun a regular shipping service between Le Havre and Senegal. Beginning in 1787, it fitted out slavers for Senegal, and by the end of the old regime, it had sent out a total of almost ten slavers, of which only two continued on to Guiana, the rest going to Saint Domingue. The company obviously failed to achieve its stated goal, preferring instead to concentrate on the large Saint Domingue market. This, of course, was exactly what independent traders were doing, much to the chagrin of planters on Martinique and Guadeloupe. The emphasis on Saint Domingue was almost total, with up to 99 percent of all French slaves going there.[11] Nonetheless, French merchants never ceased complaining about the measures taken to encourage either privileged French or foreign slave deliveries to other colonial destinations. The French traders went so far as to blame the new government regulations for the dangerous concentration on Saint Domingue, saying that the English so thoroughly dominated the Lesser Antilles that the French had no choice but to deal with Saint Domingue.[12]

The government still thought in terms of commercial monopolies and proceeded to allocate another section of the African coast to another company. This time there were no conditions imposed, even theoretically, on the site of delivery; the government merely granted one area of the coast to a company for the purpose of trading slaves. On May 27, 1786, Brillantais Marion and Company, merchants in Saint Malo, received thirty months' exclusive trading rights to the Benin River region of West Africa.[13] Beginning on July 1, the company exercised a monopoly over trade in the area in return for constructing a fort on the river; the post would revert to the crown after the expiration of the monopoly, at which time the trade there would be open to all Frenchmen. As usual, the reaction among independent merchants was as strong as it was bitter. This time the Nantais led the attack with a brilliant memoire criticizing the entire project, from the personality of its creator down to the evils of monopolies in general.[14] The complaints went unheeded in Versailles, but for a reason which was probably unsuspected by the merchants in the ports. The episode did not merely represent the attempts of a provincial parvenu to deceive the government into important concessions; it was more than likely an example of an influential government figure using his high office to advance his own business ventures. Brillantais Marion was not just a captain with two unfortunate slaving expeditions to his credit, as the Nantais claimed; he was a supplier of wood to the French navy and an associate of Claude Baudard de Saint-James, *trésorier général de la marine*. According to the balance sheet he produced on the occasion of his 1787 bankruptcy, Baudard had more than 350,000 livres invested in another of Brillantais Marion's companies.[15] Thus, it is highly probable that Baudard's influence secured the monopoly for Brillantais Marion and that Baudard figured to make a profit.

Besides reacting to personal interests and colonial complaints, the government also had to consider its own finances when dealing with the slave trade, and the result was yet another minor blow to the traders. The system of partial duty exemptions had been most lucrative for the traders and a source of considerable dissatisfaction for the tax collectors. On paper, millions of livres were lost to the tax farmers: a ship selling 300 slaves at 1,000 livres each could buy about 15,000 hundredweight of sugar at 20 livres per hundredweight, and thereby avoid paying about 40,000 livres in taxes.[16] Fifty-five slavers a year could cost the tax collectors over 2,000,000 livres; 110 ships could cost over 4,000,000 livres; figures far too high for a government on the verge of bankruptcy. Hence, in an effort to save money, the government decided to abolish the entire exemption system and substitute a simple premium based on tonnage; this it did in the decree of October 26, 1784.[17] Pretending to be concerned with the well-being of the traders, the preamble stated that the increase in the number of slaves sent to the French Antilles was greater than the increase in the quantity of sugar consumed in France, and that the traders were therefore losing the full benefits of the duty exemptions. To improve this situation and to encourage a greater participation in the trade, the decree ended the exemptions. Instead of duty rights, all traders now received 40 livres per ton of slave shipping. Needless to say, the government had less-generous motives, including a projected annual savings of some 3,000,000 livres: a ship of 180 tons would receive 7,200 livres in grants, and 110 ships would get about 800,000 livres, a far cry from the 4,000,000 livres currently being lost in taxes.

The traders reacted with predictable acerbity to this decree. They wrote numerous pamphlets to the responsible ministers, predicting the demise of all French commerce with Africa and the West Indies. Besides merely complaining, the traders found ways of using the new regulations to their own advantage, namely by augmenting the tonnage of their slaving ships. In some cases, this was probably an honest tactic, and the reported increases were undoubtedly valid. At Le Havre, for example, slave ships grew from a 183-ton average from 1763 to 1777 to 215 tons from 1783 to 1792, an increase of 17 percent. Merchants in other ports were either less honest or far more industrious: Nantes and Bordeaux slave ships suddenly grew by 55 percent, while those from Saint Malo were up by 40 percent. And in La Rochelle, slave traders imposed no limits on their imaginations; slaving ships there supposedly grew by no less than 230 percent, from 192 to 634 tons. Evidence of fraud went beyond the circumstantial and became clear in other ways; different tonnages were reported for the same ship, for example. Daniel Garesché's *Cigogne* measured 160 tons on February 26, 1784, but registered 493 tons on December 24, 1785,[18] while the Weis Brothers' *Treize Cantons* managed to grow from 500 tons in 1783 to 1,021 tons in 1786.[19] Even more revealing were the listings of two different tonnages at the same time. Among the papers found aboard the *Pauline* of Le Havre was this note: "The ship is for slave trading . . . at port is 280 tons and measured for the slave trade at 450 tons."[20] Similarly, the Chaurands' *Louis* measured both 660 and 880 tons, depending on the purpose of the document used.[21] There was one basic reason for these discrepancies: the traders knew well that taxes could be paid to the Admiralty based on the smaller figure but that premiums could be received for the larger one. The differences in figures came from differences in measuring the ship—either ignoring (for tax purposes) the *entrepont,* the between-decks, or counting it (for premiums).[22] The authorities knew of the fraud being perpetrated but were apparently at a loss to combat it. By 1788, the traders considered the new system essential.[23]

Having managed to neutralize or even profit by the October 26, 1784, decree, the traders continued their impressive pace until the Revolutionary wars. The problems posed by the government were for the most part minor, and official policy on admitting foreign slaves to the Lesser Antilles, granting new privileges along the coast, and suppressing the duty exemptions had little direct effect on the trade. The period from 1783 to 1792 was by far the most productive in the French slave trade's history, as merchants in most of the major ports expanded their activities noticeably. Nantes was still the most important slaving port, with an average of thirty-nine departures annually, but the Nantais' share of the French trade dropped to 35 percent, as merchants in other ports turned to slaving at an accelerated rate. Bordeaux merchants in particular engaged in the slave trade at this time, sending out twenty-five ships per year, or 23 percent of the French total. Most of Bordeaux' growth was the result of a sudden concentration on the East African slave trade, as an average of ten ships per year left Bordeaux for Mozambique.

If the minor obstacles posed by the government did not hinder the trade's development, the very growth of the trade created an important financial problem for the traders. During the American Revolution, the French planters were able to sell goods freely to the Spanish colonies. Since the Spanish still possessed large reserves of silver, and since they always paid for their purchases in cash, the French colonists succeeded in accumulating an abundance of cash.[24] They used this money to buy slaves from the French traders immediately after the end of the war. Soon, however, the supply of silver ran out, and purchases had to be made on credit. By the end of the old regime, credit alone was supporting the system, with the colonists deeper and deeper in debt to the metropolitan merchants. The planters owed the Nantes traders alone some 45,000,000 livres just for slaves delivered after 1783,[25] but there was no way to pay the debt. The French colonies were importing nearly twice as many slaves as before, while production of sugar and coffee was up by less than half.[26] Even the increase in price for colonial commodities failed to help, since it was largely offset by rising costs elsewhere.[27] Hence the new balance struck in 1783 between French supply and colonial demand was a precarious one, and the traders were in danger of losing the initiative to the planters. These latter were themselves in danger of suffering the same fate on Saint Domingue as their British counterparts had already suffered on Barbados: ruin by soil exhaustion. Even the lushest of the sugar islands could be exhausted by overplanting, thereby forcing the planters to accept diminishing returns on their slave purchases. The problem was not yet critical in 1792 but weighed upon the future.

The trade was not allowed to develop ''naturally,'' as war once again intervened to halt it. Since the end of the American Revolution, France had suffered serious financial hardships and political upheavals, which ended with the outbreak of revolution in 1789. As the French Revolution progressed, European powers led by Austria and Prussia became increasingly concerned and openly threatened intervention; this inspired the French declaration of war on Austria on April 20, 1792. Fighting for its life, the Revolutionary regime became more radical during the course of 1792, until the newly created Convention proclaimed the Republic on September 22, 1792. Finally, on February 1, 1793, eleven days after the execution of Louis XVI, France declared war on Britain and Holland, an act which for all practical purposes ended the eighteenth-century French slave trade. As in 1755 and 1777, the trade began to slow down in 1792, a year before the formal declaration of war on Britain. The traders knew that even with an outstanding performance by the French navy, slaving would be extremely difficult during a maritime war, and so they took the appropriate precautions. When war finally began, they ceased their operations almost immediately: the last slaver left France within weeks of the declaration of war. As during the other wars of the eighteenth century, the slave trade all but vanished during the Revolutionary wars; only between 1801 and 1803, that is, when peace was restored briefly between France and Britain, did French merchants send out some twenty-six slavers. No other slave ships left until after the Napoleonic wars.

There was one technical difference between the disappearance of the trade during the Revolution and during the earlier wars: now the trade was illegal. On February 4, 1794, the National Convention abolished slavery and the slave trade in the French empire, an act replete with revolutionary symbolism but having little practical effect. French merchants had already ended the trade when it became too dangerous to continue, and the Convention merely sanctioned the status quo. In fact, the treatment of the trade by the revolutionary governments was remarkably circumspect from the beginning. As early as 1788, liberals, including Brissot, Sieyès, Condorcet, Lafayette, and Mirabeau, followed the recent English precedent and organized the Société des Amis des Noirs, which had as its goals the abolition of slavery and the slave trade. Although the club published an impressive quantity of antislavery propaganda, it was singularly impotent on the political front. In spite of its lobbying, no references were made to slavery or the slave trade either in the reforms adopted on August 5, 1789, or in the Declaration of Rights of Man and Citizen. The government considered slaves to be different from citizens; hence, they could not enjoy the rights now guaranteed to all Frenchmen.[28] Any fears that civil liberties might be extended to slaves were at least temporarily dispelled on March 8, 1790, by decree: "The National Assembly declares that is does not intend to innovate, either directly or indirectly, in any branch of commerce with the colonies. It places the colonies under the special protection of the Nation."[29]

A year later, the National Assembly discussed the colonial problem against the background of growing chaos in Saint Domingue. The central issue this time was the status of the free coloreds. On May 15, 1791, the Assembly decreed "that colored men born to free mothers and fathers will be admitted in all parish and colonial assemblies, if they have the requisite qualities."[30] Although this decree also confirmed Paris' right to impose its will on the colony, and although the status of only a few hundred people was directly affected, the French traders were strongly opposed. Writing only five days before passage of the bill, Nantes merchants condemned its proponent, Jean Pierre Brissot, who "with his incendiary sect would like to make active citizens of free Negroes and coloreds."[31] The Nantais claimed the usual disasters if the bill were passed: an end to commerce and navigation, an increase in unemployment, and a loss of national revenue. But after a relatively long debate,[32] the motion was carried, and as the traders had predicted, civil war followed on Saint Domingue.

It is possible that the May 15 decree was not even a factor in the events which occurred after its promulgation, but the slave traders saw it as the main cause. In a petition presented to the Assembly, "thirty-six commercial citizens of Nantes" condemned the decree in no uncertain terms as leading to these "dire consequences."[33] Apparently the Assembly agreed, for on September 24, 1791, the "fatal decree"[34] was rescinded and jurisdiction over the status of colored returned to the renovated colonial assemblies. At the same time, the expiring French legislature reserved for itself all powers over the colonies' external affairs and commercial relations. The mother country was desperately attempting to regain control over the island, but was unable to keep abreast and could act only in response to decisive events such as the great slave revolt of August 22, 1791.

All was now set for the debate on abolition, but the debate never occurred. After again reversing its position on the rights of the free coloreds,[35] the Assembly seemed singularly unwilling to discuss the slave trade or slavery itself. Almost furtively, and again without debate, the government ended the premiums for the trade, at first suspending them and then stopping them officially on September 9, 1793.[36] Finally, on 16 Pluviose Year II (February 4, 1794), fully six months after the Convention's main representative on Saint Domingue, Leger Sonthonax, had unilaterally abolished slavery on that island, the National Convention officially emancipated the slaves. Again, there was no debate in the legislature, and as Deschamps noted, "such a decision, taken so abruptly, although the revolutionary assemblies had until then rarely been interested in the question, is surprising."[37]

In a sense, there was no need for a debate. To begin with, the Convention was merely sanctioning a *fait accompli* with regard to the trade, and as it developed, it was up to the slaves to gain their own freedom. Further, there was no one to debate the issue. In early 1794, the traders and other important merchants were uncomfortable and in no position to defend their currently unpopular views against the powerful radicals. Finally, a debate would have been superfluous, as the positions on both sides had been clearly expressed many times before. Since 1790 the Nantes traders had been carrying on a verbal battle with the Société des Amis des Noirs. In various dispatches the Nantais had reiterated their arguments with little variety. Typical was the August 28, 1790, letter to the Saint Domingue representatives in Paris:

> The sanguine projects of the Friends of the Blacks will, in suppressing the trade, tend only to destroy navigation and maritime commerce in the Kingdom, to deprive our colonies of the labor indispensable for their cultivation, to ruin our colonial landowners . . . and even expose them to be butchered by their slaves, to deprive the state of a major share of its revenues. . . . It must not be thought that these new apostles are unaware of the terrible ills which would result from the abolition of the slave trade. . . . It would do them too much honor to believe that humanity alone excites them to support such a cause. That would be a gross error, because if they were simple humanitarians they would find a thousand opportunities to exercise their good will among their indigent fellow-citizens . . . rather than among men who live in another hemisphere. They must be unmasked . . . and portrayed as they merit it, these incendiaries, these troublemakers, these national enemies.[38]

Repeating similar opinions would not have convinced many members of the Convention in early 1794. To the very end, the slave traders viewed the colonists only as debtors in a business relationship, and questions of humanity were irrelevant.[39]

Eight years later, the traders were more successful. Shortly after the Treaty of Amiens (1802) ended the fighting between France and Britain, Napoleon reinstituted slavery, legalized the slave trade, and even made an abortive attempt to regain Saint Domingue.[40] Thirteen years after that, the same man abolished the trade, this time in a vain attempt to appease the British.[41] Finally, Louis XVIII bowed to British pressure and accepted abolition formally, thus forever making the French slave trade illegal.[42] It was not stopped, however, nor even diminished until much later, for the law was not enforced.[43]

The history of the abolition of the French slave trade reflected the importance of economic factors and the relative weakness of ideology. The Revolution did put the trade in a precarious legal position, but war with Britain made maritime commerce almost impossible. Ultimately, it was the British blockage which proved decisive for the traders, as British warships were harder to evade than French laws. Although the periods of slaving inactivity corresponded roughly to the times when the trade was illegal, they corresponded even more closely to the periods of war with Britain. The last slave ship to leave France in 1793 departed within weeks of the declaration of war with Britain; it took five more months for the premiums to be suspended and a full year before the trade itself was abolished. Slaving began anew when the war was halted temporarily in late 1801, half a year before Napoleon legalized the commerce. The trade returned after the conclusion of a lasting peace in 1815, despite the fact that both Napoleon and Louis XVIII had outlawed it.

The eighteenth-century slave trade ended for France in 1793, although there followed a long transitional period before the illegal nineteenth-century trade began in 1815. In the eighty years succeeding the Treaty of Utrecht, French merchants had sent more than three thousand ships to Africa in search of slaves. These vessels loaded almost a million and a quarter captives and delivered over a million of them to the French Antilles; the rest simply died. Ultimately, all owed their fate to the vagaries of European taste which determined that sugar and coffee should be necessities and not mere luxuries. Using black slaves was simply the cheapest means of producing colonial commodities, and the slave trade arose to supply the plantations with laborers. At first the trade was important only as a service to the colonial planters, but soon it became a profitable commerce in itself and attracted the interest of merchants throughout the coastal regions of France. From then on economic factors dictated the scale of its growth. As Europe grew richer, demand for sugar and coffee increased, and the slave trade grew proportionately. There was a close relationship between the value of French commerce with the islands and the slave trade. This relationship worked in both directions: as colonial commerce grew in value, it caused the slave trade to grow, while a larger slave trade led to increased colonial commodity values.

The demand for sugar and coffee stimulated the trade's growth, but wars shaped much of that growth. The economic impact of the eighteenth-century wars was critical, and each period in the French trade's growth reflected war's influence. The War of the Austrian Succession brought to an end a long era of stability characterized by balanced growth in both French imports to the Antilles and exports from Africa; it began forty years of imbalance most notable for the intrusion of British traders. The Seven

Years' War crippled French shipping and reconfirmed the role of foreigners in the French colonies. The American Revolution ended the domination of the British traders, created reserves of risk capital in both France and the Antilles, and led to a larger demand for slave imports. The French Revolution ended the eighteenth-century trade by once again making transatlantic shipping too dangerous. Thus, besides halting the trade for several years at a time, the century's wars influenced the nature and extent of the trade's growth during the ensuing periods of peace. War was the economic weapon par excellence, although its use and its consequences could scarcely be controlled.

In the face of these economic imperatives, including war, the government could hope to control only what were in effect the details—however important—of the trade's development. Versailles could try to determine whether great companies or individual merchants could participate in the trade, but if the one was inadequate, the other inevitably replaced it. The government might also encourage the delivery of slaves to certain parts of the empire, but only favorable market conditions could insure the arrival of new slaves. As the century progressed, the government's main role evolved in the direction of mediation: it was up to the crown to protect the colonies from the narrow ruthlessness of the traders, and to guarantee the traders a good market in the colonies. That the slave trade and colonial commerce in general managed to grow so rapidly was a measure of the government's success in realizing its goals.

PART II
The Slaving Triangle

5
The Triangle

A migration as great as that achieved by the slave trade implied a sophisticated organization. As chaotic as individual expeditions might have been, the French slave trade on the whole followed a definite pattern which fit well the economic and technical limitations of the day. During the sixteenth and seventeenth centuries, merchants from all over Western Europe experimented with different possibilities for arranging the regular transport of slaves from Africa to the West Indies. The Spanish first tried to take slaves already established in Spain to the colonies. At first this meant shipping them to the Canary Islands, but shortly after 1492, the New World became the principal destination. Spanish merchants shipped slaves from the Canaries or all the way from Spain itself directly to America. This method turned out to be inadequate to meet the tremendous labor demands of the new colonies, and Spain began to supply them directly from Africa. The creation of a direct maritime link between the African coast and the New World meant that the third side of a potential triangle was finally in place: more or less regular services already existed between Europe and America, as well as between Europe and the African coast. The new route established between Africa and America had important consequences for Europe. Merchants in Liverpool, Nantes, Lisbon, or Seville could now engage in a commerce between two continents they would never see, and it remained only to decide how best to take advantage of the new situation. The ultimate result was the creation of the slave-trading triangle, with merchants in Europe sending ships laden with a diverse cargo to Africa. There the ships' captains exchanged the goods for slaves, who were then transported to the New World and sold for colonial produce. From the New

51

World, the ships returned home with sugar, coffee, and other colonial commodities, which the merchants sold to clients from all over Europe.

The creation of this triangle was not inevitable, however, and merchants tried other systems to get Africans to America. One method was simple plunder, with Europeans carrying off hapless Africans found near the ship's landing site. This had obvious disadvantages, and although Europeans did occasionally carry off blacks in such a manner, a regular system based on conquest was never established. Instead, the Europeans bought their slaves, and since they needed something to buy them with, a two-way commerce became necessary. Because black Africa was an exporter of precious metals, European currency was out of the question as a medium for commercial exchange. Only a barter system would suffice; goods had to be taken to Africa and exchanged for slaves. As the American colonies produced virtually nothing besides tropical produce and their by-products—all of which could be grown or made in Africa, and many of which had actually originated in Africa—only Europe or Asia could furnish exotic wares of interest to African buyers. Thus two sides of the triangle became necessary: Europeans shipped European or Asian merchandise from Europe to Africa,[1] traded it for slaves, and delivered the slaves to the Antilles. The third side of the triangle was relatively independent of the slave trade, as a large commerce existed between Europe and the West Indies irrespective of slaving. In fact, the traders would have been only too pleased to sell their slaves for cash in the Antilles and be done with the affair, but this was usually impossible. Owing to the nature of the colonial system, the islands were perpetually without specie, and the colonists had to use credit backed only by sugar and coffee. Therefore the traders had to accept produce in return for the slaves, usually with some of the produce returning to Europe aboard the slave ship itself, thereby completing both the geographic and commercial triangles. Some large slaving companies had tried to dispense with the third side of the triangle, but with little success; colonial economic weaknesses were always too great to allow for such a system.[2] The failure of the great companies and the triumph of the independent merchants confirmed the status of the entire slaving triangle, with expensive cargoes carried along each side to be followed by important sales at each vertex.

The success of the classic triangle encouraged some French traders to establish a second triangle either independent of the original or in conjunction with it. This new triangle had one major difference from the original: the second stop for the slavers was in the Mascarene Islands in the Indian Ocean and not in the West Indies. For technical and economic reasons, merchants interested in this destination usually substituted East Africa for West Africa as a trading site, but the change was not compulsory. French ships left Europe, stopped in Mozambique or Madagascar to exchange manufactured goods for slaves, and then sold the slaves on Reunion or Mauritius. A particularly enterprising trader might then proceed to purchase a second load of blacks in West Africa for delivery in the Antilles. Direct evidence for this double trade is exceedingly rare, but such a practice was by no means inconceivable.

Whether in its classic West African form or its East African variant, the slaving circuit demonstrated certain characteristics throughout the century. The starting point was always a French port, where a merchant interested in the slave trade organized a slaving expedition. This was a complex procedure revolving around two major occupations: the trader had to raise the money necessary to finance the expedition and he had to fit out the ship. Locating investors was a delicate operation that usually depended on a merchant's family and social connections: only rarely did a trader look beyond an intimate selection of relatives or friends for major investments. Fitting out the ship was an equally delicate task which demanded the most refined business skills; picking an unattractive cargo or spending too much on it could doom an expedition to financial disaster before the ship even left France. The merchant also had to deal with the various formalities required by government administrators. But the most important task facing an armateur was the choice of a captain, the man responsible for the physical and economic well-being of the expedition from the moment it left port. A competent captain with good business sense was well worth his high salary, for he frequently made the difference between success and failure.

Once in Africa, the captain was in complete control, and it took all of his naval and business acumen to produce a successful trade. Even the choice of an African destination was important: some regions were traditionally better than others, but short-term trends brought on by local wars or by the sudden arrival of several ships from Europe could change conditions radically. Sometimes it took a captain several months to find a good site for his trade. Once the ship docked "permanently," the trade began. Usually, the captain had to buy slaves one at a time from African middlemen, although French or European outposts occasionally offered large groups of Africans for sale. In either case, the purchase of slaves was a painstaking process, with merchandise offered by both sides subject to the most intense scrutiny; only when buyer and seller were completely satisfied was the sale possible. While on the coast, the captain often encountered many problems related to his main task; disease, revolt, and most important, foreign interference could all cause significant loss in time, manpower, or money.

As soon as the trade was concluded, the ship set sail for the Antilles. This "middle passage" across the Atlantic was fraught with danger; illness and rebellion could take a terrible toll among crew and human cargo alike. Although losses of 10 to 15 percent were normal, some ships lost well over half their crewmembers and slaves. It was imperative to reach the Antilles as quickly as possible to avoid a crippling mortality rate which could ruin an expedition's chances of profit. Once in the Antilles, the slaves were sold to planters and townspeople recommended by a colonial merchant in touch with the French trader. Usually the captain and colonial agent, in a hurry to complete the sale and thereby limit expenses, offered the purchasers generous credit allowances. Whatever was paid on the spot was converted into sugar and other commodities for shipment to France aboard the slave ship. Other payments extended over long periods of time and were also made in tropical produce. Finally the ship returned to France, where the armateur sold its exotic cargo and saw the first returns on his investment. It generally took about two years to receive this first payment and several more years before a profit accrued. Many traders died long before all payments were made.

6
In France

The Ports

Although the edicts of September 30, 1741, and October 31, 1784, opened the slave trade to merchants living in all but the smallest French ports, four ports which had enjoyed the right to trade slaves since 1716 dominated the commerce throughout the eighteenth century. Merchants in Nantes, Bordeaux, La Rochelle, and Le Havre fitted out nearly 2,700 slaving expeditions between the Treaty of Utrecht and the end of the old regime. This was over 80 percent of the entire French trade during the eighteenth century. One port alone, Nantes, accounted for more than 1,400 slaving expeditions, or almost 45 percent of the national total, a feat which earned the town the infamous epithet "city of slavers." We have already seen the reasons which prompted Nantes' concentration on slaving: its early commerce with the Antilles, the encouragement given by the Compagnie des Indes, and the overwhelming competition in direct shipping offered by Bordeaux. No other French city even approached Nantes' slaving activities, which reached a peak in 1790, when 49 ships left the port for Africa. The results of this frenetic commerce were great riches for the city. As Arthur Young commented in 1788, "This town has that sign of prosperity of new buildings, which never deceives. The quarter of the *comédie* is magnificent, all the streets at right angles and of white stone. I am in doubt whether the *Hôtel de Henri IV* is not the finest inn of Europe."[1] Situated on the Loire a few miles from the Atlantic Ocean, Nantes boasted a population of around eighty thousand on the eve of the Revolution, and its riches stood in sharp contrast to the poverty of the surrounding Breton countryside. "What a miracle," wrote Young, "that all this splendor and wealth of the cities in France should be so unconnected with the country!"[2]

A distant second to Nantes in slaving activity, the port of Bordeaux nonetheless witnessed the departure of more than 450 slave ships during the eighteenth century. Most of this commerce came late, as Bordeaux merchants dispatched over 250 ships to Africa in the last decade of the old regime. The sudden interest displayed in slaving by the Bordelais accompanied the leveling off of colonial commerce in general, and represented an attempt by local merchants to continue to expand their businesses. Slightly larger than Nantes, Bordeaux dominated the French colonial trade from the 1730s on; merchants had the advantage of superior local produce to ship to the West Indies, with flour and wine the most important. By the end of the old regime, profits from this commerce had created one of the richest towns in Europe. "Much as I had seen and heard of the commerce, wealth, and magnificence of this city," wrote Arthur Young, "they greatly surpassed my expectations. Paris did not answer at all, for it is not to be compared to London; but we must not name Liverpool in competition with Bordeaux."[3]

The other two major slave-trading ports paled in comparison to Nantes and Bordeaux. La Rochelle and especially Le Havre were not poor by any means, but neither had the evident riches of their great eighteenth-century rivals. La Rochelle suffered a tragic history, as its residents engaged in politically and commercially disastrous ventures. A prosperous fishing port, La Rochelle became the center of Protestantism in the west of France, and the Rochelle fleet helped win Protestants important concessions from the crown late in the sixteenth century. The city then enjoyed a brief period of semi-autonomy as a Protestant stronghold, only to fall to the siege mounted by Richelieu from August to October, 1627. From then on, La Rochelle was politically like any other city in the kingdom, and it came to depend economically on transatlantic commerce. Throughout the eighteenth century, La Rochelle merchants participated in the slave trade, sending out just over 400 slavers; during the last decade of the old regime, some 12 ships per year left the port for Africa. As was the case with the Nantais, La Rochelle merchants apparently used the slave trade to participate in a colonial commodities' trade which might otherwise have eluded them. Le Havre dispatched almost as many ships to Africa as La Rochelle during the century, but sent out an average of 17 per year from 1783 to 1792. This increased activity reflected the sudden growth of the port late in the century,

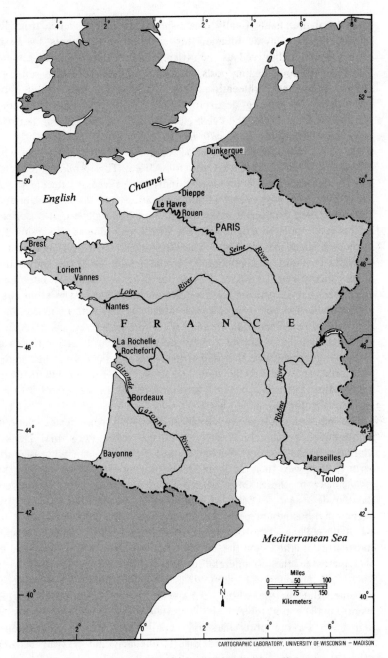

1. France: Ports for the Slave Trade

when local merchants finally established their independence from Rouen. Previously, Le Havre, founded for all practical purposes by Francis I around 1500, had served as the Atlantic port for the Norman capital.

Besides the four leading ports, at least ten others witnessed some slaving activity during the eighteenth century. Only four of these lesser ports had more than 100 slaving departures—Saint Malo, Lorient, Honfleur, and Marseilles. Saint Malo, the celebrated fishing and privateering port (known however misleadingly as *la ville des corsaires*), displayed an early interest in the slave trade, but was most active between 1763 and 1769, when an average of 7 slavers per year left for Africa. This probably reflected the boost given the local economy by individual successes during the Seven Years' War; in any event, famous corsaires such as Chateaubriand and Surcouf played prominent roles in the Saint Malo slave trade. Lorient was the home port of the Compagnie des Indes, and almost all slaving activity there took place before 1744. The interest shown by the merchants from Honfleur was quite exceptional, given the small size of this port across the Seine estuary from Le Havre. It was due in large part to the importation of investment capital from Le Havre, Rouen, and Paris. The Honfleur trade itself was carried out so as not to compete directly with its more illustrious rivals; Honfleur merchants specialized in unpopular regions of Africa, for example.[4] For the Marseillais, the trade was more a diversion than a necessity, as commerce with the Mediterranean world far outweighed trade with the Caribbean. Only at the very end of the old regime was there a concerted effort to trade slaves at Marseilles, when an average of 5 to 8 ships left annually for Africa.[5]

The remaining ports played an insignificant role in the slave trade, accounting for scarcely 2 percent of the total. Ports like Dunkerque, Morlaix, Brest, Vannes, Rochefort, and Bayonne each witnessed the departure of fewer than 25 expeditions during the entire century, and a good many of these ships belonged to merchants in larger cities. The slave trade was too costly an enterprise to be undertaken with any frequency by businessmen in the lesser ports, and armateurs there had to ask their colleagues in other cities for capital. Occasionally, special circumstances might favor the minor ports in small ways. War, for example, increased the commercial activity of military sites like Brest and Rochefort, although the slave trade itself remained insignificant during wartime. But on the whole, the departure of a slave ship was a rare event in all but a few of the largest Atlantic ports. Merchants in the four great slaving ports had little competition from businessmen elsewhere, and the Nantais, Bordelais, Rochellais, and Havrais became the strongest opponents of company privileges.[6]

Fitting Out

Organizing a slaving expedition was generally a complex, time-consuming affair except when undertaken by the Compagnie des Indes. Because of its large capital resources and its international commercial organization, the company was able to avoid many of the problems which beset independent merchants fitting out slavers. The company had a fleet of ships at its disposal and could order new ships to be constructed at its convenience in Lorient or elsewhere. The company also maintained a number of ship's captains and so did not have to waste valuable time searching for them. More important, the company had a monopoly of trade on the items most desired by slavers for their outgoing cargoes: printed cloths (or calicoes) from India. From the time that commerce with the Indian Ocean countries began on a regular basis in the late seventeenth century, it was the exclusive preserve of chartered companies like the Compagnie des Indes Orientales or the Compagnie des Indes itself (Law's company). The Compagnie des Indes used this monopoly to benefit its own slave trade, assuring for itself an adequate supply of textiles demanded along the African coast. Perhaps the greatest advantage of the company was its tremendous size. Involved as it was in extensive commercial activity, it did not have to agonize over each slaving expedition as did many smaller armateurs. For it, the trade was a relatively minor operation, and the failure of one or two expeditions did not spell financial disaster. The capacity to absorb losses, however, could have its negative side, leading the company to tolerate inefficient and even self-defeating practices. Only the Compagnie des Indes could have allowed its captains to leave the African coast without making real efforts to fill their ships with slaves. In short, the company fitted out slavers easily and as a matter of course; but if it had fewer problems in organizing and financing expeditions than did independent traders, it also had less incentive to make any particular expedition a success.

The Compagnie des Indes accounted for fewer than 5 percent of all French slaving departures in the eighteenth century. The other 95 percent were organized by independent merchants, ranging in size from a ship's captain risking his life and fortune on one expedition to men like Antoine Walsh or Gabriel Michel, founders of companies large enough to challenge the Compagnie des Indes for part of the trade. With the partial exception of the Walshes and the Michels, the independent traders ran highly unstable businesses and viewed the organization of a slaving expedition as a unique event which could be of critical importance to the trader's financial future. Most traders had to struggle with this commerce, and every step in the process presented new problems. From the original search for capital to the long wait for final returns, the trader had to be patient and skillful in business. Even maintaining what appeared on paper to be a losing business demanded a fine sense of timing and balance; expanding that apparently losing affair required an intimate knowledge of the credit mechanisms of the day. To be successful, a trader had to know how to turn every setback to personal advantage, particularly towards the end of the century, when a trader might try to become so vital to local business that his success became a community responsibility. In this vein, one Nantes merchant contemplated the ruin of another with anxiety: "Michel and Ducamp . . . have just been obliged to suspend payments . . . the whole town has come to their aid and we hope that in a bit they will begin anew.[7]

Once he decided to organize a slaving expedition, a merchant had to deal with two sets of problems, one financial, the other mechanical. In the broadest sense, financial problems claimed his attention first: he had to place the expedition on a firm financial foundation if it were to take place at all. The first step in the process was the formation of a company which would be responsible for the entire affair. This was done for good business reasons. Slaving was an expensive operation, and few men had the means or the will to assume all the risks without partners. The simplest way to limit one's involvement from the very start was to establish a commercial company or *société*. Although there were two or three examples of joint-stock companies designed for the purpose of trading slaves,[8] the vast majority of slaving companies were simple partnerships of from two to five members. This was ideal for the founder, allowing him to retain a dominant role as active associate but with a much-reduced financial commitment. The other member or members had varying duties, depending on the structure of the company. In a two-man partnership, both men were usually active, one handling the books and the other all outside business; but if one partner were much richer than the other, the poorer one might contribute more time and expertise to balance his partner's larger investment. When there were more than two partners, one usually ran the business while the rest remained in the background.

To establish a company legally, the partners had to agree to and sign an *acte de société*. Although varying widely in exact contents, most actes de société shared certain characteristics, including a brief preamble outlining the reasons for the association, and articles dealing with the name of the company, its duration, the division of capital, labor, and profits, and the resolution of potential problems. Most companies engaging in the trade were formally created for various commercial enterprises and not specifically for trading slaves. For example, the largest slaving company in Bordeaux failed to mention the slave trade in the company charter. "Between us, Paul and Elysée Nairac the undersigned, was concluded that which follows to serve as the rule for the company which we contract together for commercial affairs."⁹ This was a typical omission, since direct references to slaving were rare in the actes de société and usually came as part of a familiar phase, "for the slave trade, American commerce, and fishing."¹⁰ Business reasons and not humanitarian principles were behind this apparent obfuscation: very few, if any, small companies devoted themselves exclusively to slaving, for the very structure of the trade made other commerce almost inevitable. Only the large companies relying on Parisian capital specified the slave trade as the primary venture. This was necessary because of the relative inflexibility of large associations: silent partners in Paris did not wish to give a provincial ship armateur complete freedom in using their investment capital.¹¹ Parisian associates were equally unwilling to commit themselves to a long-term investment, and companies based on Parisian investment were of exceptionally short duration. The Société d'Angole lasted five years, Begouen Demeaux and Company only four, a considerably shorter time than the seven years usually called for in the standard contract between provincial merchants. In all cases, however, one fact stands out: although indefinitely renewable, partnerships were basically short-term arrangements designed to expedite the business at hand.

Who formed partnerships? In a word, relatives. Although religion and geographic factors often entered the picture, by far the most important consideration was family relationship. In a world dominated by uncertainty and change, only family ties could be trusted to endure. Thus most companies included at least one pair of relatives, although it was not at all uncommon to find unrelated "hidden" partners. The most common form of family company was a partnership between father and son or sons. David Gradis and Son at Bordeaux, Guillaume Bouteiller Father and Son at Nantes, and Jacques Rasteau Father and Pierre Isaac Rasteau Son at La Rochelle were among the largest slaving companies in France; each relied on the paternal link. This type of company almost always represented an attempt by the father to guarantee the continuation of hitherto successful efforts, and the preeminence of the father was usually clear. Meyer called Guillaume Bouteiller's contract with his sons "draconian," an apt description of a document which placed all powers in the father's hands and demanded uncompromising obedience from the sons.¹² Only the death or the unlikely retirement of the father could allow the son(s) to assume real responsibility in the company. Almost as popular as the paternal companies were partnerships between brothers, and many of these had begun as paternal associations but changed when the father died. This was apparently the case with Paul Nairac and Older Son of Bordeaux,¹³ which became in 1767 a partnership between Paul Nairac and his younger brother Elysée. The brothers were not perfectly equal in the new company, as the older furnished some 60 percent of the capital and received five-eighths of the profits; disputes, however, were to be arbitrated, and not resolved by the eldest's pronouncements.

Partnerships between in-laws were the third major form of family company. Marriage and business were intimately related in the old regime, and it was common for merchants to consider weddings almost as business mergers. The formation of a partnership could come either before or after the signing of the marriage contract; in either case, the offer of a daughter and the acceptance of a wife insured the loyalty of two merchant families. At Nantes, Peltier and Michaud, and Giraud and Raimbaud, were formed between brothers-in-law, while the partnership of Plombard and Le Gris was established before the marriage links were forged. Successive marriages could relate more than two families and provide the basis for larger partnerships; this was the origin of Canel, Meslé, and Bernard of Nantes.[14] Other family ties led to different business configurations. Widows often replaced their dead husbands as active members of commercial companies including son(s), son(s)-in-law, or both. The Nantes company of Veuve Le Masne and Son and Jean Praud, for example, included Marguerite Le Masne *née* Praud, widow of Jean Baptiste Le Masne, her son Jean Baptiste, and her brother Jean. The permutations were virtually endless, but they always included some family tie, however fragile.

Partnerships formed by non-relatives had to find a different basis for trust, and here a common religion could be vital. In the larger ports especially, communities formed by Protestants or occasionally Jews led a more or less independent existence. Within these communities, relations were apt to be close, with a dense network of marriages and business partnerships. Even where no marriage tie existed, there was enough common ground between members of either of these minorities to warrant the creation of partnerships, particularly if one of the partners were a recent arrival to the port. This was the case with Riedy and Thurninger, the largest slave-trading company in Nantes at the end of the old regime. The Protestant Georges Riedy arrived in Nantes from Switzerland around the middle of the eighteenth century and formed a partnership with an earlier foreign arrival, Deutscher. When Benjamin Thurninger came from Alsace towards the end of the 1770s, he was welcomed by Riedy as a fellow Protestant, and the two men formed a partnership. Other Protestant companies at Nantes worked in similar fashion, as the partnerships of Pelloutier and Bourcard, Philippe and Amyrault, and Schweighauser and Dobrée united otherwise unrelated Protestant businessmen. Most if not all of these companies had ties with the international community of Protestant merchants and bankers, and the creation of several of these Nantes companies may have reflected a conscious attempt by the Swiss to participate in the Nantes slave trade.[15] Unrelated Catholics had to rely on less-certain grounds for formal business association. Mutual recognition in the business world was frequently a basis for partnership, as merchants established companies with former employees. The Nantes firm of d'Havelooze and Dumaine included a major slave trader and his former clerk. Tourgouilhet and Rousseau represented the union of a clerk and a ship's captain, both of whom had worked for the same merchant, Larralde. And if merchants were desperate enough, they could associate with strangers, as did several new arrivals to Nantes during the last decade of the old regime.

Establishing a partnership was only the first step towards financing a slaving expedition; the trader still had to locate investors for his project. This could be done in two ways: either the partnership could expand to include a silent partner who would be committed over a relatively long term to all the ventures of the company, or investors in particular expeditions could be found. Several companies had hidden partners in many instances living far from the port where the partnership was based. In these cases of dispersion, the local firm was often a subsidiary of a larger, sometimes international organization. Henry Romberg, Bapst and Company, a prominent Bordeaux slaving company of the 1780s, depended on silent partners in Brussels for its financial backing,[16] while the earlier Nantes partnership of Michel and Grou was in reality a front for the Société de Guinée, which was in turn dominated by Parisian investors.[17] Silent partners could also reside in the ports. There they could witness first hand the operations of the visible partners without having to engage directly in an active commerce. Occasionally a hidden partner was one who had been an active associate at one time but whose status had changed; Antoine, a silent partner in Boittard and Company, had been a participant in Antoine and Boittard.[18] Or members of the trader's family might be passive shareholders in the company, either because of the vagaries of inheritance or because of a desire to help out a relative. Thus Jean Joseph Arnous owned a fifth of Nicolas Arnous Father and Son, which was run by distant cousins.[19]

The most common way to raise money was by searching for investors for each expedition. Few merchants cared for long-term investments, especially in something as uncertain as the slave trade; they preferred instead to invest in one expedition at a time when they saw fit. Although this proved more expensive because of the commission fees levied by the outfitting company, it was preferred by the majority of merchants, those who demanded flexibility in their investment portfolio. Thus the need for capital complemented the desire for "liquidity," and the practice of selling shares in slaving ships was born. Technically speaking, the armateur sold "parts" of the ship or expedition in question, and investors actually owned the vessel and all its contents. Once he had sold several shares, the armateur was no more than an associate owner responsible for arranging the ship's use, and even then he might have to obey the wishes of his investing colleagues.[20] In effect, the outfitting firm and the investors together constituted a new company for each slaving expedition, a fact recognized by Saint Malo port authorities, who spoke of *sociétés des navires*.[21]

At Nantes, where administrators were particularly careful to record sales of ship interests,[22] armateurs kept an average of slightly less than 40 percent in their own ships during the last decade of the old regime and relinquished over 60 percent to other investors. Because the other three-fifths were almost always divided among five to ten investors, the armateur usually remained the dominant figure in the slave trade, although his power was far from absolute. The great majority of the hundred outfitting firms at Nantes did keep from 30 to 50 percent of the shares in their ships, besides investing rather heavily in other armateurs' expeditions. In fact, armateurs constituted one of the best sources of investment capital for each other: local armateurs purchasing shares in each other's ships accounted for one-fifth of all the investments made in the Nantes slave trade from 1783 to 1792. Of course, not all armateurs retained a two-fifths share in their own ships; it was not unusual for an especially rich or adventurous merchant to keep from 50 to 100 percent interest in his affairs. Many of the most active armateurs, in particular, regularly exceeded the two-fifths average investment, but rarely invested in their colleagues' ventures. These men were generally quite independent and rarely associated with other merchants for purposes of mutual investment. At the other exteme were those armateurs who invested little if anything in their own ships. Although most of these men were relatively unimportant and fitted out only one or two ships during the entire decade, a few sent out several slavers. These latter relied heavily on their colleagues for capital and invariably associated closely with a group of trading merchants for reciprocal investment purposes.

Businessmen who did not fit out ships took most of the remaining shares. Local merchants of this type owned a bit more than one-fifth of all slaving interests. Most of them also dealt in colonial commodities, and some had even fitted out slave ships at one time or another. Obviously, the sums risked in this way varied from investor to investor, with some men taking just one small interest during the decade and with others committing hundreds of thousands of livres. Non-residents held about one-tenth of the slaving shares at Nantes from 1783 to 1792. Parisians and colonists were responsible for half of this total, while the rest came from all over France. It was technically illegal for foreign residents to invest in French shipping,[23] but merchants easily and frequently evaded this rule by employing indirect means. As we have seen, it was common, particularly after the

American Revolution, for foreign firms to establish subsidiaries in the French ports. These new ''French'' companies had the right to participate in French transatlantic commerce, even though all financing came ultimately from abroad.

To attract out-of-town investors, French armateurs published prospectuses describing the proposed expeditions in considerable detail.[24] Since the prospectuses had a definite purpose, they were always written in the most glowing terms and reflected the optimism underlying the traders' outlook. A typical prospectus promised a minimum gain of some 30 to 50 percent, and hinted at even greater profits,[25] which would accrue inevitably if the captain simply followed the armateur's instructions. In composing a prospectus, armateurs occasionally gave free reign to their imaginations and made all-but-impossible claims. One proposed to dispatch three slavers to the African coast simultaneously.[26] The ships would dock in different ports but would work together to trade some 1,400 slaves, presumably in a few weeks' time. After a safe voyage to the Antilles marked by a mortality rate of only 7 percent, the slaves would be sold for 1,600 livres each, making for a minimum net profit of 30 percent upon the return to Bordeaux. Although almost all of these figures were grossly exaggerated and virtually impossible to realize, they were typical of the claims made by slaving armateurs attempting to lure investors from beyond the port.

There existed yet another category of investor in the slave trade, the captain and crew. In more than one-half of the expeditions recorded, the captain held anywhere from a nominal share to one-third or even five-eighths, while the crew occasionally had small parts as well. Although the captains often sold pieces of their larger interests, they nonetheless ended by keeping about one-tenth of the whole expedition. At least one captain invested all his savings in one voyage: ''I invested more than 70,000 livres in the ship, or the total of my father's legacy and the product of twenty years of work.''[27] Not infrequently a captain would virtually be forced to take an interest by an armateur in search of capital. On August 26, 1789, the armateur Baudouin declared ''that I give to Pradelaud the commander of the aforementioned ship, the *Gardes Françaises* . . . sent to the Coast of Angola for 200 blacks . . . 200 livres per month and 5 percent commission on the sale of the blacks at Saint Domingue and two young Negroes.'' The captain replied, promising to ''take an interest of 30,000 livres in the entire fitting out and cargo of the said ship.''[28] Similar agreements existed between other officers and the armateur; in return for slaves or a commission on the sale of slaves, an officer could either invest in the expedition or give the armateur money outright.[29] Getting the captain and the crew to invest was a convenient and perhaps an economical way to raise money for the expedition; it also insured their loyalty to the success of the voyage.

Besides being exchanged for services, parts were also sold for goods received. Instead of paying cash for merchandise, armateurs could offer shares in their ships. C. G. Petit received a one twenty-fifth share in Nau's *Antenor* in return for 6,000 livres' worth of carpentry,[30] while Brée de la Touche got a one-eighth share in the *Oracle* in exchange for rope he supplied.[31] Traders may have discounted the shares when using them as payment, hoping to defer real payment until the ship returned in two years.[32] These parts, like all the others, were exchangeable, and there was a brisk trade in them. Indeed, shares were marketed almost like modern stocks, complete with "blue chips" (shares in ships fitted out by large, established firms; such shares were difficult to obtain) and more speculative issues (shares in ships sent out by smaller merchants, usually cheaper and less secure). Even the equivalent of preferred shares existed in the *grosses aventures* or *cambies,* a practice with elements of insurance, loan, and investment.[33] In return for a usually large sum of cash which was, at least in theory, taken on board the departing slave ship, the insurer-lender-investor received a 25 to 30 percent premium the moment the ship returned. If the ship failed to regain port, however, the money was lost. Thus the slave trade offered a wide variety of possibilities to the investor.

While searching for adequate financing, the armateur organized the slaving expedition. Here the merchant had only one consideration, economy; he did everything in his power to limit expenses. The preparations usually took several months and consisted of three main tasks: assembling a crew, obtaining a ship and cargo, and fulfilling certain formalities. An example of the time involved came from Bordeaux.[34] Before the beginning of the summer of 1743, Elie Thomas, recently arrived from La Rochelle, decided to fit out a slaving expedition, and on July 8 he bought a one-half interest in the *Amiral,* owned by its captain, Richard Mollard. By early October, Thomas had purchased most of the cargo, apparently from the Compagnie des Indes. At the same time, he was looking for investors, and Mollard was recruiting the crew. This done, the ship set sail for Africa on November 7, although Thomas did not actually receive the money invested until two days after the departure. Thus, from four to six months had passed between the original decision and the sailing. These months were filled with hectic activity: Thomas had to order cloths from Hamburg, ropes and iron from Amsterdam, and general merchandise from Nantes; he had to find investors in Bordeaux and purchase insurance in Nantes; his captain had to hire a crew and oversee the refurbishing of the ship. The slave trade demanded complete attention from all but the largest participating merchants.

Except for the unusual cases when the captain came along with the ship, the armateur had to find a good captain.[35] Choosing a captain was not a decison to be undertaken lightly, for no single person besides the armateur himself had as much influence over the expedition's ultimate success as did the captain. To begin with, the captain had to be an excellent sailor to guide the tiny ship safely on a 7,000 mile voyage which included two crossings of the Atlantic Ocean. Even to become a captain, he had to have experience on transatlantic voyages and pass an examination on ocean sailing. A typical captain might have ten years of sailing experience before reaching the coveted rank at the age of twenty-five or thirty. As important as his nautical abilities was a captain's business ability. The captain alone was responsible for conducting the slave trade along the African coast; he had to choose the trading sites, deal with the African chieftains, and trade with the African merchants. These skills were uncommon and commanded such high salaries that a commander who did not succumb to disease or slave revolt could count on amassing a respectable fortune after leading only two or three expeditions. Typically, a captain received a monthly salary of 100 to 200 livres, which was in reality a minor consideration compared to the other benefits he earned. Most armateurs either gave the captain 2 to 5 percent of all income from slave sales in the Antilles or allowed the captain to trade a few slaves on his own account in Africa. The Compagnie des Indes gave bonuses of up to 12 livres per slave to the captain and the principal officers for achieving low mortality rates among the slaves on the middle passage.[36] When all the incomes were combined, a captain could earn over 20,000 livres on one expedition, a prospect which encouraged some to specialize in commanding slaving expeditions. Captain Maniable of Le Havre led six slaving expeditions between 1763 and 1774; another Havrais, Captain Barbel, took five ships to Africa from 1774 to 1787.[37] Sometimes a captain remained faithful to one outfitting company; four of Maniable's ships belonged to Mouchel and Beaufils. But, sometimes a captain preferred to change employers; each of Barbel's ships had a different armateur. This concentration on slaving could be most lucrative, and many big armateurs were sons of ship's captains.

Other officers did not fare so well financially, but they did not share the captain's responsibilities. A typical slave ship carried from four to ten staff officers depending on the size of the vessel. Assisting the captain were the second captain and up to three lieutenants, all of whom were active, especially along the African coast. While the captain was ashore conducting the trade, the second captain remained aboard the ship, and the lieutenants guarded the trading merchandise which had been unloaded. Occasionally, the lieutenants and second captain disembarked with some merchandise to trade slaves at a secondary site while the ship continued on to the primary trading area. Away from the African coast, these officers had little specific to do and even had to work like simple sailors in case of rough weather.

Since their positions were directly related to the trade, they received handsome wages—from 50 to 100 livres monthly—often augmented by small commissions and bonuses. The other members of the staff concerned with sailing were the ensign, the pilot, and the apprentice pilot, who was optional. These men received modest wages of less than 50 livres per month, but they could look forward to promotions on future expeditions. As officers, they were capable of estimating the ship's position and could keep a logbook, skills learned at an officers' training school such as the one run by the Jesuits at Nantes.[38]

The other members of the staff were the doctor (surgeon) and his assistant or assistants. The presence of at least one doctor was mandatory, and some armateurs hired two or more, depending on the size of the ship. Although responsible for health and hygienic conditions on the ship, the ship's surgeon, like his terrestrial colleagues in eighteenth-century France, disposed of only the most rudimentary weapons for the fight against disease.[39] The doctor aboard the *Phénix,* which departed from Bordeaux on October 14, 1740, had about 150 different "remedies and medicines" of which only a handful probably had any healing properties.[40] Divided into cordials, syrups, waters, oils, balms, plasters, salts, unguents, spirits, and drugs, the doctor's medicine cabinet included everything from almonds and dates to peach syrup and cinnamon water. Learning to use these remedies was a lengthy if not exacting process, and it was one of the surgeon's duties to teach students in the art of healing. The Compagnie des Indes "wanting with all its power to work for the conservation of the men it employs on its ships" was particularly interested in training new doctors, and required each ship's surgeon to devote an hour daily to medical instruction.[41] The company asked each doctor to give practical lessons in diagnosis and treatment of the "diseases he had to treat, at sea or in port, even of those of the Negroes."[42] For his efforts, the doctor received about 50 livres monthly.

Beneath the staff officers were two groups of petty officers, the *officiers-mariniers* and the *officiers-non-mariniers.* There were up to seven officiers-mariniers, although only three were essential, the master, the bosun, and the carpenter. The master—aided by the bosun—was responsible for discipline and for the performance of the captain's orders; this merited a respectable salary of over 50 livres per month plus the odd commission or bonus. Besides incidental repairs, the carpenter (or carpenters on a large ship) had two important tasks to perform: he had to transform the emptied cargo area into a hold for the slaves, and he had to construct the temporary post where the captain would trade slaves in Africa. Other officiers-mariniers included cannoneers, long-boat operators, and sail-makers. On average, a ship had between five and six officiers-mariniers, and they earned about 40 livres per month each. Of the six officiers-non-mariniers, only two appeared on every ship, the cook and the barrel-maker or cooper. The cooper, and on larger ships, his assistant(s) performed one of the most vital duties on ship: he was in charge of the water supply. Assuring an adequate supply of water for four hundred people for sixty days was a demanding task which the cooper accomplished by using emptied gunpower or liquor barrels. The other officiers-non-mariniers could be bakers, gunsmiths, and even chief stewards.

There was one other person whose presence was required by law but who rarely if ever sailed on a slaving ship—the chaplain. Usually the church "could not find a priest to go as chaplain aboard" the ship in question.[43] This dearth of priests was not caused by religious scruple—missionaries regularly sailed to Africa aboard slavers; it reflected the extreme danger and the large number of ships participating in the trade.

Officers comprised almost half the crew, sailors the other half. There were four groups of sailors, distinguished more by experience than by function. Almost all were of local origin. The most senior group consisted of *matelots,* able-bodied seamen who earned between 20 and 30 livres monthly. Then came the novices, who received somewhat less than 20 livres per month, and the ship's-boys, *mousses,* who earned less than 10 livres. Finally, there was the occasional volunteer, a young boy willing to work for nothing just to escape his native poverty. The life of these sailors was wretched; the ship offered no comforts, and death rates were alarmingly high. Even if the sailors managed to survive the voyage, they had little hope of making much money. Novices, mousses, and volunteers were particularly poor, and most owned nothing but the rags on their backs. Georges Rivière, novice aboard the *Prince de Paix,* died at sea on September 27, 1789, and left nothing, "having rotted everything during his illness."[44] Another novice, Martial Foudron, left behind only "three bad shirts, two pairs of long pants, one pair of stockings, and one African outfit"; all this was worth 3 livres.[45] Some sailors, usually matelots, fared somewhat better, but the poverty was nonetheless obvious. Martin Arpogens, matelot, died on Guadeloupe on December 24, 1768, while in possession of "five shirts, three vests, three pairs of pants, one jacket, one silk handkerchief, and one chest" worth a total of 32 livres.[46]

In spite of the poverty of the average sailor, the high salaries of officers combined with the senior command's taste for luxury to make the crew's wages an important expenditure for the armateur. An average slaver carried from thirty to forty whites during the eighteenth century, as growing ship sizes offset increased efficiency in terms of the ratio of men to tons. Since these crews cost the armateur over a thousand livres per month with three months paid in advance, and since the Admiralty forced the armateur to pay the crew the rest in cash almost immediately after the ship's return to France, a quick expedition became a major goal. Armateurs never tired of exhorting their captains to complete the triangle as rapidly as possible, and the merchants complained incessantly about what they considered to be the undue slowness of each step in the slaving operation. Normally, a few thousand livres would not upset the armateur too much, but any unnecessary cash outlays posed problems. Outside of the crew's wages, little was paid for in cash, and the merchant did everything in his power to limit these expenditures. Many armateurs found it easier to commit tens of thousands of livres in credit than to distribute thousands or even hundreds in specie.

Of course, the armateur never wanted to waste money and always tried to economize. This was especially true in the selection of a slaving ship. Once the armateur had a clear idea of the size of the operation he was planning, he bought an appropriate ship. Most seemed to have little if any interest in the ship, wanting only a vessel which could sail from France to Saint Domingue via Africa; even the return voyage to France was not critical. Armateurs appeared ready to use any ship available, and one merchant seemed content with a ship that would carry "400 to 450 Negroes, even 300 if the outfitting company has such a vessel."[47] This nonchalant attitude was quite extraordinary, as armateurs usually took an almost obsessive interest in every aspect of their work; apparently, they believed that the ship itself had little influence on the success of the expedition. Thrift was the true guiding light in choosing a ship, and judging from the lack of complaints about a shortage of used vessels, it seems that there was no problem in finding the "ideal" ship, one relatively old and large. Only occasionally did an armateur order a new slaver to be constructed, but again only the largest merchants could do this. Most traders wanted simply to refurbish an old vessel.

There was no such thing as a specialized slaving ship: any ship capable of transatlantic sailings was appropriate for the trade.[48] Since "ship techniques remained stable during the eighteenth century,"[49] merchants used the same basic type of ship throughout the century. The ships had either two or three masts and three levels: the hold reserved for food and water, the between-decks for the cargo or slaves, and the top-deck for the crew and officers. Owing to the ever-present danger of war or even of hostile native activity, the ships were quasi-military and carried several cannons. But the most salient characteristic of slave ships was their small size. The largest eighteenth-century slaving ship leaving France to sail the triangular route measured only 1,667 tons, and the average slaver before 1783 was only slightly more than 150 tons.[50] Actually, these already small figures have to be halved, because an eighteenth-century nautical ton was but half a modern one, measuring only 1.44 cubic meters instead of 2.83.[51] Thus in twentieth century measures, the average French slaving ship was less than 100 tons; it was some sixty-five feet long, nineteen feet wide, and ten feet deep. Given these dimensions, the celebrated drawing of the English slaver the *Brooks* seems most reasonable.[52]

The preoccupation with saving money so apparent in the dealings with the crew and in the selection of a ship also appeared in the purchase of "accessories." Even though the cargo always accounted for more than half the total expenses, traders believed that "it is not merchandise for the trade which makes outfitting expensive, it is the accessories like food for whites and blacks. . . ."[53] Nowhere was this implicit call for frugality better heeded than in the selection of equipment to be used by various members of the crew.[54] Only the most basic necessities found their way aboard a slaver; except for certain items bound for the captain's table, all luxuries were banned from the ship. The pilot, for example, had at his disposition only a few compasses and clocks to enable him to navigate between three continents. Navigation was more art than science in the eighteenth century, with guesswork and estimation far more common than precise calculation. We have already seen the meager contents of the surgeon's medical chest, which was equalled in its simplicity by the carpenter's toolbox and by the cook's kitchen. The food provisions were similarly frugal.[55] The slaves ate beans and rice, while the sailors and minor officers had a diet of crackers, salted meat, and salted cod, relieved only by a large reserve of wine and spirits.[56] Only the major officers enjoyed a varied regime including live poultry and animals, cheese, numerous vegetables, and spices. The captain's table reflected the sole true luxury aboard a slaving ship.

The money saved by purchasing only the most basic nautical necessities was used in the selection of a trading cargo. Frugality in this domain could hurt the expedition, so the slaver carefully supplied his captain with enough merchandise to ensure an abundant trade. The cargo could cost well over 200,000 livres, but it could bring commensurate returns. It was up to the individual French armateur to assemble a cargo which would appeal to African tastes. This was a sensitive business, given the variety of African demands: depending on the time and place, African sellers of slaves preferred a wide variety of European or Asian goods. African merchants normally bought four types of merchandise from French traders— cloths, jewelry, arms, and alcoholic beverages, valued in that order. The textiles, known by such exotic names as *guinées, liménéas, indiennes,* and *neganépaux,* were usually of Indian origin and imported by the Compagnie des Indes or by the Dutch; only towards the end of the old regime were some produced in France. Most of the material was cotton, and it came in white, in various solid colors of which blue was the most popular, and imprinted with striking designs. For the most part, jewelry meant brightly colored beads—*rassades* or *cauries* (cowries)—used in making necklaces, bracelets, and earrings and serving as money along the African coast; the French usually procured these in Amsterdam. The French had to turn to England to find rifles to trade with the Africans; those manufactured in Saint Etienne were considered inferior and more expensive than their British counterparts.[57] Other armaments sent to Africa included pistols, swords, knives, and ammunition. French slavers also traded large quantities of local spirits, or *eaux-de-vie*, for slaves, and even wines were occasionally sold.

After having purchased a ship, recruited a crew, and assembled a cargo, the armateur finished his preparations by completing certain formalities and by purchasing insurance. The admiralty required him to obtain a series of documents before the ship could legally sail. These administrative obligations—the record of which form the bulk of the extant documentation for the trade—had various purposes. One protected the interests of the investors by recording all sales of ship interests; another protected the sailors by registering the names and salaries of all who worked on ship. Other procedures enabled the government to collect different taxes and to verify the armateur's compliance with certain regulations, such as the transport of *engagés* on ships bound directly for the Antilles. Then (during most of the century) the armateur had to receive from the Compagnie des Indes the permission to trade slaves along the African coast. And finally, the armateur almost always insured his expedition,[58] even if he occasionally waited until after the ship's departure.[59] In times of peace, insurance was cheap, costing less than 5 percent of the estimated net worth of the expedition. During wartime, or even on the eve of war, insurance premiums soared, occasionally reaching 50 percent of the expedition's estimated value. In the larger ports, insurance was usually available locally, provided by groups of merchants banded together in numerous and invariably short-lived insurance companies. Some merchants, however, insured their ships abroad, and there were even instances of French merchants insuring their ships in England during periods of war with that country.

7

In Africa

The Voyage to Africa

After months of preparation the ship finally left the dock. If departing from Nantes or Bordeaux, another few days or even weeks might pass before it was able to leave the Loire or the Gironde and enter the Atlantic. Bad weather in the North Atlantic could cause grave problems, and many slavers never succeeded in leaving European waters. The ninety-ton *Chercheuse* left Nantes on March 7, 1754, and was immediately caught in a violent storm. Six days later, the ship sank off the Spanish coast, killing four of the crew and losing most of the cargo.[1] To avoid such dangers, armateurs preferred to schedule their departures for the calmer summer months, and about 55 to 60 percent of all slavers left France from May 1 through October 31. May, June, and July were the most common months to leave in, and December, January, and February the least popular; but slaving was a year-round commerce and even mid-winter departures were far from rare. This was because fall and winter sailings, though more dangerous, tended to be faster: leaving after October enabled slavers to sail directly to Africa along the European and African coasts, a voyage which took about a month less than the longer, circular route approaching the Brazilian coast.[2]

The choice of route to Africa was usually the armateur's and he transmitted it to the captain in the form of written orders.[3] Outside of specifying the basic plans for the expedition, the independent armateur gave few precise instructions; only the Compagnie des Indes, relying on its agents in Africa, could realistically be exacting in its directives. Individual merchants told the captains in which region to trade slaves, how many slaves

73

to trade, and which colonial commodities to buy for the returning cargo. They then filled their instructions with general observations on slaving. Typical were these remarks of an eighteenth-century armateur:

> The captain will begin to trade at the top of the coast and will go from coastal port to port, stopping for appropriate lengths of time where he expects to do some business. . . . He will take only young, good, and healthy [slaves]. . . . He will not go beyond Popo unless he has been well assured that business is good at Juda. . . . We approve of all the stops and dealings which he will effect for the good of our interests.[4]

The armateurs would then stress the importance of a quick trade and advise the captain to prevent the crew from mistreating the human cargo. He would last of all list the merchants with whom the captain was to consult if necessary. A captain leaving from Nantes, for example, would know whom to contact if he had to anchor in La Rochelle, Bordeaux, Lisbon, Cadiz, Martinique, each of the Saint Domingue ports, Brest, or Lorient. Given the primitive state of eighteenth-century communications, the armateur had to plan for every eventuality.

The typical voyage took from 80 to 130 days, or from three to four months. But some sailings were much shorter or longer. The *Superbe* left Le Havre on April 30, 1790, and arrived in Senegal only 29 days later,[5] but the *Heureux Captif* took more than six months to sail from Saint Malo to Angola.[6] One reason for the variation was the need for some ships to stop along the way. Ships leaving northern French ports often visited Lorient or Bordeaux to augment their cargoes. Similarly, many French slavers anchored at Lisbon or Cadiz in order to purchase more exotic trading merchandise. Further south, stops were often required for food or repairs; the Canary Islands were a favorite destination of French ships. Depending on conditions, these stops could add several weeks to the slaver's sailing time, besides costing the expedition thousands of livres.

There were a few hazards on the voyage to Africa, but these were well known. One navigational problem arose near the Canary Islands, where many ships ran aground in the channel between the islands and the mainland. To avoid further losses, the French government proposed a safe route and then instructed all captains to follow it.[7] Only sudden, violent storms caused real danger to the Africa-bound expedition, and life aboard ship was as near to pleasant as it could ever be on a slaver. Sailors did not have to fear slave revolts or diseases carried by tropical waters, and although crew mortality would rise to one in six before the end of the expedition, deaths were relatively rare on the first side of the triangle. Safe for the moment from death, crew members could "enjoy" a standard of living which was higher than the poverty they left behind in Brittany. Even if the sailors had no comforts and lacked blankets, beds or hammocks, and cabins, they still received enough food to keep them alive and healthy. This was already a great advance over their prospects in poverty-stricken France. Each sailor was entitled to a quart of wine daily, while each week they ate four meat meals, three of fish, and seven of vegetables.[8] During the voyage to Africa, most of this food was still in a reasonably decent condition. The water in particular was good, having come from France and not having had time to spoil.

On the African Coast

The voyage ended when the ship finally arrived in African coastal waters south of the Sahara. In the eighteenth century, the coast was the only part of Africa most Europeans ever saw. Although the Atlantic slave trade influenced the development of many interior African societies, few Europeans ventured far from the shore. Hence the slavers knew Africa only as a giant port or trading post abounding in gold, ivory, gum, and especially slaves. Commercial considerations were paramount in eighteenth-century European-African relations: while local conditions occasionally enabled or even encouraged European involvement in local politics, colonization was not the major goal at this time.[9] Even the forts established in Africa by various European maritime powers were mainly to facilitate commercial relations with the natives. The outposts had little military value and did not serve as bases for the conquest of the interior.

Upon arriving in African waters, the captain had to decide where to conduct his trade. Unless he worked for the Compagnie des Indes, the captain had in practice almost complete discretion in choosing a trading site. This was a difficult decision depending on several considerations. Two negative factors set some limits to the range of possibilities: foreign domination and French governmental regulations. The French had little power in Africa. Although they claimed to have been trading with black Africa since the fourteenth century,[10] it was not until the late seventeenth century that commerce in slaves and gum led France to take a serious interest in the continent. But by the time the French "returned" to Africa, much of the coastal trade was under the domination of Portugal and England, and France never succeeded in establishing itself as an African power during the old regime. French weakness was a perennial source of difficulty for French merchants trading along the coast. Harassed by the Portuguese, British, and Dutch, the French had to avoid confronting their European competitors, and fear of foreign interference influenced the captain's decision of where to dock. Besides fear of hostile foreign activity, restrictive government regulations affected the choice of a trading site: at any moment the government might declare certain regions closed to independent French traders in order to protect the exclusive privileges of the large companies. This happened in 1786, when independent French trade near the Benin River region was banned so that Brillantais Marion might exercise a monopoly there. Usually, however, the government interfered with commerce only in Senegal, the center of most chartered company activity.

These negative factors merely set limits to the slave trade, and a captain based his choice of a trading site on positive considerations such as traditional reliability and current conditions. By the middle of the eighteenth century there was a wealth of information available about the African coast. Several decades of slaving had forced the French to acquaint themselves intimately with the sub-Saharan coast, and the results of their activities were frequently published. Former captains wrote memoires or even guide books describing the coast in detail and giving precise information about the art of trading. There thus developed a fund of common knowledge which armateurs and captains used in planning expeditions. The French learned to view the African coast with a discerning eye, and they distinguished between regions, preferring some and avoiding others. The planter Moreau de Saint Méry was merely echoing popular opinion when he described the characteristics of various tribes whose members might be purchased by Europeans. For example, Moreau liked the Senegalese, whom he found "big and well made . . . intelligent, good, faithful . . . very sober and very calm,"[11] but he condemned slaves from the Gold Coast as "liars . . . and drunkards."[12] Captains were well versed in this common knowledge and usually tried to act in accordance with the popular dictates; only the most desperate of traders would accept a cargo of Mousombés, "cannibals" from the interior of the Congo who possessed the "most hideous personalities."[13]

Of course, the armateur had given the captain vague intructions, but once the ship was actually on the coast, these general instructions had to be interpreted in the light of specific conditions. An armateur might have ordered a captain to conduct his trade along the Angolan Coast, for example, but the captain still had to decide between Luanda, Cabinda, and Malimbe. Occasionally armateurs specified more exact locales—for instance, Honfleur merchants insisted on Gabon because of the lack of competition[14]—but such precision was rare, and the captain usually had to learn the situation obtaining on the coast and act accordingly. He had to find out how many slave ships were in port, how many slaves had been delivered recently, what quality and quantity of slaves were still available, and how much they cost. On the basis of these investigations, he chose his primary trading site, although he was well aware that many sites might have to be visited before the trade was concluded.[15]

Not counting the modest, and only recently developed, trade in East Africa, the French traded slaves in four regions extending from Senegal to Angola. Although the boundaries between these regions were reasonably well delineated on maps, they tended to blur beyond recognition in written accounts of the trade; expeditions marked on certain documents "to the Guinea Coast" might proceed to the Gold Coast or even the Angolan Coast, thereby rendering a precise statistical study of individual slaving sites all but impossible.[16] Only the trade with Senegal was closely regulated by the French. The nearest region to France, Senegal was more properly a part of the Guinea Coast region, but it always stood apart for administrative reasons; as Rambert noted, "Senegal constituted a forbidden zone for independent traders."[17] In fact, Senegal was the private preserve of the chartered companies almost from its "discovery" by France in the mid-seventeenth century.[18] This was not a consequence of the slave trade but of the lucrative commerce in gomme; companies were given a monopoly over the Senegal slave trade almost as an afterthought. The first company to acquire exclusive rights in Senegal was the Compagnie des Indes Occidentales in 1664; it was succeeded in 1672 by the Compagnie du Sénégal, and in 1719 by the Compagnie des Indes. Although the Compagnie des Indes continued to exercise its Senegalese privileges long after it had all but abandoned other African rights, it finally ceased slaving operations there after the War of the Austrian Succession. Then, as a result of the Seven Years' War, France ceded most of Senegal to England, retaining only the island of Gorée and its continental dependencies. With the subsequent death throes of the Compagnie des Indes, the Senegal trade was finally opened to all Frenchmen in 1767, a rather specious concession in view of the English control over most of the mainland. Even this limited freedom was revoked in 1777, when the French government gave the exclusive slave rights at Gorée to the Compagnie de la Guyane, rights the company kept until the end of the old regime.[19] In spite of all restrictions, the company outpost at Gorée was still important to independent French traders; not only did the company fort signify a French presence in the area, it also served as a convenient and secure resting place for French ships, particularly those on the way south along the direct route.

Just beyond Senegal was the Guinea Coast, at first glance the most popular destination for French slavers. This was illusory, for "Guinea Coast" was used in many eighteenth century documents to represent any portion of the African coast where slaving operations might take place. In reality, the Guinea Coast was of secondary importance. Extending from the Senegal River to Cape Palmas, near what is now the Liberia–Ivory Coast

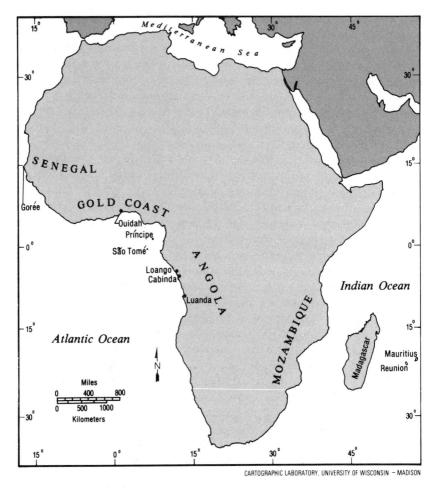

2. Africa: Major Trading Sites for the French

border, it had two major parts, the Senegambia region and the Sierra
Leone region. As we have just seen, Senegambia included the coast between the Senegal and Gambia rivers and was treated as a separate trading
zone by the French. The Sierra Leone coast went from the Gambia River
to Cape Palmas and contained two important trading sites, one at the
mouth of the Sierra Leone River, the other on the Iles de Loos.

East of the Guinea Coast was the Gold Coast, one of the two major trading
regions for French slavers. Although the Gold Coast also belonged to the chartered companies for most of the eighteenth century, it was usually open to all
French merchants upon payment of a nominal imposition. The Gold Coast
welcomed about half of all French slave ships and was especially popular dur-

ing the earlier part of the eighteenth century. As defined by eighteenth-century French merchants, the Gold Coast had three sections with rather uncertain frontiers. The first section was along the shores of what is now Ivory Coast; but this area was largely ignored by French captains continuing to the Gold Coast proper. Including modern Ghana, Togo, and part of Benin, the Gold Coast was renowned for its markets at Accra and Grand-Popo. A bit further came the geographic and perhaps numerical center of the French trade, the Slave Coast. Located on the Bight of Benin, the Slave Coast was composed of most of modern-day Benin and western Nigeria. This area boasted active sites like Badagri and Porto Novo, and it contained the only permanent French outpost in black Africa, Ouidah.[20] Founded in 1671, Ouidah was one of several French outposts established along the African Coast, but the only one to function without interruption until the end of the old regime. It was the largest of the European forts in the area and was run by eleven whites, who oversaw the labors of over a hundred blacks. Situated in a highly productive slaving region, the outpost at Ouidah served the needs of a large number of French slaving ships, and it was quite normal for most slavers to make at least a stop there. When conditions were reasonably favorable, captains preferred the security, comfort, and stability of Ouidah to the uncertainties of other sites.

The last major slaving region was the Angolan Coast, which ran from the Bight of Biafra to the southern boundaries of present-day Angola. The Angolan Coast had two parts: the north, including what are now Cameroon, Rio Muni, and Gabon; and the south, Angola itself. Although the northern section was not particularly popular—Honfleur merchants traded at Gabon because of the lack of competition—it did have a major site at Galbar. The southern portion was probably the most visited area in Africa during the second half of the eighteenth century. Pushed further and further south by aggressive foreigners along the Gold Coast, French traders began to concentrate heavily on the Angolan trade.[21] Although Portugal theoretically controlled maritime commerce along this section of the African coast, the French usually managed to conduct their business there unhindered. Indeed, when Portugal did decide to enforce its claims to the area, French traders were genuinely surprised and upset.[22]

Having arrived at the chosen destination, the captain prepared to trade for slaves. If the captain worked for the Compagnie des Indes, he had little to organize himself, since most eventualities were explicitly covered in his detailed instructions from the company. Captain Le Seure, for example, was told exactly what to do:

> He will leave from the port of Lorient at the first favorable wind, to go to Ouidah on the coast of Guinea. He will stop at Goreé in order to deliver to the island governor a package from the company, as well as beans and porridge; he will also pick up fresh water and wood. The

company is writing to the governor, requesting him to supply any
needed goods to the captain, who will remain at Gorée as briefly as
possible; it being necessary for him to go to Ouidah as soon as he can.
Upon his arrival at Ouidah, he will unload the merchandise, food, and
other items which were loaded aboard his ship, and he will give them,
together with the company package, to Mr. Derigoin, or in case of his
death, to Mr. Detchegaray, assistant director of the post. Captain Le
Seure will be sure to get a receipt for the unloaded cargo. . . . Mr.
Derigoin is supposed to put together a cargo of blacks as well assorted
as possible; the company does not order Captain Le Seure to take a
certain quantity, but nonetheless estimates that he can take at least
400. The company advises him to load as many as he can and to take
great care of them during the crossing. . . . The intention of the company is that Captain Le Seure obey the orders given him by Mr. Derigoin, director at Ouidah. . . . Captain Le Seure will not leave the
coast until the director visits the blacks on the ship.[23]

Thus, a captain working for the Compagnie des Indes, particularly during the
brief period of active monopoly (1722-25), had merely to report to his superi-
ors in Africa and follow their directions. He took no real part in conducting
the trade and could do little but complain when his African contacts failed to
do an adequate job.[24] The advantages of such a system were obvious: by maintaining outposts in Africa, the Compagnie des Indes greatly facilitated its
trade and thereby saved money. On the other hand, it was expensive to man
trading posts on a permanent basis, and any lapse by the local managers could
throw several expeditions into chaos. In the long run, the company had to
abandon the slave trade, very possibly as a result of the outpost system.

Independent armateurs wishing to expedite matters occasionally copied
the company's system and arranged for agents to deliver slaves along the
coast. This was the system used in the Senegambia area by some Honfleur
merchants after the Seven Years' War.[25] Although the decline and ultimate
demise of the Compagnie des Indes left the Senegal slave trade open to all
Frenchmen, English control over most of Senegal meant that French traders
had to use the services of English agents living in Africa. The Honfleur-
based Compagnie pour la Rivière de Sierre Leone signed a contract with
some of these English intermediaries, agreeing to purchase slaves in British
outposts at predetermined prices. Merchants in other ports followed the
Honfleurais' example, and after 1770, contracts of this nature multiplied.
Although the French had to pay relatively high prices, they were assured of
an adequate and quick trade. The security of this system kept it alive even
after the 1783 Paris Treaty reestablished French rights over Senegal.

If the armateur had no prior contracts arranged, the captain was free to
trade in any fashion he desired. Some captains decided to try to make their
own arrangements with merchants in Africa. Mathurin David, for example,

captain of the *Comte Dazamar,* left Nantes on November 12, 1763, and stopped at Gorée for repairs thirty days later.[26] After a few unsuccessful attempts to trade slaves along various sections of the Guinea Coast, his ship entered the Gambia River on January 23, 1764. While there, Mr. de Batt, governor of Fort Jacques, proposed to sell David a total of sixty-five slaves: thirty-five men, twenty women, and ten children at least four feet two inches tall, all in good condition. David accepted the offer, and on March 10, a contract was signed in English, with delivery promised within two months. Such arrangements had the advantage of facilitating the trade, but they were singularly unreliable. Accords signed on the coast were scarcely binding in practice, and unscrupulous merchants might simply disappear after receiving advance payments. This, in fact, happened to David. The only sure way to avoid fraud in local arrangements with European merchants was to purchase slaves already on hand. Thus Captain Jean Arnoult purchased twenty-nine slaves from Mr. Bauduchiron, former employee in the royal stores at Ouidah, for 11,600 livres;[27] delivery was immediate. This rare type of cash transaction all but eliminated the possibility of cheating.

If the captain did not enter into any comprehensive agreements with white merchants along the coast, he had to conduct his trade in a more piecemeal and time-consuming fashion. Once he found the "ideal" location, he stopped his ship and began a long series of preliminary operations designed to assure a favorable trade. As soon as the ship docked, the French were truly in Africa and had to respect local customs. Failure to heed these could spell disaster for the expedition; a gaffe at a particularly critical moment could leave the captain with no market for his wares and hence with no slaves. Customs varied from site to site, but the general idea remained the same almost everywhere: the Europeans were on foreign soil and they had to acknowledge the supremacy of their African hosts. Satisfying the egotistic as well as the economic needs of the African kings and merchants was the surest way of guaranteeing an abundant trade.

Thus the wise captain sought the blessing of the native ruler even before dropping anchor "permanently." For example, the *Grand Duc de Bretagne,* whose captain was Achille La Vigne, arrived in the Loango harbor on May 31, 1715.[28] In spite of the fact that other ships were already engaged in the trade there, La Vigne went ashore "to see the king of the said place and obtain the permission to trade slaves." This was granted, but only after La Vigne paid the king and his sons gifts worth six or seven slaves. Occasionally, this first meeting with the king gave rise to an elaborate ceremony. When Captain Foures was about to encounter King Pepel of Bonny, the Frenchman ordered a cannon salute, which was heartily welcomed by the monarch. Then the captain was invited to drink a glass of "poison" to prove his confidence in his royal host. As the captain recorded, "I proudly took the brew and, full of confidence, I swallowed it with one gulp. Afterwards, the king's officials began to laugh over the trick they thought they had played on me. . . . The king solemnly rose; someone announced that I was agreeable to Pepel; and the farce of introduction was over."[29]

However important the psychological ramifications of the dramatic encounters between European and African, what really mattered was the barter. Here the differences between the whites and the blacks became most apparent: the slave trade brought together two civilizations with different notions of commerce.[30] In the end, the European conception of a profit-oriented trade won out over the African ideal of a fair trade, but in individual transactions Africans usually had the upper hand: they were at home, and they knew that the Europeans were invariably in a hurry and therefore inclined to accept any vaguely reasonable offer. The most obvious manifestation of the superior bargaining position of the Africans was the Europeans' need to offer gifts to most of the blacks involved in the trade. Depending on the circumstances, Europeans saw these gifts as either service charges or bribes demanded by local officials; the Africans may have considered gifts as proper features of trade. In any event, failure to provide enough free merchandise could lead to a virtual boycott of the culprit's wares. Since in many places the king was ultimately in charge of the trade, his favorites usually received the lion's share of the gifts. The presents could be expensive, and it was not unusual for a captain to part with a significant portion of his cargo merely to keep the king and his entourage happy.

Having gained official permission to do business in the area, the captain prepared his trade. There were numerous ways in which the actual trade was conducted, depending on the time and place. It was quite common, for example, for a captain to enter into a relatively long-term agreement with an African official or merchant. In exchange for immediate payments in merchandise, the Africans agreed to furnish a given number of captives by a certain date. Unfortunately, like the impromptu arrangements with resident European merchants, agreements with the Africans were unreliable. Most of the time, therefore, the captain had to purchase slaves one at a time from African merchants or officials. This usually meant that he had to establish an office or trading post, either by renting an existing building or by constructing a new one. Captain La Vigne, for example, paid for the right to trade slaves and then "took a store in the town and placed his merchandise in it in order to conduct his trade."[31] Captain Foures, on the other hand, ordered his carpenters to construct a new *baraquon* where he would do his business;[32] this was a two-story structure made of wood. The ground floor served as a storage chamber where the newly purchased slaves were placed each day; the trading merchandise was stored on the upper level. Once the cargo was moved ashore, the captain was ready to begin his trade. The gong was sounded, and the trade was officially under way.[33]

The trade moved slowly at first, and the French trader needed much patience. Since all depended on African merchants, there was little a captain could do besides wait for slaves to be offered to him. This was especially unnerving later in the eighteenth century when, as Raynal noted, the Africans began to take full advantage of increased European competition.[34] To overcome the problem, the French could only resort to further gift-giving. For example, when Gaspard Le Blanc, captain of the *Blazon,* had a great deal of difficulty in attracting Africans to trade with him, he credited the local king with seventeen captives "in order to facilitate the trade."[35] Bribery was necessary in virtually every phase of the trade, but nowhere was it more effective than during the actual trading process. Generous payments to the right men could win a ship priority in the presentation of slaves and thereby expedite the operation.

Where did the slaves come from? Depending on the region, they came either from coastal areas near the trading sites or from the interior of the continent. Although most whites remained confined to the ports, the Atlantic slave trade affected large areas of Africa, with the Africans themselves handling the mechanics of delivery. Here the European demand for slaves frequently meshed with existing African trading networks to provide an efficient slave marketing operation.[36] The African merchants who used these networks— which may or may not have been used to provide slaves before the advent of the Europeans[37]—could reap large profits for their efforts,[38] a fact which goes far towards explaining the success of the trade in Africa.

Besides enriching some kings and merchants, the transatlantic slave trade influenced the development of African societies. The exact nature of this influence, however, is unclear. Slavery and an internal slave trade certainly existed in Africa before the Europeans arrived; indeed, "the Portuguese first became involved in the slave trade as middlemen for internal West African demand."[39] What is not clear is the nature of this indigenous slave system. Some historians claim that particularly African notions of slavery obtained and that they were far more benign that their New World counterparts; slaves in some areas of Africa could achieve positions of considerable wealth and prominence in spite of their legal status.[40] This view has been challenged, and significant regional differences make it impossible to draw any firm conclusions.[41] It does seem clear that the sale of slaves in the seventeenth and eighteenth centuries was normally limited to people having no positive bonds with the seller, namely prisoners of war (particularly in West Africa) and criminals (especially in Angola).[42] As European demand increased, more and more of these rootless slaves were required, and many areas of Africa were consequently afflicted with endemic warfare and lawlessness. While it cannot be proven that the Atlantic slave trade was exclusively responsible for African warfare, the trade certainly encouraged it: Africans were now being enslaved for the sole purpose of being sold ultimately to whites.[43] Thus, the Atlantic slave trade did not, as its defenders maintained, merely sift off surplus Africans and transport them to the Antilles; it imposed significant change on many African societies and economies.

After acquiring captives, the African merchants conducted them to the trading site. When a merchant—or, indeed, anyone possessing captives—arrived at a trading site with his slaves, he was approached by a broker, who offered certain indispensable services.[44] Having the exclusive right to present slaves to the captain, the broker occupied a particularly powerful position. The captains appreciated the powers of the brokers and did not hesitate to bribe them in order to improve the trade. The brokers thereby profited doubly from the trade: not only did they receive bribes from the Europeans but they also kept a large percentage of the merchandise intended for the African merchants in payment for their slaves.

Once the merchant confided his captives to a broker, the latter began the actual trade.[45] Entering the chosen outpost's grounds, the broker approached the captain, who was sitting in front of the building. The broker brought only one slave at a time, and this slave was subjected to an extremely careful inspection by the ship's doctor. Knowing the exigencies of the colonial market, the French traders in Africa demanded perfection in their slaves, and the slightest faults diminished the captive's value. After the doctor gave his expert opinion on the condition of the captive, the captain began to bargain with the broker. This bargaining procedure was made especially difficult by the complex barter system employed. First, especially in Angola, the slave's sale value had to be established with reference to an abstract measure, and then an appropriate amount of varied merchandise had to be exchanged. Once the bargain was struck, the captain ordered his officer to pay the African. No less carefully than the surgeon had examined the slave, the broker scrutinized the merchandise. He then accepted it on behalf of the slave's seller. By this lengthy procedure the captain acquired one slave.

How much did the slave cost the French captain? Depending on the time, the place, and the bargaining abilities of the captain and the broker, slaves sold for 100 to 600 livres. Although the long-term trend was probably inflationary, variations could be so great at any one time or place that generalizations are almost meaningless.[46] There were several systems of calculation used in the sale of slaves, of which the best known were the ones prevailing at Ouidah and along the Angolan Coast. At Ouidah, the trade was controlled by the indigenous rulers, who set the prices. Late in the eighteenth century, the official prices were 11 *onces* for an adult male, and 8 onces for women and children.[47] An once, however, was a purely local measure used in barter and had nothing to do with French values; it represented an assortment of goods which the Africans desired.[48] One once, for example, could be worth one *ancre* (six gallons) of spirts, or four iron bars, or one piece of Guingamp cotton from India, or one piece of Siamese cloth, or two printed cloths from Anjou, worth in France 13, 23, 50, 55, and 56 livres, respectively. Obviously, local taste and the captain's cleverness were decisive. Along the Angolan Coast, the basic unit was the *pièce,* but there were several types of pièces. The most important was the *pièce d'Inde,* the theoretical value of a perfectly healthy, young, adult male; all slaves sold were evaluated in terms of the pièce d'Inde. A *pièce d'Inde* was worth a certain number of *pièces de cargaison,* each of which included a definite quantity of the various items of the cargo. Hence, the pièces de cargaison did not vary in value as widely as did the onces. On the Angolan Coast, the crucial bargaining came more over the number of pièces de cargaison granted for a pièce d'Inde than over the assortment of pièces de cargaison to be delivered. To take an example, in February 1768 an unknown captain purchased a total of seventy-eight African slaves— forty men, fifteen women, and twenty-three children.[49] Together these cost 2,452 pièces de cargaison: 1,425 for the men (or 36 each), 478 for the women (32 each), and 558 for the children (24 each). This worked out to two rifles, four power barrels, and about a dozen cloths for each pièce d'Inde or average man. Of course, if the African proved too demanding, the captain could always refuse to purchase the offered slaves. The log-book of the *Africain,* for example, reads "We traded for only one male captive, as they were too dear. . . ."[50]

The sale completed, the surgeon placed a distinctive mark on the captive's shoulder or thigh to signify ownership. These brands were useful in retrieving escaped slaves, and they also helped identify the captives' status. Most slaves belonged to the ship or expedition, but some belonged to the captain or officers; a few were even traded on behalf of merchants in France or the colonies. Hence, each class of slaves was marked somewhat differently, either by using a special symbol or by stamping them on different parts of the body.[51] With proof of servitude thus established physically, the slave was led into the post's "prison" to await transfer to the ship later in the evening. While the trade was going on, the carpenter had remained aboard the ship in order to modify its hold to accept the human cargo.[52] Basically, a new deck was constructed to accommodate the captives. The deck was divided into two chambers to separate the males from the females.

The bargaining system prolonged the trade for several months. The French were well aware of their reputation for slowness along the coast, but they attributed this to their discriminating tastes. As Nantes merchants wrote in 1762, "If our colonies would take defective blacks from us as they do from the English, our trade would be neither more difficult nor less abundant than theirs."[53] In any event, the trade usually dragged along painfully before all the merchandise was exchanged. The average French slaving ship spent about five months in Africa, although there were wide variations in the time spent by individual ships. The *Duchesse d'Orléans,* for example, left Le Havre on October 17, 1788, and arrived on the Gold Coast on December 30; only thirty-two days later, Captain Marcy finished his trade, having purchased some 338 captives.[54] This was in marked contrast to the *Belle Nantaise,* a forty-ton ship which departed from Nantes on June 14, 1764.[55] The ship reached Gorée on July 16 but subsequently encountered great difficulties; some twenty-nine months later, on December 10, 1766, it finally left Africa with a cargo of 45 slaves, or about 1 slave for each three weeks along the coast. During more typical voyages, about 2 slaves were procured daily. This was the case with one expedition in 1767-68.[56] The captain managed to purchase slaves on nineteen of February's twenty-nine days, and on each of those days he bought an average of 4 captives. Although he did succeed in acquiring 21 on February 3, he never again exceeded 6 in one day, and the median was 3. Unless prior arrangements had been made, slaving was invariably a time-consuming operation, even when only one site was visited. Finally, when the captain sold the last of his merchandise, or in the case of exceptionally favorable conditions when the ship was full of slaves, the trade ended. Amidst a certain fanfare, the captain distributed gifts to local authorities and prepared his ship for departure.

Usually, captains had to visit more than one trading site to complete their trade. A captain could either visit several sites in succession or he could let his officers conduct a separate trade at one site while he himself ran the primary trade elsewhere. In either case, the result was the same: one expedition took advantage of differing conditions along the African coast. Sometimes, however, this involved seemingly interminable sailings up and down the coast, such as those of the *Aigle,* commanded by Joseph Fougas.[57] After leaving Nantes on January 20, 1750, the ship arrived on the Banana Islands on February 28. Three weeks later, following a rest stop at Mazurade, the *Aigle* left for Namabou, where it arrived on April 15. After trading slaves there for over a month, the ship went to Accra and then to Ouidah. Fougas sent 54 slaves from Ouidah to Saint Domingue as freight aboard another slaver and then continued his coastal trade down to Cape Lobo. He returned to the Banana Islands on November 18 "to recommence his trade.'' This wandering continued almost without interruption until July 16, 1751, when the *Aigle* finally set sail for the Antilles with 176 slaves aboard. The disadvantages of this type of trade were obvious. It was clearly slower and more inefficient than the stationary trade, and it could take a high toll of crew and captives. On the other hand, a more mobile trade was necessary if few slaves were available at the initial site. Furthermore, a captain saved by not having to construct elaborate stores or give expensive gifts. Usually, however, a succession of moves indicated difficulties and was to be avoided if possible.

It was also common for an expedition to conduct two or more trades simultaneously. Usually this meant setting up one or more minor outposts under the direction of the second captain or a lieutenant, before the captain himself proceeded to establish the major trading post elsewhere. This was the procedure followed by Antoine Perroty, commander of the *Aimable Française* from Nantes:

> He arrived at Gorée on June 8, 1776. After having learned about the business situation there, he decided with the unanimous consent of his officers to establish a post at Portudal, near Gorée. As a result of this agreement, they left Sieur Liot, second captain, to run the post and conduct a trade there; and to this end, they gave him enough merchandise from the cargo to trade ten blacks. Having left Sieur d'Impre, ensign, at Gorée with other merchandise to trade as well . . . Perroty continued with his ship to Gambia . . . to conduct his trade.[58]

The chiefs of the two subsidiary outposts were instructed to work closely together and to obey any instructions which might come from the expedition's leader.

Often, to increase the expedition's chances of finding the best possible trading sites, the captain would leave the ship, and with a few men and some merchandise, take a small boat to sail independently along the coast. Usually the secondary vessel traveled in the opposite direction to that taken by the main ship, but occasionally it simply went up a narrow or dangerous river. For example, Captain Blanchard took four men with him in a launch to trade along the coast,[59] while Captain Lavallée took his launch up a small river.[60] Both captains left their ships to trade independently whenever the occasion might arrive; they thereby improved the chances of finding a truly advantageous trade. Similarly, multiple-ship expeditions enjoyed great freedom of movement under the command of one supreme chief. Auguste Seigne's *Entreprise, Union,* and *Concorde* sailed together to the African coast during 1769.[61] The three ships gave each other considerable aid when necessary, exchanging food and merchandise, but they also managed to separate to search out the best trading sites. Chance encounters along the coast between ships belonging to the same armateur could have similar results, although not having a commander in common hindered coordinated activity.[62]

No matter which trading methods were employed by the captain, life along the coast was scarcely enjoyable. The primary concern of the sailors was survival: keeping healthy in the unfamiliar tropical environment was difficult, and many died in Africa. Probably the single most important influence on health was the quality of the water, and almost every captain's report referred to the painstaking efforts taken to ensure a decent water supply. African water was notoriously foul, at least as far as European stomachs were concerned, and only few sites offered acceptable reserves. The oppressive atmosphere along the coast helped foster a spirit of camaraderie among slaving crews working on different ships from France or even from abroad. When peace reigned in Europe, slavers from different countries could deal with one another amicably, and food, merchandise, and slaves were exchanged without problem between ships flying different flags. Usually such transactions were carried out through barter, but sometimes letters of exchange were used, with payment deferred until the safe return of the creditor. Even a sort of rough postal service was provided by ships about to leave African waters. Captain Foures of the *Africain,* for example, asked a friendly English captain to carry some letters to Barbados and then to post them to France via London.[63] The Englishman agreed.

Occasionally, more selfless aid could be given, especially in cases of nautical disaster. When the *Roi Morba* went aground in a small African river, its captain Adrien Doutran asked for assistance from Captain Penny of the English ship *Cavendish.*[64] Penny promptly ordered his second to take five men in a dinghy and attempt to extricate the French ship. But the most compelling force for unity was fear of the Africans. In the face of the common black enemy, Europeans of all nations joined together for mutual defense. On one occasion, Captain Luc Jolly left 116 slaves aboard the *Bienfaisant* under the eyes of six sailors and went ashore with the rest of his crew.[65] This prompted the captives to revolt, take over the ship, and kill the six whites. Seeing the trouble and responding to Jolly's pleas, a neighboring English ship began to fire on the *Bienfaisant.* Although the gesture proved futile—most of the slaves managed to escape and the ship was lost—it reflected the natural bond which linked white slavers of different countries.

Friendly relations with other Europeans did not solve all the problems of the African coast. As we have seen, simply staying alive was not something to be taken for granted. Besides falling victim to poisonous waters, French sailors were continually menaced by contagious diseases. Indeed, so great was the fear of epidemic that captains risked immediate loss rather than expose the expedition to a communicable malady. Captain Mathurin David of the *Eole* alleged that on one occasion he ordered five captives suffering from scurvy to be taken ashore in order to keep the disease from spreading (!) to the other slaves and to the crew; poorly guarded, the five quickly escaped.[66] Although David might well have fabricated this story to account for a deficient trade, it still reflects the great fear of contagion: David's action was accepted as perfectly natural. Diseases threatening slave ships included malaria, yellow fever, smallpox, scurvy, and dysentery, but there were undoubtedly a good many other, and more peculiarly African, diseases. Any combination of these ailments could be devastating, as it was for the *Deux Pucelles*.[67] Within a four-month period in 1751, the crew lost its captain, second captain, and two lieutenants, and an officer from another French ship had to take command of the expedition.

In addition to serving as a fertile ground for microbes, slaving ships were dangerous from a strictly nautical point of view. The African coast was as dangerous, if not actually more dangerous, than the high seas, and many a ship met with disaster in the treacherous currents and winds of West Africa. Although government directives and guidebooks aided the captains in their struggle against the elements, few French slavers left the coast unscathed. Most damage was relatively minor, but occasionally a ship had to be abandoned. Such was the case of the *Jeune Reine* in 1769: "They left for Gambia where, having struck a bank at the mouth of the Gambia River, the ship was lost."[68] Usually, however, rocks or storms claimed a mast or an anchor or caused more or less serious leakage. Minor damage could be repaired immediately by the carpenter, and new parts could often be purchased from passing ships.[69] More serious repairs might necessitate a journey to a European, usually Portuguese, outpost with proper dock facilities. The need to work constantly on the ship was apparently considered normal, especially given the antiquated nature of most slaving vessels. Indeed, it may be that the very inevitability of damage influenced the outfitters' decision to employ used ships.

Almost all the other problems encountered by French expeditions along the African coast were more closely related to the slave trade itself. Even disciplinary difficulties usually stemmed from the trade. Although general mutinies were not unheard of,[70] they were certainly rare and much less important than the problems brought on by the practice of trading *pacotilles*. A pacotille was a package of merchandise carried aboard the slave ship but having nothing to do with the expedition's cargo. It belonged to either an officer or to a French merchant, and it was to be traded by an officer for his own account or for the account of his associate in France. The practice of permitting these separate trades led to conflicts of interest which were inevitably resolved in favor of the private trade. Given a choice between working for his own account or for the good of the expedition, the officer with a pacotille sacrificed the armateur's interest. A classic case of the problems posed by this type of private trade occurred aboard the *Aimable Française*.[71] As we have seen, Captain Perroty ordered his second, Sieur Liot, to remain in the Gorée area while the ship continued on to Gambia; Liot was to trade for slaves until recalled by Perroty. On July 28, 1777, some five weeks after leaving for Gambia, Perroty wrote to Liot and requested the second captain to finish his trade and continue on to Gambia. When Liot ignored this command, Perroty sent a small boat to fetch him, but Liot refused to go, saying "that he had a lot of money to collect for a pacotille which he had taken aboard furtively and that he could not go right away." Preoccupied with his private trade, Liot did not rejoin the ship until December 28, thereby causing "considerable loss to the expedition." To combat the negative effects of these private trades, many armateurs explicitly forbade their employees to take pacotilles on the ship. The Compagnie des Indes, for example, warned Captain Le Seure against such practices: "Captain Le Seure will not conduct any private business either directly or indirectly during the expedition. He will prevent his officers from conducting any on any pretext. He will not allow any merchandise not belonging to the company to be taken aboard the vessel."[72] To compensate for this prohibition, the major armateurs paid their crews bonuses based on the number of slaves traded or on the mortality rate during the middle passage. Armateurs unable to pay such premiums often had to sanction private trades.

Disciplinary problems were relatively minor, compared with what might be termed political problems. The French in particular had no end of difficulty in Africa, in large part because of their military shortcomings. In some areas, effective local administrations spared the French many problems, but not all of the coast was well governed. Where strong kingdoms did prevail, the French, as the weakest of the foreign visitors, benefited the most from the rule of law. This was apparently the case of Ouidah in 1704, when the powerful king "imposed" a peace treaty on the British, Dutch, and French, and thereby saved the French from an obvious military disaster.[73]

African strength was not always so great, however, and in many areas the blacks had to be content with getting the Europeans to acknowledge formally African sovereignty. In these places, the French were at a marked disadvantage, not only militarily but commercially. In areas where effective government was lacking, all agreements, however "correct" technically, were particularly tenuous, and any contracts signed were subject to instant disavowal. Captain La Vigne suffered from this uncertainty: he arrived in Loango shortly after the signing of the Treaty of Utrecht but still found competition from a large number of ships already in the Angolan port.[74] To improve his position, La Vigne agreed with a Dutch and an English captain to pay the Africans a fixed amount for each slave offered; any captain breaking the agreement had to give his two colleagues four slaves. Although La Vigne and the Englishman kept their word, the Dutch captain soon broke the pact but refused to pay the penalty. Further, seeing La Vigne continue to conduct a prosperous trade, the Dutchman threatened any black merchants who persisted in trading with the French captain. La Vigne complained to the local ruler, who was incapable, however, of acting against the Dutch ship. Finally, La Vigne's outpost was burned to the ground, and in spite of the king's order that the Dutch captain should give La Vigne 200 captives, the French ship had to depart without any compensation. The African ruler had no desire to embroil himself in a battle with the Dutch, and the matter was presumably dropped.

The gravest dangers facing the French traders in Africa came when war broke out or appeared likely to break out in Europe. Where African authority was weak, coastal waters turned into European battlefields, and France lost many slaving ships caught in "neutral" waters when war erupted. Most disturbing were the measures taken by Britain to destroy French shipping even before war was declared. On July 15, 1776, for example, the *Lord of Dartmouth* dropped anchor alongside the *Grue,* trading in Gambia.[75] The British captain then presented the French captain with a letter from the British governor of Senegal ordering the seizure of all French ships in the area. In this manner, Britain interfered with French commerce more than a year before declaring war. Similar hardships were suffered by French slavers immediately following wars, for primitive communications kept enemy ships ignorant of the peace.[76]

Even when there was no threat of European war, encounters between French and foreign slavers could hurt the French. It was not unusual for French captains to find traditionally open areas suddenly closed by a competing power. Typical was the case of the *Venus,* whose story was told by its armateur in a letter to the Guienne Chamber of Commerce (Bordeaux).

Jean Auger, merchant in this city, has the honor of reporting to you that on March 11, 1737, he sent his ship, the *Venus* of Bordeaux under Captain Jean Cordier, to the Guinea Coast to trade slaves and to enjoy the privileges accorded by His Majesty. He arrived on the Guinea Coast on April 27 of the same year and continued to Anamabou, where he found twelve English vessels trading. Sieur Cordier, captain of the *Venus,* began to conduct his trade there in spite of the opposition of the English. He stayed for twenty-one days with the twelve English vessels trading there. On August 17, two coast guard vessels of the King of England arrived in the harbor. As soon as they anchored, all the captains of the English merchant ships went aboard to complain about Sieur Cordier, commander of the *Venus* of Bordeaux. Then the English commander took his launch to board the *Venus* to oblige it to leave, saying that the port was not for the French, that they had paid large fees to the King of Anamabou to trade there alone, that the French had paid no such taxes. . . . In spite of all the entreaties made to the English commander, Captain Cordier was forced to raise anchor and leave the harbor, together with the greater part of the merchandise brought from France. He went to Saint Domingue, not being able to go elsewhere, given the wars taking place down the coast at Petit and Grand Popo, Juda, Appa, and Patagris. He was obliged to leave on August 27 for the French colonies in America, where he arrived on January 20 of this year, with 198 blacks. During the crossing, 180 died, since he was not able to load enough provisions for 378 blacks. . . .

Since the Guinea trade is the principal source for the introduction of blacks whom our colonies need every day, I hope, sirs, that you will tell my lord Count Maurepas of the wrong perpetrated by the English, and that it is in His Majesty's interest that his subjects have the liberty to trade in the port of Anamabou and that they enjoy the privileges accorded them.

[Signed] J. Auger[77]

Obviously, Cordier could do little in the face of overwhelming British naval power. He had to trade elsewhere and save his complaints for French authorities in France; no local British administrator would have supported his claims.[78]

Although they were too weak to challenge their European antagonists with arms, the French were prepared to resort to armed force against Africans displaying overt hostility towards the whites. One such incident occurred on April 27, 1770, and was reported by Captain Hardy of the *Marie*.[79] On that day, the King of Dimby, along with some retainers, asked permission to board the ship in order to sell two slaves. The captain allowed them to come aboard, but as soon as they did, they began to shoot all the whites. They succeeded in killing every Frenchman on the ship except for the pilot, the master, and the carpenter, who saved themselves by means of the launch. Meanwhile, when Africans on the shore saw what was happening, they came out to the ship, evacuated the slaves, and hid them in the woods. Although one of the three eye-witnesses blamed *un anglais* for the events, the wholesale slaughter of the French plus the liberation of the slaves probably reflected at least one African's feelings towards the trade.[80]

The Africans welcomed the opportunity to rob all Europeans, and ships in difficulty were vulnerable. The French were particularly vulnerable because of their weakness in Africa, and Africans may have preyed on them, knowing the unlikelihood of retaliation. When the *Cote d'Or* was stranded on a sand bank near Bonny in 1768, it was approached by "over one hundred rafts" each with "thirty to sixty blacks" carrying sabers, knives, and rifles.[81] The captain later reported that "more than 3,000" of the Africans boarded the ship and stole everything in sight. Only the appearance of two English ships saved the crew; the English rescued the French from certain death and took them to safety on São Tomé. Although the captain was perhaps exaggerating, the broad outlines of his story were undoubtedly true, as was the conclusion that troubled French ships were considered fair game for aggressive Africans.[82]

Although the trade encouraged hatred which could provoke armed conflict, relations between the French and the free Africans were usually peaceful albeit cold. Economic interest dictated accommodation, and the French were even hopeful that contacts realized through the slave trade would lead ultimately to a certain Europeanization of Africa. The French believed that once the Africans came to depend upon European commerce, it was only a matter of time before the blacks—like European peasants—would learn "true civilization." Thus, when considering trade with Madagascar, the Nantes merchants dismissed fears of barbarism:

> The same thing used to be said about the blacks along the African coast, but nevertheless, commerce in general civilized them in such a manner that the Europeans can deal and trade with them in confidence. The same thing will happen with the men from the interior of Madagascar if they are treated well and if one trades with them in good faith. Soon they will come of their own to offer their slaves, their beasts, their food, and their merchandise in exchange for those of Europe and Asia. . . . Instead of being our enemies, they will become our friends.[83]

The traders clearly hoped that business comradeship would overcome difference in skin color and culture.

Although no such understanding was conceivable between white owner and black captive, necessity nonetheless encouraged these implacable enemies to co-exist on peaceful terms. The trader wanted his captives to survive in good health, at least until they landed in the Antilles, while the slaves usually submitted from fear of horrible reprisals. It was precisely the twin sentiments of humility and hatred which gave rise to the conflicting views of the eighteenth-century African slave. On the one hand, there was the image of the submissive slave, an image reinforced by the claim that the Europeans were actually saving the Africans from an even more cruel fate.[84] Like sheep going to the slaughter, these docile slaves went unprotesting to the end. Even when they expected a fate worse than servitude, the humble Africans submitted.[85] On the other hand, there was the fierce rebel determined to resist the white in every way. While the ship remained on the coast, the captives had a positive goal, escape. Some slaves managed to evade their new owners even before boarding the ship; these escapes were made quickly and bloodlessly, the captives simply vanishing into the forest. Slaves who had already been taken had to gain control over at least a part of the ship before they could flee to safety; this usually involved violence and often ended in the death of one or more crew members. If escape was impossible, some slaves apparently resorted to self-mutilation or suicide. According to popular belief, the danger of such self-destructive actions were greatest while Africa was still in view, and knowledgeable writers urged a rapid departure. As Savary noted,

> it should be said that the moment one has completed one's trade and loaded the Negroes on the ship, one must set sail. The reason for this is that the slaves have such a great love for their land that they despair to see that they are leaving it forever, and they die from sadness. I have heard merchants who participate in this commerce affirm that more Negroes die before leaving port than during the voyage. Some throw themselves into the sea and others knock their heads against the ship; some hold their breath until they suffocate and others starve themselves.[86]

How many slaves succeeded in regaining their freedom or in killing themselves is unknown, but the number was probably not large. Captains reported few evasions or suicides, even though such events would have made excellent excuses for poor trades.

8
Completing the Triangle

The Middle Passage

With Savary's admonition in mind, the captain prepared to leave Africa immediately upon completing his trade. The armateurs always stressed the need to depart as quickly as possible from the coast, since they feared everything from contagious disease to mass suicide. As one armateur wrote, Captain Hamont "will leave the coast as promptly as he can and he will set sail for Cap Français without wasting time."[1] The Captain could not, however, simply set out for the colonies the minute the last slaves entered the specially constructed hold; he had to make certain that the ship had adequate provisions for a transatlantic crossing and that the captives were in a reasonably good state of health. For these purposes, a stop on the Portuguese coastal islands of São Tomé or Príncipe was especially useful. To begin with, the islands had abundant reserves of acceptable drinking water, a vital commodity for the more than three hundred people making the two- to three-month crossing. Since the French could not safely drink the water found along most of the coast, visits to São Tomé or Príncipe became quite common for French slavers. A slaving ship might spend from two to six weeks in the Portuguese islands while the cooper painstakingly sealed one barrel of water for each passenger and then stored the barrels in the lower levels of the ship's hold. Needless to say, armateurs reminded their captains of the high costs involved in lengthy stays on the Portuguese islands, but the captains were not willing to leave before they were fully prepared for the long voyage.

Besides providing water for the slavers, São Tomé and Príncipe offered

French ships an abundance of cheap food, albeit of apparently dubious quality.[2] Although some food for the slaves was taken from France, most had to be purchased in Africa; after several months on the coast, not enough remained to feed a large number of people for eight weeks. This was especially true because, as Rinchon established, approximately ten tons of food were needed during the crossing for each one hundred slaves.[3] But, as was the case with water, acceptable food was not easily found along the coast, and thus a stop at the Portuguese islands became even more necessary.

While visiting the islands, the French captains made the most of their time by "refreshing" their slaves. Giving the captives exercise, in fact, was sometimes the only reason for a stop, as it was for Captain Arnoult of the *Diamant*. After the captain had finished his trade at Ouidah on June 10, 1774, he "made for Príncipe in order to refresh his blacks there."[4] The ship remained on the island for over thirty days. It was important to return the slaves to good health before beginning the crossing; since some of the captives may well have been confined on the ship for more than a year already, they undoubtedly had need for considerable conditioning if they were to survive the rigors of the middle passage.

Having reloaded the slaves, and with adequate reserves of food and water, the captain finally gave the order to sail for the West Indies. Thus began the infamous middle passage, almost legendary in its horrors; it was traditionally known as the scene of bloody revolts, devastating contagion, and unimaginable cruelty. How true is this portrait of the crossing? In exceptional cases, it is very true: some voyages led to hideous fates which fully realized the wildest nightmares. But in most cases, the middle passage was not nearly as spectacular as imagined. Death was far more subtle in its methods: for each ship struck by a contagious disease or a bloodthirsty rebellion claiming more than 50 percent of the passengers, dozens experienced an "acceptable" death rate of 5 to 15 percent. The middle passage had its own norms for mortality, which over the century felled hundreds and thousands of people. Indeed, it was precisely this acceptance as unavoidable of a one-in-twenty to a one-in-five mortality rate which ultimately made the crossing so inhuman; merchants considered such losses tolerable and planned for them in their original calculations.[5] Even the Compagnie des Indes, which offered its captains bonuses based on low mortality rates, decided that a one-in-five death rate was commendable and worthy of financial support.[6]

Nautically, the middle passage was a simple affair. Ships leaving the African coast followed the currents westward to near the Ascension Islands and then turned north towards the Antilles. There were only three dangers to be faced on this route. First was the risk of encountering the doldrums, the windless area near the equator. Drifting aimlessly was catastrophic for a slaver because of the relationship between time at sea and mortality; hence experienced captains always steered clear of potentially wind-free areas. Second was the opposite danger of tropical storms, particularly near the Antilles. The third and most serious risk was that of Portuguese attack off the Brazilian coast. French slavers were virtually defenseless against such attacks, and captains had to leave the South Atlantic current before approaching too closely to Brazil. All told, however, the middle passage was not difficult technically, and almost all the important problems resulted from events on board ship.

A normal voyage from the African coast to the Antilles lasted from two to three months. Average sailing times from Africa to the West Indies remained fairly constant throughout the century, in spite of the growth of the French slave trade and the increased knowledge of the slaving captains. Le Havre average sailing times, for example, were very constant, ranging from sixty-one days at mid-century to sixty-four just before the French Revolution. This constancy reflected the lack of progress in French merchant shipping techniques during the eighteenth century.[7] As usual, there were wide variations in sailing times, with voyages taking anywhere from less than a month to over a half-year. The *Castries* of Le Havre made the short voyage from Senegal to the Antilles in only twenty-eight days, leaving on March 3, 1788, and arriving on the 31st.[8] At the other extreme was a second Le Havre ship, the *Frère et Soeur,* which left the Gold Coast on July 7, 1766, but did not reach Saint Domingue until January 8, 1767, some 185 days later.[9]

Although sailing time affected mortality rates, the relation between time at sea and death was apparently not as intimate in the French trade as it was in the Portuguese.[10] Herbert Klein has shown clearly that mortality rates on Portuguese slaving ships climbed sharply when the ships failed to arrive in Brazil within a certain time. He attributed this rise to diseases caused by bacteria-laden drinking water; after so many days at sea, the stagnating water became dangerous for human consumption. Such a clear-cut conclusion cannot be drawn about the French trade, perhaps because of the nature of existing documentation: there are no records of slave mortality during the middle passage alone. The captains' reports, which are the most comprehensive and presumably the most reliable documents available, regularly mention the number of slaves traded and the number delivered alive to the Antilles. But the captains did not specify where the slaves died, saying only that so many perished "either on the coast or at sea." Hence an epidemic on the coast could severely decimate the ranks of the captives even before the ship left African waters. An example of this was provided by the *Roi de Louangue* of Nantes.[11] This ship arrived on the coast on September 10, 1765, and left on August 15, 1776, for a stay of 339 days. The ship traded 401 slaves but delivered only 193 to Léogane (Saint Domingue) on October 4; in spite of a quick crossing of only 50 days, the mortality rate was over 50 percent. It seems probable, however, that the middle passage did not claim all or even most of the victims; the captain reported that twenty-one of the ship's thirty-four crew members died along the African coast, including eight in one five-week period. Since only one sailor died during the middle passage, it is likely that the majority of slaves also died before leaving the coast and that the quick crossing cost few lives.

Records from the Compagnie des Indes reveal somewhat more about slave mortality during the middle passage, and company statistics tend to confirm the importance of mortality along the coast.[12] Although the company's papers, like the captains' reports, mentioned only the number of slaves traded and the number delivered, the unique African organization of the company gave the figures a slightly different significance. Company ships did not usually have to spend much time on the coast, because resident agents accomplished the actual trade before the ship even arrived. Thus the ships set sail for the Caribbean shortly after loading the cargo of slaves, and almost all the captives who died while in the captain's possession did so during the voyage. This was particularly true after 1725, when the company no longer exercised its monopoly rights over the French slave trade. Sending only a few ships to Africa each year, the company did not overburden its African agents, and company captains were reasonably sure of finding a cargo already assembled. Slave mortality on company ships leaving Lorient from 1730 to 1739 was only 7 percent, exactly half the figure registered on non-company ships at the same time. Unfortunately, the company sample is limited to only twenty-two examples while there are more than one hundred for independent slavers, but the data are nonetheless instructive. Encouraged by offers of attractive bonuses for low mortality and exempted from long sojourns on the coast, company captains achieved remarkably low mortality rates after 1725. It is significant, though, that on company ships of the 1722-25 period—or during the days of active monopoly when company captains had to act much the same as independents—the mortality rate on company ships was only marginally lower than on non-company ships. This increased company rate was probably the result of a longer stay in Africa and not of any radical changes in the toll wrought by the middle passage. The statistics from the company suggest that the middle passage was responsible for about half the African deaths, the other half occurring before the ship left African waters.

Another indirect method of establishing the geography of slave mortality is by studying crew mortality. As implied earlier, conscientious captains noted the dates of death of their hapless sailors. An analysis of these dates shows the relative importance of the African coast as a place of death. On fifty-three ships returning to Nantes from 1764 to 1767, for example, 7 percent of the crew members perished during the middle passage. Many more, however, had died before the ship even left the African coast. Thus by the time the ship arrived in the Caribbean, over 17 percent of the sailors embarking in France had succumbed. On the same ships, some 16 percent of all slaves traded never reached the West Indies, and a large percentage of the captives undoubtedly were dead before the ships departed from Africa, their weakened bodies falling victim to unfamiliar diseases. But in spite of the statistical similarities, there were probably important differences between crew and slave mortality. Although the overall death rates of the two groups were similar—and the Nantes statistics are confirmed by Saint Malo records—it is very likely that the middle passage took a heavier toll among the blacks, while the coast was relatively more deadly for the whites. By the time the French slaving ship set sail from Africa, its crew members had been living on ship for several months, mostly in the inhospitable tropical environment. Since approximately one sailor in ten had already died, those who remained were in a sense the strongest and the most likely to withstand the rigors of the Atlantic crossing. In other words, life on the African coast represented a severe selective process, which claimed the weakest members of the crew. This weeding mechanism may not have affected the Africans so strongly. More familiar with the food, water, and climate of the region, the Africans could better tolerate life along the coast. Further, the blacks spent much less time on the ship before the crossing than did the white sailors. Thus the Africans faced a shorter and milder selective process on the coast and probably suffered more during the middle passage itself.

During the eighteenth century, nearly 150,000 captives died in French ships, either along the coast or while crossing the Atlantic. Of the 1,150,000 taken aboard French slavers, only 1,015,000 reached the Antilles; the rest simply perished—the century-long mortality rate was in the neighborhood of 13 percent. The rate, however, was far from constant, displaying a generally downward trend from 1713 to 1792. From the signing of the Treaty of Utrecht until the period of company monopoly, 18 percent of all captives purchased in Africa by the French failed to reach the Caribbean. The Compagnie des Indes managed to reduce this figure to 13 percent while exercising its monopoly over the French trade, and subsequent low company figures kept the toll at 13 percent from 1726 to 1736. Decreased company activity caused a slow rise during the next two periods, to 14 percent from 1737 to 1743 and 15 percent from 1749 to 1754; but from the Seven Years' War to the American Revolution, the rate declined sharply to 12 percent, where it apparently remained until the French Revolution.[13] The average mortality rates were far from universal, however, and some groups registered radically different figures. Slavers from Saint Malo, for example, consistently had lower than average rates, recording losses of 12 percent for the 1710 to 1734 period, 9 percent from 1747 to 1756, and 7 percent from 1763 to 1777. La Rochelle, on the other hand, had exceptionally high rates; the limited data from this port show 20 percent losses from 1763 to 1777 and 17 percent from 1783 to 1792. Individual variations were of course even wider. Several ships lost fewer than five slaves, and occasionally a ship would not lose any. At the other extreme were the disastrous losses suffered by the most unfortunate expeditions. Losses of more than 50 percent were not unknown, and several ships failed to complete the voyage to the French West Indies.

Most slaves fell victim to diseases, the most serious of which were scurvy and dysentery.[14] Both were slow to strike, hence the time element was vital. Scurvy became dangerous after four to six months of vitamin C deprivation, and amebic dysentery had a sixty-day incubation period. The slave ship was a floating time bomb primed to explode some six to eight months after arriving in African waters. An analysis of mortality rates aboard more than two hundred Nantes slavers from 1764 to 1777 confirms this conclusion. One out of every nine slaves traded by the French captains (11.4 percent) and one crew member in ten (10.5 percent) died either on the coast or during the crossing, with slower expeditions showing a markedly higher death rate among captives and crew alike. Ships taking less than seven months to conduct the trade and cross the Atlantic lost only 6.0 percent of the slaves; seven to nine months in Africa and on the middle passage meant a 13.5 percent loss; more than nine months yielded an 18.3 percent loss. Similarly, 7.7 percent of the crew died when the ship spent less than nine months either in Africa or on the crossing, but 15.1 percent on longer expeditions. Time, by aggravating vitamin deficiencies, by allowing diseases to incubate, and by provoking food shortages, was the most important element in determining slave and crew mortality.

There were other influences on the death rates, but they were felt in more ambiguous ways. For example, the number of slaves traded and the size of the ships used seemed to affect the death rate among the slaves, but not quite in the expected manner. In other words, there was no evidence that overcrowding led directly to higher mortality. Although smaller ships carried more slaves per ton than did larger ones, the small vessels had slightly lower mortality rates.[15] On the other hand, expeditions trading larger numbers of slaves also had lower mortality rates. The captain therefore was not afraid of loading the maximum number of captives; indeed, it appeared that the best policy for a slaving captain was simply to procure as many slaves as possible and sail west immediately. An abundant trade usually meant a quick trade and thus a relatively benign trade, whereas expeditions having trouble assembling their human cargo stayed far too long on the coast and suffered heavily for it.

Besides disease, brutality on the part of the crew could occasionally lead to slave deaths. The crew kept the captives under close surveillance at all times, and this position of authority could lead to abuses. For obvious business reasons, such mistreatment was universally condemned, with armateurs explicitly warning their captains to prevent it. As one armateur wrote, "During the crossing, the captain will always be on guard for some revolts and he will give such good orders to his officers that the said Negroes will not be mistreated."[16] But the very frequency of the condemnations suggested the persistence of the abuses. Although instances of mortal abuse were undoubtedly rare—the similarity between black and white death rates reflected the lack of fatal mistreatment—many crew members took advantage particularly of the female slaves' defenselessness. Second Captain Liot, whose insubordinate actions along the coast had already cost his expedition much time, was also guilty of rape. In spite of warnings to improve his conduct, Liot

> mistreated a very pretty Negress, broke two of her teeth, and put her in such a state of languish that she could only be sold for a very low price at Saint Domingue where she died two weeks later. Not content, the said Philippe Liot pushed his brutality to the point of violating a little Negro girl of eight to ten years, whose mouth he closed to prevent her from screaming. This he did on three nights and put her in a deathly state. . . . This Negro girl . . . finally admitted . . . that the said Philippe Liot had descended into the hold and had forced her by putting his hand over her mouth to prevent her from screaming, and that he had done this for three nights. This mistreatment and violence did so much damage to this Negro girl that she was sold in Saint Domingue for only 800 livres instead of the 1,800 livres she would have been worth.[17]

Since personal contempt for Liot, along with a desire to justify a poor trade, were behind the captain's decision to report the incident, it can only be imagined how many similar attacks went unreported.

Life aboard the fully loaded slave ship was tense, with both the crew and the captives living in fear of disease and revolt. In order to lessen the apprehension, a strict routine prevailed on ship; this also discouraged rebellions and inhibited the development of certain diseases.[18] Every morning, except of course during storms or after revolts, the captives were taken onto the deck, one at a time. As each slave appeared, the carpenter checked his chains, while the surgeon quickly examined his body and inquired about his health. He was then given something to stave off scurvy, such as vinegar or lemon juice, and allowed to use the toilet and to wash. The slaves then had their breakfast, the first of their two daily meals. While attached to a chain linking their feet, they consumed a quart of soup each. The soup, composed primarily of beans and rice, was prepared fresh for each meal. Occasionally corn meal, hot peppers, or salt were added to the mixture to give it more nutritive value or simply a better taste. The slaves also received water to drink three times daily, and on special occasions they were given a few drops of spirits. Around 4:00 P.M. they ate their second and final meal for the day, a virtual copy of the first. Then, after a bit of singing, they returned to the hold, where they were locked in for the night.

The main activities on board the slaver centered on cleanliness. Personal hygiene was important: healthier slaves lived longer and fetched higher prices in the Antilles. Hence efforts were made to keep the slaves in good physical and emotional condition. The male captives, who were kept naked in order to avoid vermin, showered at least twice weekly on the deck; they could also wash whenever they wanted. The female slaves, clothed in a minute piece of cloth which they washed daily, were ordered to wash themselves in semi-privacy each morning. From time to time all the slaves were given some oil for their skin, although this was most important just before the arrival in the West Indies. Every two or three weeks, the surgeon supervised the cutting of the male captives' hair from all over their bodies; the female captives were allowed, in groups of eight, to scrape off their hair themselves. In this manner, captains sought to prevent the spread of contagious diseases.[19]

Besides guaranteeing the personal hygiene of the captives, slaving captains paid attention to the cleanliness of their ships, and the major occupation of the slaves was cleaning the ship. The anonymous author of the "Observations touchant le soin des nègres dans un voyage de Guinée"[20] recommended that three squads of blacks be formed to clean the vessel. The groups would first divide the work equitably and then proceed to accomplish their respective tasks under white supervision. For the most part, cleaning the ship meant scrubbing and scraping everything from the decks to the hold, and this was done every two or three days in good weather. If the weather was bad, the hold where the slaves were kept had to be perfumed with anything from vinegar to incense, and any period of relative calm was used to wash the hold. The slaves had to wash out the toilets twice daily, and wash the entire vessel each evening. The foulness of the air breathed by the captives while in the hold caused some concern, and pains were taken to ventilate the slaves' quarters properly.

Even with all the required cleaning, the slaves had little to do most of the time, and it was the captain's responsibility to prevent a destructive or self-destructive restlessness from developing. The most important pastimes to engage the captives' attention were singing and dancing, activities which had the advantage of putting them in a good humor while giving them much-needed exercise. The slaves were encouraged to sing virtually at all times—during their work, after meals, before going to sleep—and some ships even provided a pair of drums to accompany the singing. Besides helping the slaves pass the time agreeably, wise captains also tried to give them something to look forward to as a reward for good behavior. Thus on Thursdays and Sundays, well-disciplined slaves were offered a small glass of watered-down spirits or a little morsel of beef, favors which gave them both pleasure and hope. Slaves were occasionally given a bit of tobacco to prepare and to chew, since the smoking of pipes aboard the wooden ship was strictly forbidden. According to the author of the "Observations," a clever captain could keep his slaves healthy and content merely by bestowing small gifts at judicious intervals.

Such niceties could not mask the fact that the ship was divided into white owners and black slaves, with the latter always seeking to overthrow the former. Little was or could have been known of the attitudes of the African captives toward their French masters, for the illiterate and possessionless slaves were truly a "people of silence."[21] Only in their actions did they display their true feelings, and it is in the records of slave revolts that their deepest sentiments are reflected. In fighting these nearly hopeless battles, the captives exposed the violence, cruelty, and despair engendered by the trade. But whereas rebellions along the African coast could succeed, with the rebels managing to flee the ship and win their freedom, success was almost impossible at sea. Even if the crew were massacred, the Africans still had to sail the unfamiliar vessel to safety, a feat far beyond the ability of most men without specialized training.

It is impossible to know the number of revolts aboard eighteenth-century French slaving ships, but it seems likely that they were common, so common in fact that they scarcely merited mentioning in the captains' reports. Sometimes revolts which would have been completely ignored were referred to almost accidentally: a captain occasionally registered the death of a sailor who was "killed by slaves,"[22] or mentioned that so many slaves had died "during a revolt."[23] For each detailed description of a slave rebellion, there were several brief references to other revolts; for each uprising mentioned in passing, there were undoubtedly numerous forgotten challenges to white authority. Slave revolts were expected and accepted as integral parts of the triangle.

Revolts aboard ship usually began when observant captives took advantage of a crew member's negligence. The armateur and the captain demanded constant vigilance from the crew to prevent such attempts. Strategically placed sailors guarded the slaves carefully as they worked, and any utensils which could be used as weapons were systematically denied the captives. Occasionally, however, a careless sailor would leave a potentially dangerous tool within reach of a slave, who would then seize it and hide it for use at the appropriate time. The attack usually came during the night, when most of the whites were asleep and when panic and confusion could easily spread. The slaves first had to gain control over the hatch to win unlimited access to the deck. This was usually done without difficulty; the lone sailor on night watch was invariably taken by surprise and unable to react. Then came the crucial battle for possession of the ship's arms supply. It was at this stage that most rebellions ended; the aroused sailors usually managed to capture the supply room and beat the captives into submission. Very rarely, the slaves gained the upper hand, seized the rifles and powder, and forced the whites to abandon ship in utter terror. Most of the time the sailors easily dominated the situation and put a quick end to the revolt, which explains the laconic remarks in captains' reports like that made by Adrien Doutran, commander of the *Roi Morba*. "Thirteen days after the departure from the coast, the Negroes revolted, seeing the small size of the crew. The said revolt was nonetheless suppressed without much bloodshed."[24] Although in this instance the unsuccessful rebels were merely kept in irons until their arrival in Saint Domingue, serious rebellions were treated much more harshly.

One of the rare successful revolts occurred on the *Diamant* in September 1774.[25] This small, 120-ton ship carrying four cannons and twenty-nine members of the crew left Príncipe for Saint Domingue on August 23, 1774, with a cargo of 244 slaves. Three weeks later, because of calm winds and adverse currents, the ship anchored off Corisco, a small island near the Gabon coast, where the revolt erupted on September 15.

> All the said slaves being in irons and the quarters very well closed, the captain ordered the women's quarters to be opened around 11:30 P.M. in order to empty the toilets. But just then, three blacks, *pièces d'Indes*, having mounted onto the quarter deck by way of the hatch and armed with an axe-handle and logs, struck the crew members within reach. The crew, rising to their defense, injured the said three Negroes, who threw themselves into the sea. The hatch was closed for the moment, but the black men who were below, having broken through the partitions separating the [men's from the women's] quarters, went out the back and wrenched off the iron bars which were on the storeroom gratings. They took the carpenter's tools in the said storeroom, as well as three rifles remaining from the trade and a sixty-pound barrel of powder which they drew from the bread room. The captain and his crew fired on the said blacks without being able to stop them; they also fired on the crew. Most of them having climbed

onto the deck, they threw themselves into the sea and climbed up again by the port and starboard sides to master the crew and the ship. Then they decided to set sail, and the next day at 4:00 A.M., having noticed two ships downwind, they went in that direction but could not reach them. The Negroes took over the helm and set the ship adrift. Finding it impossible to resist further . . . the captain embarked in the dinghy with fourteen of his crew.

After abandoning the ship to the captives, the whites attempted to reach the two other ships, but leaks in the dinghy forced them to head for the nearest shore, where they arrived the next day. When they landed near the St. Benito River, they were immediately captured and enslaved by Africans. Only in October did they regain their freedom: a Dutch captain redeemed the French, and a French captain later reimbursed the Dutchman for the ransom money.

Much more typical was the unsuccessful revolt aboard the *Africain* on November 27, 1738.[26] In his journal, Lieutenant Dom Jeulin wrote:

The Negroes revolted.

Last night before prayers, the slaves were talking and apparently arguing. It was difficult to silence them. All night long, there was quiet. This morning at 5:00, two of them, seemingly chained, came through the hatch. They approached the guard, as if to ask his permission to light their pipes. With a knife in his hand, he refused. Seeing the knife, they jumped on him and killed him. Then they all came out—furious, unchained, and armed with bits of iron bars which they had broken off in silence. They were unchained. . . .

Two others, including one who had sailed with the English, jumped onto the quarter deck. Being quick and cruel, they wreaked havoc. One had a knife, the other a log, a cutlass, and an unloaded pistol. . . .

Seeing the door open, the Negroes headed in a fury to take the room where the arms were held. We barricaded the door well with trunks and boxes piled up to secure it.

We found the arms. . . . I loaded four pistols and fired from the room's windows. The arms worked wonders . . . we certainly would have had trouble containing them if we had not taken the arms room. We succeeded in taking it at the beginning of the revolt when we were half asleep. . . .

Seeing themselves scalded from the left and fired upon from the right, they jumped into the sea. . . . Thereupon we battened down the hatch with the trunks and a thousand other things found on the deck. . . .

No longer having any Negroes to watch on the deck, we only placed armed guards on the hatches.

The officers then subdued the two most dangerous slaves.

> The defeat of these two Negroes ended the revolt. The English one asked for pardon. . . .
>
> When peace returned, nine Negroes were missing. Three were killed by pistols . . . one was strangled, two others were killed by blows from an iron bar, and one by a log . . . and finally, two drowned. For now, we are letting the Negroes alone. Tomorrow, the guilty ones will be punished.

The punishment for the leaders was harsh, designed to set an example for their comrades.

> Yesterday at 8:00 A.M., the most guilty Negroes were taken onto the deck, where they were spread out on their stomachs. We whipped them and we also scarified their buttocks to make them feel their faults better. Once bleeding from the lashes, we rubbed the wounds with cannon powder, lemon juice, and brine of peppers, mixed together with a drug prepared by the surgeon. This mixture prevents gangrene, and also has the advantage of cooking their butts [*leur cuire sur les fesses*].

After four days of such treatment, the slaves' leader died, the tenth black to lose his life. Only two whites had perished, the captain and the guard whose negligence had led to the rebellion.

Thus in spite of the occasional success, most revolts at sea were doomed to failure. Slaves faced a very powerful opposition: the crew had firearms and other dangerous weapons, and the nervous sailors were not at all unwilling to resort to violence. Further, the slaves lacked almost any sort of organization. Speaking a wide variety of languages, they could not adopt a common strategy, but had to rely first on the independent actions of two or three bold leaders and then on the momentary advantage gained if the sailors panicked in the face of a mass uprising at night. Surprise was the captives' greatest weapon, but it was of little use against a well-disciplined enemy. The crew knew what to do if confronted with a rebellion: they knew which stations to occupy, and they took care to capture the weapons room. With the crew rallying, the slaves had three possible courses of action: they could continue to fight, they could submit, or they could jump overboard. Here the lack of communication hurt the captives. Some slaves chose each alternative, and even those who continued the battle could not launch a coordinated attack. Individual slaves fought valiantly, but were easily cut down by the well-armed, well-organized French. The revolt quickly subsided, and those who had jumped into the sea simply drowned.

Fear of slave rebellions helped to keep discipline strict aboard the slave ship, and instances of disobedience or mutiny were rare.[27] As we have seen, even mistreatment of the slaves was uncommon, except of course when it came to sexually abusing the defenseless female slaves. Economics prevented the crew from disabling the slaves, and fear kept the sailors from rebelling against their officers. Indeed, most of the few problems with discipline encountered aboard eighteenth-century French slavers resulted from the bad conduct of certain individual officers. For example, one of the most important complaints against Second Captain Liot was that "he continually threatened the crew and even struck the sailors."[28] Similarly, the new captain of the *Deux Pucelles* had to put the master in irons because of incompetence.[29] But such examples of officers' arrogance or failings were infrequent. Even more unusual were mutinies, and there was only one clear case of a captain being challenged by mutinous crew members. That happened in June 1754 aboard the Nantes ship *Hazard,* when the pilot and the surgeon attacked the captain physically.[30] According to the injured captain, English meddling provoked the entire affair. With the captives presenting a constant threat, members of the crew were careful to band together.

In the Colonies

After two or three months of sailing, the ship finally arrived in the Antilles. Entering the Caribbean Sea from the southeast, the ships always sailed near Martinique, where many stopped for a much-needed rest. Of course, Martinique itself was often the final destination, particularly before the Seven Years' War, but even towards the end of the century it was common for French ships to stop there if only to "refresh" the captives, who were always weakened by the long journey, and to purchase fresh food. A short stop either on Martinique or on any of the myriad small islands in the area could prove most efficacious in reviving the captives. Since healthy looking blacks commanded much higher prices, it was clearly in the captain's interest to spend the time exercising his human cargo. Extreme care had to be taken to prevent escapes at this point. After having successfully brought his captives across the Atlantic, the captain took every precaution not to lose them now.

The slaves now looked more presentable and the ship continued on to its final destination. Although the vast majority of French slavers went to the French Antilles, a few managed to go elsewhere. With a handful of exceptions—one or two French slaving ships went voluntarily to Brazil,[31] while several were seized by the British or Portuguese—the sole foreign colonies visited by French slavers were Puerto Rico and Cuba. Since such practices were forbidden by the French government, captains always had to provide excuses to the authorities upon returning home. That these excuses were singularly implausible apparently bothered nobody. In 1769 and 1770, for example, four ships belonging to the Nantes merchant De Guer

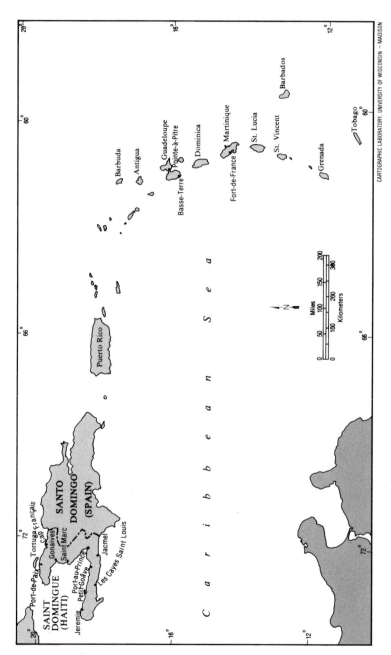

3. The West Indies

"had to" go to the Spanish colonies because of "currents" or "technical problems,"[32] although it was common knowledge that De Guer had a contract to deliver slaves to the Spanish.[33] Since the Spanish always paid in cash, doing business with them was a temptation for the French slave merchants.

Ninety-nine percent of French slaving ships sailed to the French colonies of Saint Domingue, Martinique, Guadeloupe, Cayenne (Guiana), and Louisiana. For all practical purposes, however, they had but two destinations, Martinique and Saint Domingue. Early in the century, Martinique was the destination for up to three-fifths of French slaving ships, and Martinique retained its privileged position until the 1730s. Not only was it the richest French colony at that time, it also served as an obligatory depot for slaves destined for Guadeloupe. Until the Seven Years' War, direct commerce between Africa and Guadeloupe was illegal, and Martinique merchants had a monopoly of trade with the island. Thus any slaver wishing to deal with Guadeloupe had to deliver his slaves first to Martinique and use the services of a local businessman; the slaves were then carried to Guadeloupe aboard a small craft designed for local services.[34] In effect representing the two oldest colonies, Martinique, which was itself the most productive French island at the time, dominated the slave trade until the second quarter of the eighteenth century. Then it was the turn of Saint Domingue. Much larger than Martinique, Saint Domingue was relatively slow to realize its potential worth as a producer of cane sugar. Once the colony began to grow, however, it quickly surpassed in value all the other French colonies and indeed all the other Caribbean islands, until it was reputed to be the richest colony in the world. Saint Domingue's growth was reflected in the number of slave ships sent to the island: in 1720 and 1730, about 40 percent of all Nantes slavers sailed there, but in 1740 and 1750 the proportion was more than 70 percent, and after 1760 it rose to more than 90. So complete was Saint Domingue's domination, that French slavers began to ignore the demands of the Lesser Antilles, with the result that these smaller markets were virtually ceded to the British, following the 1744-48 and 1756-63 wars.[35]

Upon arriving in port, the slave ship was treated as a potential carrier of disease and therefore forced to anchor far from the other ships in the harbor. According to the ordinance of April 3, 1718, nobody was allowed to disembark until local health authorities had issued the appropriate authorization. To prevent this law from being circumvented, the government proclaimed on July 25, 1724, that neither could anybody board the ship until the medical permit was obtained.[36] These decrees, of course, were designed to prevent the introduction of contagious diseases into the colonies, but captains considered such formalities mere hindrances to commerce, while administrators saw in them an opportunity to fill the public coffers as well as their own pockets. It cost the captain over 100 livres to obtain the certificate, but even then the right to trade in peace was not guaranteed.[37] Arrival in port meant the paying of bribes, and local officials could have voracious appetites. Captain LaVigne of the *Grand Duc de Bretagne* had to pay 2,750 livres to Mr. Duquesne, general of Martinique, 3,000 livres to M. de Naueresson, intendant, and 108 livres to M. Meunier, commissaire, "for which they did not want to give any receipts, in spite of the verbal requests made by the captain."[38] Similarly, the governor of Martinique relieved the captain of the *Africain* of thirty-two slaves for no apparent reason.[39] Doing business in the colonies was apparently little different from trading in Africa: all depended on buying the goodwill of powerful patrons.

With official permission to unload, the captain began his preparations for the sale. The first step was to procure yet another certificate, one indicating the number of slaves being introduced to the colonies. This document would be important later when dealing with French revenue agents and was the origin of countless disputes between the traders and the tax collectors.[40] After this final formality, the captain contacted a local merchant for help in selling the slaves. Whereas the English captains commonly sold their entire cargo to colonial merchants, who then concerned themselves with reselling the slaves individually, French captains usually sold directly to the slave owners.[41] To do this, however, the French needed the services of someone familiar with both the colonial market and the capacity of the potential buyers to pay. This was the job of the colonial agent, a man whose intimate knowledge of local conditions made him an indispensable and expensive addition to the slaving triangle.[42] Taking a 1 to 5 percent commission on all transactions, the agent was probably the only person certain to make a profit out of the slave trade, and many French traders actually got their start as colonial merchants. The choice of the agent was not made by the captain but by the armateur, who gave the captain a list of acceptable merchants to be consulted in each port. The armateur was very careful in selecting these correspondents, and he searched endlessly for someone who would give full attention to his particular problems. The only way of guaranteeing an honest and efficient colonial operation, however, was to establish a subsidiary office in the colonies, and if the French company could not afford to do so, it had to deal with strangers over whom it had little control. For example, the Chaurands, slaving merchants in Nantes, complained continually about the colonial firm of Sheridan, Gatechair, and Company, which seemed to do everything ineptly.[43] The Chaurands resolved their problems only when they purchased a one-fifth share in Guilbaud, Gerbier, and Company of Cap Français.[44]

The need to control their colonial affairs led many other French slaving merchants to open subsidiaries in the colonies, often under the direction of a relative. Jacques François Begouen Demeaux, the richest Le Havre slave trader in the second half of the eighteenth century, worked closely with his brother-in-law Stanislas Foache, one of the most important merchants in Saint Domingue.[45] Similarly, Riedy and Thurninger, the largest Nantes traders at the end of the old regime, established a company at Cayes Saint Louis (Saint Domingue) in 1791.[46] The Nantais chose one of their former employees, the clerk Charles Duvau, to operate the house, which also included Charles Hums of Bruges. The company was called Charles Duvau, Hums, and Company, and was to last for five years. As a passive partner, the Nantes company paid 60,000 livres, while the two active members contributed 30,000 livres each. The Nantais held this money at 5 percent interest, and used it to buy shares in slave ships which would be consigned to the new company. Duvau, Hums, and the Nantais divided the profits equally, thereby making for a typical division of labor, capital, and profits. The firm of Sheridan, Fitzgerald, Ducros, and Company, established for two years as a successor to Sheridan, Gatechair, and Company of Léogane (Saint Domingue), was similarly constituted.[47] The passive colonial partners, Sheridan *oncle* and Gatechair, put up 60,000 and 20,000 livres respectively, while the Nantes merchant Le Roux des Ridellières paid 60,000 livres. The active partners, Sheridan *neveu*, Fitzgerald, and Ducros, contributed about half that much (29,000, 29,000, and 25,000 livres, respectively) but took five-twelfths of the profits.

Other slave traders had to accept what was available in the colonies. If the French company were large, it could expect to be approached by colonial entrepreneurs or their French representatives. Thus the Chaurands recommended the services of their colonial agents, Guilbaud, Gerbier, and Company, to Langevin Brothers, a large Nantes trading house,[48] and Guillaume Duffour, a merchant at Cayes Saint Louis, requested the honor of handling the colonial affairs of Pierre Lalle, a Bordeaux trader.[49] Conversely, less-important French companies had to be recommended to colonial merchants. In an effort to help their new colleagues, the Chaurands wrote several letters to colonial agents: "There had been established [in Nantes] a commercial house named Tiby, Sanlecque and Company . . . the first worked for several years in the office of M. Michel and the second worked for us."[50] In the absence of credit-rating services, recommendations based on personal experience were doubly important.

The captain followed the agent's advice in selling the slaves. The agent, of course, used his own judgment, but he also had to take the wishes of the armateur into consideration. Well before the ship even arrived in the Antilles, the armateur usually conveyed his instructions to the agent, telling him to order the captain to act along certain lines.[51] Although the armateur thought that a conscientious agent should line up buyers for the arriving shipment, this was not usually the practice. Uncertain as to the date of the ship's arrival and busy with other affairs, the agent could scarcely be expected to have the buyers waiting patiently on the dock when the ship finally appeared. Instead, he would merely mention informally that he was expecting a ship to come in the near future and that prospective buyers might consider delaying purchases until this ship arrived. In any event, serious plans for the sale could not begin until the captain notified the agent that all was in order and that so many slaves were to be sold. The agent then announced the upcoming sale with posters and letters:

Cap Français, *March 27, 1785*

Sir:

We have the honor of informing you that the ship the *"Iris"* of *La Rochelle*, captain *Michaud*, coming from *Porto Novo, Gold Coast*, with a cargo of *850* blacks to our address, had just anchored *in this harbor*. We will open the sale on *Thursday, the thirty-first of the present month* and we will offer you with pleasure those slaves which you might need.

We have the honor to be

Your very humble
and very obedient servants

Poupet Brothers and Company[52]

The sale commenced as quickly as possible after the ship's arrival. Each additional day in confinement only caused the slaves' health to deteriorate even further, thereby diminishing their market value, besides increasing the danger of death or escape. Hence the captain frequently began the sale within a week of his arrival in port. The sale took place either on board the ship or in a special marketplace in town. Although local authorities much preferred to have the sale in town, the captain thought it wiser to conduct it aboard his ship, and usually did so. Besides the fact that escapes were more likely on land, the captain enjoyed a psychological advantage by forcing the buyers to come onto his vessel. He rented launches and put them, and some of his crew members, at the disposition of the buyers, who were then ferried to the slaving ship. Once on the ship, the buyers participated in a process which strongly resembled the trade which had occurred earlier in Africa. They examined the slaves like livestock and made their offers to the captain. If the captain accepted the offer, he consulted the colonial agent and proposed terms of payment; these acknowlledged, the buyer took possession of his slave and led him away. The slave now belonged to his colonial master, and even if the captive died before reaching the shore, the colonist alone would suffer the loss. As in Africa, usually only one slave was sold at a time, although the occasional major purchase, together with the large number of buyers, meant that the sale was often completed within two or three weeks.

Whites from all walks of life owned slaves in the French West Indies. Although most slaves ended up on the plantations, where they worked either as field hands or domestics, thousands found their way into the towns. Seventy-two people bought the 346 slaves offered by Pierre van Alstein, captain of the *Duc de Laval*, in 1775;[53] of the fifty-one buyers whose place of residence was indicated, twenty-nine lived in the city, while only twenty-two were from the country. Although the planters undoubtedly made much larger purchases than the townspeople—one planter bought 51 slaves—it is important to note just how widespread the institution of slavery was in the Antilles. Among the purchasers of the captives sold aboard the *Duc de Laval* were several merchants and administrators, including a royal surveyor and a prosecutor. Members of the liberal professions were also represented, with two doctors and two notaries buying slaves. Even simple artisans managed to acquire black slaves, in this case two carpenters, a shoemaker, a butcher, a tailor, and a baker. Thus, although the entire colonial economy was based upon the production of sugar and coffee and although these exotic commodities provided the sole *raison d'être* for slavery and the slave trade, all of colonial society, whether urban or rural, was permeated with slavery, and there were few whites of any means who did not own slaves. Purchasing slaves was considered proper in colonial society and posed few moral problems. For example, when Pierre Lefranc arrived in Saint Domingue to work on water distribution, he found it quite normal to buy 22 slaves for his work immediately and 118 others within six years.[54] What had begun as an economic quirk became a social necessity.

When selling his slaves, the captain had to be particularly careful in agreeing to terms of payment. Colonial debtors were notoriously untrustworthy, and captains had to take every precaution to insure payment. The basic problem was the poor economic position of the colonial planters, who were forever in debt to the French merchants. Hence the colonists had scarcely any credit reserves to draw upon in France. Worse, the colonial system forbade the export of precious metals from the mother country to the colonies, thereby encumbering the colonies with a perennial lack of specie. The only source of specie was the Spanish colonies, but illicit sales of French slaves to Spanish colonists offered only limited relief during periods of war. In peacetime, when commercial links with France were functioning normally, the French colonies served as a mere way station for Spanish silver flowing inevitably to Paris.[55] It was in establishing the terms of payment that the colonial agent earned his salary. The agent kept abreast of business life in the colony, and he knew the financial position of potential buyers. Therefore he was in a good position to recommend to the captain terms for each purchaser. Ideally, the captain accepted the agent's suggestions, but over both men hovered the image of the armateur, whose immediate preoccupation with speed and expense outweighed his concern over long-term benefits. In short, the armateur's impatience encouraged the captain to conclude a poor deal quickly rather than a good deal slowly.

At issue was the size of the down payment and the subsequent installments. Full payments upon delivery were exceedingly rare, in spite of the armateur's blind insistance to the contrary. "Sir," wrote a Bordeaux merchant to his agent and captain, "I would be most grateful if you sold these slaves for cash. Let them go rather than sell for a higher price on credit."[56] But the best the captain could realistically hope to get was a large down payment and sincere promises of future payments. Needless to say, all payments were made in kind. Although the value of the debt was expressed in terms of livres, the actual payments were made in colonial commodities having a certain market value. Usually about 25 percent was paid immediately, with the rest to be delivered within eighteen months or two years. The planter gave the agent a series of bills due on certain dates, usually at thirty-, sixty-, or ninety-day intervals, but these notes were of little real value. Most planters were either unwilling or unable to pay on time, and the creditors had little leverage against them. Foreclosures were uncommon, and colonial agents had other things to do besides pressuring delinquent debtors; even if the captain remained in the colonies, there was no guarantee that payments would be forthcoming.[57]

In most respects, the captain was at a marked disadvantage when dealing with the colonists. It was usually a buyer's market. The captain was in unfamiliar territory, relying totally on the services of a colonial merchant whose interests were frequently divided. Colonial laws regarding debts favored the debtor so heavily that creditors were virtually without legal recourse; the minute the captain set sail from the Antilles, there was a minimum of pressure on the planter to pay. And the purchasers of slaves well knew of the captain's need to leave the Antilles as quickly as possible. By the time the slave ship arrived in the Caribbean, it had been away from France for close to a year, and the armateur was very anxious to receive some returns on his investment. Besides, life in the colonies was so dear that a long stay could significantly reduce the expedition's profits, especially since purchases in the islands were in cash and not on credit.[58] The captain therefore did everything in his power to conclude his business in the colonies rapidly, but for various reasons—the need to repair the ship and to find an appropriate return cargo—a three-month stay was standard.

With the slaves sold, the captain sought a cargo for the return voyage. Since the captain had been away from France for nearly a year, he could not possibly know the market conditions there and had to rely again on the agent. The armateur wrote the agent frequently, giving him precise instructions with regard to the return cargo. "Send me indigo, cotton, and coffee and on no account sugar," wrote one armateur in 1786.[59] More often than not, however, these instructions were conveniently forgotten by the agent, who was anxious to send out whatever was available. The agent, of course, worked on a commission basis, so that it was in his interest to dispatch anything he could quickly. This gave rise to great bitterness, with the armateurs accusing their correspondents of gross incompetence. The Chaurands complained about Séguineau Brothers, who against all orders "dared to buy 25,000 livres' worth of cotton for us. For a long time we have asked only for coffee and those were our explicit orders."[60] Usually the choice was even more limited: there were only two major colonial exports, sugar and coffee, as the minor commodities such as indigo, cotton, and cocoa were never produced in sufficient quantities to fill ships regularly. The real choice was between sucre terré and sucre brut, with the more refined terré almost always in greater demand than brut.

His instructions ignored and his debtors irresponsible, the armateur developed a strong dislike for the colonists. The French merchants sincerely believed that the colonials were incapable of anything but deceit. They accused the colonists of everything from negligence to fraud, and the need to keep the colonies in line was the favorite theme of traders complaining to the government. As described by the armateurs, the colonists were perfectly unscrupulous, concerned only with their own advantage. They unilaterally imposed taxes which hurt the French merchants,[61] and to increase the weight of their imports, they even went so far as to put rocks in barrels of sugar and coffee.[62] They did everything in their power to subvert the colonial system, such as encouraging British and American smugglers while refusing to honor obligations to the motherland. Although the planters replied that foreign slaves were far cheaper than French ones, the French traders took this to be another example of colonial perversity: the planters were knowingly buying inferior merchandise.

> The English commonly trade slaves in places like Galbar and Gabon where the slaves, on no account appropriate for working, cost much less than elsewhere. Further, they then give the first choice of their slaves to the Spanish colonies, and the second to their own colonies; it is only the dregs—dregs fattened by including slaves affected by hidden diseases, rebellion, and other crimes—hurting their own colonies which they transport to and introduce when possible into our colonies.[63]

By the end of the old regime, even the pretense of a common interest between French merchant and colonial planter was dropped, and during the Revolution the two groups were openly hostile.[64]

The Return to France

Trapped between the armateur's wrath and the planter's duplicity, the captain wanted only to return to France as quickly as possible. He was prepared to leave, or at least to send the ship back under the command of the second captain, once the ship was even half full.[65] The sailors loaded the goods aboard the ship while the captain completed the formalities. Besides getting permission to sail—and many ships were no longer considered seaworthy by this time—the captain had to obtain the documents allowing the armateur to import the colonial commodities at the special-duty rate. Finally, the ship set sail for France. With a slightly altered crew, because of the new sailors who signed on in Saint Domingue to replace those who had died or deserted, and occasionally with a different commander, the ship began the two-month crossing. Except in times of war, when French ships on this popular route were particularly vulnerable to English attack, the voyage home was usually uneventful. For the first time since entering tropical waters a year earlier, the crew could relax and worry only about the business of sailing the ship.[66] During the crossing, it was common for French captains to meet their colleagues on the high seas. "On the fourteenth of the present month, being at 35° 57′ N latitude and 15° 20′ W longitude, the captain spoke to Captain Martin, commander of the *Fran-çaise*, which left Martinique thirty-four days ago, with whom he sailed until the seventeenth. . . . He spoke on the twentieth to [another] Captain Martin going to Martinique."[67] And in times of war, ships returned to France in formal convoys. The only significant occurrence aboard the returning slaver was the incidence of damage to the cargo.[68] Imperfectly packed, the crudely refined sugar was subject to losses of 10 to 25 percent on every voyage from the Antilles to France. Although the captains invariably gave dramatic explanations for the damages, such as exceptionally high seas caused by storms, the rudimentary techniques used to prepare the goods for shipment made such losses inescapable, and armateurs fully discounted the effects of spoilage when planning their expeditions.[69]

Some fifteen to eighteen months after leaving France, the ship returned home. With one-sixth of its crew dead, with its hold half empty, and with major damages to its structure, it limped into port more a survivor than a conqueror; yet each little vessel which completed the triangle represented a triumph for French business. Every ship which succeeded in delivering three hundred captives to the Indies helped consolidate a vast commercial empire relating three continents for the purpose of enriching the mother country. Nantes, Bordeaux, Le Havre, Marseilles, and the other major French ports benefited directly from the trade or from other commerce generated by the trade. Paris and the major commercial centers gained from the general increase in commercial, and to a lesser degree industrial, activity, and all Frenchmen and northern Europeans of means profited from cheaper prices for sugar and coffee.[70] At the cost of the freedom of three hundred people, each ship contributed in its own small way to the economic development of France.

Many formalities attended the return of the slaving ship. The captain had to file his official report of the expedition within two or three days of his arrival. These reports, full of information about the triangle, gave the captain the opportunity to justify his conduct during the expedition. Although he may never have lied consciously, he exaggerated and distorted the truth as he saw fit. He was concerned primarily with his armateur's reaction, and tried to show that he had done the best possible job under the worst possible conditions and that he could not be held legally responsible for any shortcomings. The captain also had to submit his copy of the original crew list to the admiralty. During the voyage he had revised the list as necessary, noting deaths, desertions, and new appointments, and when he returned his annotated list, the admiralty forced the armateur to pay the crew's wages. Since the armateur had paid three months' wages in advance, he now owed for another twelve to fifteen months, at 1,000 to 1,500 livres per month. This amounted to some 10,000 to 20,000 livres, a considerable sum to pay immediately in cash, and the armateurs complained vehemently about the crew's high wages. With the completion of these formalities, the captain's responsibilities ended, and the armateur once again took charge. He paid the duties on the commodities brought into France and arranged for storing the re-export merchandise in bonded warehouses. He also prepared to sell his produce.

His capital tied up for well over a year, the armateur desperately wanted to see some cash returns. He therefore sold his merchandise in bulk, letting other merchants sell smaller lots to retailers. This meant that the trader sold his goods in his home port and had nothing to do with their further distribution. Since the bulk of the commodities was ultimately re-exported, most of the middlemen were either of foreign origin or possessed close ties with foreign countries. In 1785 and 1786, for example, the Chaurands recorded sixty-two sales of colonial commodities, of which twenty-five were to fairly recent foreign immigrants and another eight to foreigners long established in Nantes.[71] These middlemen then arranged for the shipment of the produce abroad. In 1789, the only year following the American War for which comprehensive import and export statistics overlapped in Nantes, about 78 percent of the coffee and 63 percent of the sugar entering Nantes from the colonies were exported to non-French ports, particularly in northwest Europe.[72] Half the outgoing sugar went to Holland, while one-fifth went to northern Germany and one-eighth to Belgium, three destinations which also accounted for more than three-quarters of the coffee exports. Although shipping these goods abroad was probably a lucrative commerce, it was largely ignored by the French merchants. The great majority of ships sailing from France to Holland, Germany, and Belgium were foreign. As the Nantes merchants complained, "Almost all the goods which leave this city are carried by foreign ships;"[73] and official statistics gave French shipping as a whole less than 10 percent of the Franco-Dutch and Franco-Hanseatic traffic in 1792.[74] The slave traders wanted only to sell their goods with a minimum of delay and a minimum of effort, and did not attempt to control this corollary to the trade.

After selling his commodities, the armateur finally received his first cash proceeds, usually quite meager, representing one-fourth to one-third of the original investment and scarcely covering all the additional expenses incurred. Soon other returns arrived, and within three years of the ship's departure, the initial outlay was amortized and profits began to accrue. The payment system was painfully slow. Planters had to deliver the commodities to the agent, who, after taking his commission, forwarded the merchandise to France, where it had to be sold by the armateur. After extracting his own commission, the armateur finally distributed the proceeds to all the expedition's investors, including himself. Such payments continued at more or less regular intervals for five or six years and then slowed to a mere trickle, extending up to a quarter of a century. Many debts were never repaid at all.

9
The East African Trade

Although the Antilles formed the cornerstone of the French empire in the old regime, they were not the only tropical islands occupied by Frenchmen. Halfway around the world in the Indian Ocean the French colonized the Mascarene Islands of Mauritius and Reunion, where they introduced the institution of slavery.[1] To procure slaves for these islands, a new slave trade had to be established, one taking into account the remote geographical position of the Mascarenes. After some early attempts to carry slaves from West Africa, an East African trade developed, bringing captives from Madagascar or Mozambique to the two islands. At first, ships came all the way from France to trade slaves in East Africa for delivery to the Mascarenes, but as this proved too costly, a local trade began; residents of the two colonies gained the right to go to East Africa to procure slaves. Toward the end of the eighteenth century, the French developed yet another East African slave trade, this time for furnishing slaves to the Antilles. As demand increased for West African slaves, they became so expensive that cost-conscious armateurs believed the longer and more dangerous voyage beyond the Cape of Good Hope was justified by cheaper prices charged for East African slaves. Thus the French had four "eastern" slave trades: one based on the France, West Africa, Mascarenes triangle; one directly between the Mascarenes and East Africa; one from France to East Africa to the Mascarenes; and one designed to bring East African slaves to the West Indies. During the last decade of the old regime, when French slaving reached unprecedented heights, the four eastern trades tended to combine in a variety of fashions, yielding new and complex combinations.[2]

European links with the east coast of Africa and the southwest Indian Ocean began in 1498, when Vasco da Gama first sailed around the southern tip of Africa. The Portuguese, like their Dutch and English successors, were primarily interested in commercial routes to India, the East Indies, and China, and made little effort to trade slaves in the area. It was the French who developed slaving to a high degree in East Africa. The last of the great powers to arrive in the Indian Ocean, France began by establishing outposts along the eastern coast of Madagascar, of which the most important was Fort Dauphin, constructed in 1643. Three years later, as the result of internal dissension, the ruler of Fort Dauphin exiled twelve rebels to Reunion, an uninhabited island some four hundred miles to the east. This feeble attempt at colonization failed, as did a second one in 1654, and it was not until the 1660s that uninterrupted occupation of the island began with the arrival of a dozen French and Malagashe. While the French were slowly establishing their rights to Reunion, the Dutch were gradually relinquishing their hold over Mauritius, finally abandoning the island around 1710. Five years later the French claimed the island, and settlers began arriving from Reunion in 1721.

Lying just above the Tropic of Capricorn, the Mascarenes were slightly larger than Guadeloupe, but were uninhabited when discovered by Europeans.[3] Both Reunion and its more easterly counterpart Mauritius evolved from volcanic action, but at different epochs. The basically flat island of Mauritius was much older than Reunion, which was dominated by an active, 10,000-foot volcano. A further natural difference between the islands was in their coastlines; whereas Mauritius was endowed with several excellent harbors, Reunion had only a few of inferior quality. But the islands shared two important characteristics: they were on the French route to India, and they boasted tropical climates. If their geographical position gave them their original strategic importance, their tropical nature made them attractive to planters. Devoid of dangerous mammals, snakes, and insects, the Mascarenes were doomed to suffer the same fate as the Antilles. The Portuguese, Dutch, and French arrived, destroyed much of the indigenous flora and fauna, including the dodo, and established a plantation economy devoted to producing coffee and sugar for consumption in Europe. This economy was slow to develop, however, and it took until the fourth quarter of the eighteenth century before the Mascarenes grew significantly. On the eve of the Revolution, more than 90,000 people lived on the two islands, including 73,000 slaves.

Throughout most of the old regime the Mascarenes either belonged to or were the exclusive preserve of the great trading companies. From the creation of the first Compagnie des Indes in 1664 until the collapse of John Law's company a century later, the Mascarenes depended on the royal companies for virtually everthing, including slaves. At first the companies merely had a monopoly over commerce with the islands, but in 1721 the king actually ceded the two colonies to the Compagnie des Indes, making company domination total. The company, however, was far too concerned with India and the Antilles to spend much time or money on the Mascarenes, and soon the colonists began to clamor for the right to trade their own slaves in Africa. Reluctantly, the company acceded, and from 1742 to 1747 it authorized the colonists to conduct their own trade. At the same time, the company established free trade in the islands. The experiment failed, primarily because the colonists were too poor to pay for all the necessary services, and the company resumed its monopoly. After the Seven Years' War, the crown repossessed the colonies from the moribund company and inaugurated a new era of open trade and prosperity. The colonies remained royal possessions open to all French merchants until the end of the old regime, as the new Compagnie des Indes, Calonne's company of 1785, failed to receive a monopoly over the islands' commerce. During the Napoleonic wars England conquered both islands, and returned only Reunion at the Congress of Vienna. Reunion, of course, remained part of France, while Mauritius became an independent state in 1968.

Throughout most of the eighteenth century, the slave trade to the Mascarenes was quite small, especially when compared to the West Indian trade. According to the study undertaken by J. M. Filliot, it was not until 1767 that the Mascarenes became major importers of slaves.[4] From 1669 to 1705, there were never more than 100 slaves introduced each year into the islands, for a total of less than 1,000. In fact, there was no real slave trade at all, as ships destined for the islands merely picked up 2 or 3 slaves while passing the (West) African coast. Then a small but irregular trade developed, so that from 100 to 500 slaves entered the Mascarenes each year until 1725. After 1725, with the successful introduction of coffee, the colonists needed many more workers, and a regular trade evolved, delivering from 500 to 1,800 slaves each year until the late 1760s. Some 40,000 slaves probably entered the islands during this period, many of them aboard company ships sent out especially for that purpose. After 1770, with the lifting of all commercial restrictions, the slave trade to the Mascarenes grew impressively. Filliot estimated an annual import of from 2,000 to 5,000 slaves, which would have made the Mascarenes as important to the trade as the Lesser Antilles. Unlike the West Indies, the Mascarenes continued to receive slaves from a variety of sources during much of the Revolutionary period, with approximately 35,000 landing between 1793 and 1810, the year of the English conquest. All told, 160,000 slaves were introduced to the Mascarenes during the "long" eighteenth century.

As colonial demands for slaves grew, the responses of the government, trading companies, and French armateurs changed. While the islands were only producing small quantities of pepper or tobacco, only a few slaves were needed, and no formal trade was necessary. Then coffee production began to increase after 1720, particularly on Reunion; exports rose from 120,000 pounds in 1728 to a record 2,500,000 pounds in 1744. As the coffee plantations began to prosper, a much larger labor force was required, and the company felt obligated to supply it. Ships on the way from France to India or the East Indies were occasionally ordered by the company to winter in the Mascarenes, make the short journey to Madagascar, trade slaves, and deliver them to the islands, before resuming their voyage to their more exotic destinations. In addition to the company ships, independent armateurs in the Mascarenes organized their own expeditions to East Africa, where they were favorably received by the Portuguese governor of Mozambique, Almeida, a friend of the French governor general of the Mascarenes, La Bourdonnais.[5] Occasionally the Mascarene merchants sought slaves in India or West Africa, but these sites were unpopular: the former produced "lazy" slaves, the latter was too expensive. During the period of accelerated growth, spices competed with coffee as Reunion's most important export, while indigo was Mauritius's leading crop. Interesting, however, was the fact that a large percentage, if not the majority, of slaves employed on Mauritius worked in the port and not in the fields, as Mauritius had become not only an almost obligatory stop for French ships returning from Asia, but also a free port. To furnish the needed slaves at this time, local merchants continued to fit out their own expeditions, and they were aided by a few French armateurs who now found it worthwhile to send slavers to the Mascarenes instead of to the West Indies.

The East African slave trade was very much like its West African counterpart, although there were a few novelties.[6] Depending on their port of origin, ships used on the Madagascar/Mozambique route tended to be either larger or smaller than the West African slavers. Those ships which came from France to trade in East Africa were large, having an average capacity of almost 250 tons midway through the century and exceeding 400 tons by the 1780s. Ships based in the Mascarenes, however, were much smaller, as the short crossing and the limited financial means of the island residents kept sizes down. The voyage from France was long, taking an average of four or five months. Leaving Bordeaux, Lorient, or Marseilles (the ports of origin for more than three-quarters of the East African expeditions) during the winter in order to round the Cape by July, the ships followed the same basic routes south as did the West African slavers. They then continued along the Brazilian coast until they crossed the south Atlantic by way of Tristan de Cunha; sailing well to the south of the Cape of Good Hope, they stopped there only if necessary. Some ships, including those belonging to the Compagnie des Indes, stopped at Gorée before approaching Brazil, while others went all the way to Ouidah before heading west. Once in the Indian Ocean, the ships followed the prevailing currents and winds and landed first at Mauritius, where they arrived during late spring or summer. Most ships left the Mascarenes for France in December or January. If the captain had not traded slaves on the way to the Mascarenes, he had to undertake a separate slaving expedition to the East African coast. Usually, however, this trade was accomplished by local merchants in small ships. Because of the prevailing winds and currents, a circular route was followed, with the ships sailing north and then west to Africa, and then south, east, and north back to the islands. The slaving expedition itself took no more than three to four months from the Mascarenes, with the only extra stop being at the Seychelles—especially towards the end of the eighteenth century.

There were two great slave trading regions for the Mascarenes: Madagascar and Mozambique. Madagascar was of little interest to the French until the eighteenth century: although some Frenchmen had been on the island since the 1640s, they did not become a major force until the Compagnie des Indes was granted a monopoly of French trade with the island. As early as 1717, the new company organized an expedition to Madagascar, and the island remained the company's favorite East African site until 1769. After the disappearance of the company, the crown allowed independent slavers to trade on Madagascar, but only under certain rather trying conditions. For example, the crown opened the west coast to French traders but imposed restrictions on trade with the east coast. The French traders, however, much preferred the east coast because of its proximity to the Mascarenes and because of the lack of European competition there; and Foulpointe served as the center of French slaving operations in Madagascar. The actual trade along the Madagascar coast was unique. After a festive arrival in port, during which the French paid homage to the local ruler, the captain had to "marry" a native woman, who would later serve almost as his business representative. Since the woman was instrumental in procuring the slaves, the captain had to be careful in choosing her; he was advised to court a noblewoman, if not a princess. After a typical trade, with protracted bargaining over each slave, the captain paid his "wife" for her services, offered gifts to the local authorities, and departed for the ten- to fifteen-day journey to the Mascarenes.

The other major trading area in East Africa was the coast itself. Although the French dealt with Arabs all the way up to the Aden Gulf, most French slaving activity centered on the area south of Cape Delgado, and particularly Mozambique. The Mozambique coast had not always been of great interest to French of Mascarene traders, occupied as it was by Portugal, and only after 1770 did it surpass Madagascar. By the time of the Revolution, the French dominated the Mozambique slave trade. Using the services of Portuguese intermediaries, French slavers exported probably close to 40,000 Africans from Mozambique during the last decade of the old regime. North of the Portuguese possessions, the French encountered Arabs willing to sell slaves. Although the French never quite controlled the Zanzibar slave market, for example, they still managed to buy thousands of black slaves from the Arab merchants and more important, they "acted as an important stimulus to the demands for slaves at a period when the Arab trade was still outgrowing its infancy."[7] Thus French influence in the eighteenth century helped create the immense East African slave trade of the nineteenth century.

The relaxing of restrictions on commerce with the Mascarenes was not the exclusive cause of the sudden growth of the French slave trade in East Africa after 1769: West Indian demand also influenced its development. Particularly after the American Revolution, East Africa—that is to say, Mozambique—emerged as a serious rival to the more established regions of Guinea and Angola as a supplier of slaves to the French West Indies. It was a complicated business, however, since not all slaving expeditions merely substituted East for West Africa in the existing triangle. Some combined the East Africa–Antilles trade with either the carrying or slave trades to the Mascarenes or beyond. In such cases, the textile trade with India was probably the most important factor, as cloths produced on the subcontinent were necessary for the slave trade. Ships therefore sailed from France to India and purchased goods required in Africa; they then traveled to Mozambique or even to West Africa, exchanged the cloths for slaves, and continued on to the Antilles. This was the route followed by the *Trois Cousins*, which left Saint Malo on January 11, 1784.[8] After a trip to India and in all probability to Mauritius, the ship arrived on the West African coast on June 2, 1785. During its three month stay at Malimbe, the ship traded 888 slaves, of whom 700 survived the crossing to Cap Français. The ship arrived back in Saint Malo on March 27, 1786, some twenty-six months after its departure. At least two other ships went to India before proceeding to Africa and presumably the Antilles, but complete documentation is lacking for these expeditions; the sailing permits for the *Pauline* and the *Phénix* specified only Mauritius, India, and Mozambique.[9]

Precise data is even more limited in cases when Mauritius was apparently substituted for India as the first stop on the new quadrilateral. Mauritius was a free port towards the end of the old regime, and almost all French ships returning from India stopped there. Thus the island was well stocked with the Indian goods so useful in trading slaves. It is known that dozens of ships sailed to the Mascarenes, Mozambique, and the West Indies, but the significance of the stop at Mauritius is unclear: some ships conducted important business, while other merely rested. In 1788, for example, the Bordeaux firm of Henry Romberg, Bapst, and Company sent out the *Ville de Bordeaux* on a slaving expedition to East Africa and the West Indies by way of Mauritius.[10] The ship carried 1,234 barrels of flour, which it undoubtedly exchanged for slaving merchandise on Mauritius. On the other hand, the same company's *Lafayette* followed a similar route but transported only 8 barrels of flour; since flour was by far the most important French export to the colonies, the *Lafayette* merely used the Mascarenes as a convenient resting place before conducting an arduous trade.[11] Examples like these could be multiplied, but the conclusion is inescapable: armateurs in France occasionally combined slaving expeditions to East Africa with the carrying trade to the Mascarenes or India.

The trade about which the least is known is the multiple slave trade. Although there exists no incontrovertible evidence that certain expeditions incorporated two slave trades, there are hints that they may have. It would have been quite possible for a ship to deliver one load of slaves to the Mascarenes and a second to the Antilles. Given the time involved in the France, Mozambique, Antilles triangle, the few extra months necessitated by the extra trip to the Mascarenes would not have lengthened the expedition unduly. Cargoes posed a more serious problem: what would the slaver use for merchandise on the second trade? Since Africans were hardly interested in the Mascarenes' primary exports, coffee and spices, the trader had to procure whatever goods from India were then available in the islands. Thus the itinerary for the twin trade was complex: the ship left France filled with trading merchandise, part of which was exchanged in East Africa for cheap slaves. These were sold in the Mascarenes for Indian cloths, as well as colonial commodities to be shipped directly to France at a later date. The new merchandise and what remained of the original cargo were then traded in Mozambique for slaves, who were taken to the West Indies. Crucial to the operation were the low price of slaves in East Africa and the large size of ships going to the Indian Ocean. These enabled the captain to conduct two trades with somewhat less than two complete cargoes, for it was doubtful that island merchants had enough imported goods to assemble complete cargoes on demand. Since some ships belonging to the Compagnie des Indes did undertake two voyages between the Mascarenes and Madagascar before returning to France, the problem of replenishing trading stocks was obviously not insurmountable.[12] But if double trades to the Mascarenes and the Antilles were feasible, did they happen? One Bordeaux merchant, Pierre Lalle, spoke as if they were commonplace.[13] When writing to his agent in Mauritius, Lalle discussed the courses of action open to the captain of the *Glaneuse*, then in Madagascar trading slaves. After selling the slaves in the Mascarenes, the captain could return to Madagascar and buy a cargo of rice for delivery to Europe. Lalle approved of this idea: "I would even prefer it to carrying blacks to America because of the risks of losing money on the way." Although Lalle may have been referring to the original cargo of captives, and hence simply expressing a preference for the Mascarenes over the Antilles, it seems more likely that he was indeed speaking of a second slave trade which, like virtually everything else related to slaving, had its own uncertainties.

The development of a second source of slaves as well as the creation of a second colonial market underlined the wide range of possibilities in the slave trade. The French slaving triangle did not suddenly appear in a mature form during the seventeenth century; instead, it gradually emerged and continually evolved over a period of at least two hundred years. In fact, it was on the eve of its abolition that the French trade reached its apogee and maximum diversity. The formation of an entirely new triangle not only confirmed the success of the original but also reflected the similarity in conditions. As had happened in the West Indies, a growing colonial economy required vast labor resources, and only imported slaves seemed appropriate to meet the demands. French merchants, familiar with the West Africa–Antilles commerce, therefore established a new triangle with vertices in France, East Africa, and the Mascarenes. At the same time, however, slightly different causes produced different effects: the proximity of the Mascarenes to East Africa implied the creation of a novel slaving circuit, one based on direct commerce in both directions between producer and consumer of slaves. Being on the *route des Indes,* the Mascarene colonists had more merchandise to sell to the Africans than did the West Indians, and residents of Mauritius and Reunion could to a large degree dispense with the services of French traders. A full-blown triangle was not logical in the Indian Ocean.

The experience of the slave trade to the Mascarenes showed that only part of the slaving system was in any way inevitable. Once planters determined that colonial economies should be based on the export of tropical produce, slavery became necessary in the Caribbean Sea and the Indian Ocean. Slaves alone could be procured in sufficient numbers to support a plantation economy, and only slave labor was considered profitable to the proper degree. But the organization of the slave trade was by no means predestined. Only a combination of racial, economic, and geographic considerations imposed a triangle on the Antilles trade and a direct line on the Mascarenes trade. Always concerned with lowering expenses and raising profits, neither the planters nor the merchants were afraid to try new methods of trading slaves.

PART III
The Traders
and Their Business

10
The Slaving Business

The Place of the Slave Trade in the Maritime Economies

The slave trade was a business. With the exception of a few humanitarian thinkers active primarily following the American Revolution, any Frenchmen who bothered to think of the trade conceived of it in financial terms. To the interested merchant, the trade represented one type of investment among many, and traders were not loath to speculate in everything from government bonds to fishing in the New World. Indeed, the very structure of the slaving triangle implied close relationships between slaving and other commerce, particularly the trade in colonial commodities. So intimately related were the slave and colonial trades that the integrity of the slaving business has been questioned; it has been suggested that, far from being a separate enterprise, the business was merely a corollary to the more important one of importing and re-exporting exotic produce. The value of the sugar and coffee entering France or Europe by way of French ports far exceeded the market value of the slaves transported from Africa to the Antilles, and the French slave trade existed only because of the peculiar economic structure of the Antilles. On the other hand, slaving expeditions were organized and realized with little consideration for colonial productivity, and it was only when converting his colonial credits into merchandise that the French trader entered directly into the realm of colonial commerce. Both descriptions are therefore correct: the slave trade relied on colonial commerce for its existence, but the individual slave trader planned to make a profit solely through the sale of slaves in the West Indies.

129

The relative autonomy of the slave trade varied according to place and time. At Nantes towards the end of the old regime, for example, the slave trade held a privileged position and surpassed direct colonial commerce in capital invested. Throughout the eighteenth century, Nantes had steadily declined as an exporter of French goods to the colonies, and by the eve of the Revolution, Nantes merchants were concentrating heavily on the slave trade. This emphasis on the trade produced a specialized business which subordinated virtually all other economic activities. At Nantes during the 1780s, colonial commerce depended largely on the slave trade, and only massive investment in the trade kept the volume of colonial imports from diminishing in the port. By selling slaves to the planters, Nantes merchants succeeded in retaining or even expanding their interest in the exotic-commodities market, as colonial commerce simply followed along the paths charted by the slave trade. Ironically, the supremacy of slaving tended at the very end of the old regime to modify the nature of the trade itself. Debts arising from the purchase of slaves in the colonies became so large that many French traders had to buy or run indebted plantations. The new trader-planters then had to worry as much about procuring cheap slaves as selling slaves for a comfortable profit. It is even possible that a new system was about to be created when the French and Haitian Revolutions intervened, a system dominated by the French merchant now in control of every phase of the triangle. At Bordeaux, on the other hand, the slave trade was almost always inferior to direct trade with the colonies. Except during the final decade of the old regime when local merchants began slaving operations at an unprecedented pace, Bordeaux businessmen showed only a superficial interest in the trade. Bordeaux' maritime economy was based on the sale of local goods to the West Indian colonies and on the redistribution of colonial produce throughout Northern and Western Europe; the trade was of secondary or even tertiary importance. Whereas Nantes merchants used the trade in order to participate more heavily in colonial commerce, the Bordeaux traders' limited involvement in slaving meant that each expedition was an isolated event on the periphery of the local economy. Thus the trade could either dominate a port's life and control other forms of commerce or be a mere curio enjoyed by eccentric merchants.

Slaving played an ambiguous role in the trade of the French empire as well as in the ports of France. The traders believed it to be a business, while the planters wanted it to be a service; and the government had to satisfy both groups. Concerned exclusively with profits and losses, the independent trader could only understand slaving as a financial venture. The slaving merchant paid little attention to long-term trends or to the whole of which the trade was a part. Instead, he dealt with each expedition as a particular business affair having as its primary purpose the selling of slaves at a profit. This narrow view explains the difficulty traders had in understanding the problems faced by the planters. Uncomprehending and unsympathetic, French merchants sincerely believed that sheer avarice prevented the colonists from paying their debts; they rarely recognized that the planters were subject to contradictory forces beyond their control. The planters' perspective differed sharply from the merchants'. Preoccupied with rising overhead, the planters desperately wanted more and cheaper slaves to produce greater quantities of expensive commodities. The conflict between the two groups was clear, and it centered on the question of slaving profits. The merchants reasoned that since the trade was a business, profits should be as high as the market would allow; and that the well-known risks run by the traders justified large profits. The planters replied that the trade should be considered an essential service to the island communities and that French merchants should be satisfied with earning commissions on the re-export trade. The colonists believed that the government should release the colonies from the tyranny of the French traders: either the trade should be controlled by the government to assure all areas an adequate supply of slaves at reasonable prices, or the colonial slave markets should be opened to foreigners. In the end, neither group was completely satisfied, as the government decided to permit foreign traders to operate within selected areas in the French West Indies. This gave some relief to the more-oppressed planters, but it still guaranteed the French traders control over the best colonial markets. Many planters remained in an impossible situation and were forced to renege on part of their debts. At the end of the old regime, it was considered standard for 10 to 20 percent of the slaving debts to go unpaid. In this manner, a temporary *modus vivendi* was realized between merchant and planter, with the traders' paper profits remaining respectable while the colonists' real costs stayed reasonable.

The Trade Supreme: Nantes, 1783-92. After nearly a century of growth, the slave trade reached its apogee at Nantes during the final decade of the old regime. The most remarkable indication of the ever-increasing interest in slave trading was the growth in the number of African expeditions fitted out by Nantes merchants. Local businessmen were already sending out an average of fifteen ships a year to Africa between 1713 and 1722. The number increased irregularly throughout the century until it reached an average of thirty-nine ships a year following the American Revolution (see table 10.1). Although the Nantais fitted out only 35 percent of all French slavers after the American War, as opposed to over 50 percent before the Seven Years' War, they still had no serious rivals in the trade, and with almost forty departures annually, remained far ahead of all other French merchants. The sharp increase in the number of slaving expeditions fitted

Table 10.1
Nantes Slaving Departures

Years	Average No. per Year
1713-22	15
1726-35	12
1736-44	24
1749-54	31
1763-77	24
1783-92	39

out at Nantes from 1783 to 1792 altered the relationship between the trade and colonial commerce at Nantes. Direct commerce between Nantes and the Antilles did not expand appreciably in the second half of the eighteenth century, that is, during the period of Bordeaux' ascendancy. According to Jean Meyer, some seventy-five ships left Nantes each year for the Antilles between 1733 and 1744, while only seventy-seven left from 1783 to 1792, for an annual increase of less than 1 percent.[1] At the same time, slaving departures nearly doubled, significantly lowering the ratio of ships *en droiture* to those *en circuit,* from three to one to two to one. There was therefore a clear shift in emphasis which justified the subordinate role ascribed to direct shipping by the traders. As one slaving merchant wrote, "The armateurs were forced to send out large ships to the colonies to bring back the goods realized from the sale of slaves."[2] Once the triangle was firmly established, direct trade between Nantes and the colonies was more dependent upon the slave trade than upon supplying the islands with French goods.

An analysis of the cargoes carried by ships engaging in the two branches of commerce underlines the increasing importance of the slave trade at Nantes during the second half of the eighteenth century and particularly after 1783. The crucial question is one of size: how many slaves were carried to the colonies and what quantity of goods returned to Nantes? Not surprisingly, the number of slaves transported aboard Nantes ships from Africa to Saint Domingue varied directly with the number of expeditions sent out. This is especially clear because of the stability of slaving cargoes. Although slave ships increased in tonnage by some 50 percent from 1749 to 1792, they still delivered almost the same number of slaves each; at most, the pre-Revolutionary ships carried only 10 percent more slaves per ship than their mid-century counterparts, a fact which may well have affected profits adversely. Thus, just as the average annual number of expeditions increased by almost 50 percent from 1748-55 to 1783-92, so did the number of slaves taken to the colonies, in this case from 8,500 to 13,000 annually. Since the price of slaves had risen markedly as well, the nominal value of this human commodity soared. Trade between the Antilles and Nantes developed along similar lines, at least as far as the relationship between cargo and ship size was concerned. Shipping directly from the

Antilles became no more efficient than did slaving, as each ship returning from the islands from 1771 to 1789 continued to transport between 400,000 and 500,000 pounds of sugar and coffee.[3] If anything, the average probably declined by 10 to 15 percent towards the end of the century. Since the number of ships arriving in Nantes from the colonies increased only modestly throughout the second half of the century, the total annual volume of colonial goods arriving at Nantes did not alter appreciably, although the value of those goods increased. This stability in volume was all the more surprising in light of the tremendous growth in average ship size, from 251 tons in 1749-54 to 363 tons in 1783-92.[4] At the end of the old regime, ships were filled to only two-thirds capacity instead of to over nine-tenths as before.

By 1789, the Nantes economy relied on the slave trade. Not only did investments in slaving exceed investments in other forms of commerce, but the trade was instrumental in keeping Nantes a major distributor of colonial commodities. Towards the end of the old regime, at least one-third, and possibly as much as one-half, of all exotic produce entering Nantes represented payments for slaves bought from Nantes merchants. Even ships sailing directly between Nantes and the Antilles returned to Nantes with large portions of their cargoes representing slaving payments. The basic reason for this was evident: direct ships leaving Nantes after mid-century usually carried small cargoes which scarcely paid for expenses in the islands, let alone the purchase of large quantities of exotic produce. While in other ways costing almost as much to send out as a slaver, the direct ship had a small cargo which could not possibly allow for any significant investment in colonial commodities.[5] Even though selling the merchandise in the Antilles normally made a respectable profit, the amount involved was too small to be of more than secondary importance.[6] Hence the typical captain of a Nantes direct ship had to concern himself primarily with locating freight for shipment back to France, and the success of the voyage depended on the size of the cargo he found and on the time he took to find it. Much of this freight represented payments for slaves delivered earlier. Freight, incidentally, was doubly important because it attracted hard currency. As one agent wrote, "You ask me, sirs, to stipulate in my bills of lading that the freight or a part of it shall be paid for in paper. . . . You can well believe that a captain would never agree to that proposition. It is in his interest to have the freight paid in silver, and he will never sacrifice this interest to the rivalries of the loaders. If he did so, he would be wrong."[7]

Only the slave trade kept Nantes from declining to the level of a minor provincial port. Given Bordeaux' supremacy in supplying the islands with flour, wine, and other essentials, a supremacy which provided Bordeaux merchants with huge commissions on the massive re-export trade, Nantes merchants had to invest great sums in the slave trade. The Nantais could not limit themselves to the role of middlemen in the re-export commerce, and had to risk their own capital in order to make large profits. The Chaurands understood this principle well when they wrote, ''The new out-fittings are crushing us, for do not believe that we work by commissions; on the contrary, we have very few investors in our ships, and you would be amazed at the capital which we invest.''[8] Only large risks could yield the desired returns: the Chaurands earned 100,000 livres on their 170,000-livre investment in their slaver *Brune*.[9] Nantes merchants found it necessary to invest heavily in the slave trade if they were to continue to take advantage of the opportunities offered by transatlantic commerce.[10]

Dominating Nantes' maritime commerce, the slave trade also had an important role to play in Nantes' industrial development, as merchants invested in related enterprises. Sugar-refining, the manufacture of hardware, shipbuilding, and the making of printed cloths were all aided by the trade. Although Nantes' position outside the main French customs union tended to discourage local sugar-refining and favor processing either further up the Loire or in foreign lands, there were several working refineries in Nantes during the eighteenth century. Similarly, local hardware manufacturing helped supply the slave ships, although most of their hardware was bought elsewhere. On the other hand, the trade was a decisive influence on local shipbuilding, and on the eve of the Revolution, Nantes led all French ports in ship-building activity.[11] One of the most important traders after 1783 was Nicolas Arnous, himself a former shipbuilder. Another branch of the Arnous family was based in Lorient and supplied the Compagnie des Indes with timber, if not constructed vessels; René Arnous Brothers went bankrupt shortly after the company's end.[12]

The most significant slave-related industry to arise in Nantes was that of *indiennage*, or the manufacture of printed cloths used to purchase slaves in Africa. Legalized in France in 1759—before which only calicoes brought from Asia by the Compagnie des Indes could be used—the printed cloth industry got its start that very year when the Langevin brothers began to produce brightly patterned textiles. By the time of the Revolution, the industry was the most important in Nantes, and it still existed almost exclusively to serve the slave trade, as its directors well knew.[13] At least a dozen factories were established in Nantes before the end of the old regime, all attempting to provide a necessary commodity at a competitive price.[14]

The link between commerce and industry was not limited to the use of indiennes on slaving expeditions: many of the prominent factory owners were deeply and directly involved in the trade, and by 1789 almost all of them were slave traders. The most important factories were owned by Swiss Protestants, including Benoit Bourcard (Burkhardt), partner in Pelloutier, Bourcard, and Company, a major investor in the trade. Using cheap labor, including that of children, the printed cloth manufacturers at Nantes were like their counterparts in eighteenth-century Lancashire,[15] but the advent of the Revolution prevented further development along those lines. In any event, it was clear that eighteenth-century Nantes manufacturing reached its peak at the end of the old regime, and that it was largely based on the needs of the slave trade and financed by men who were directly involved in slaving.[16]

The Inconsequential Trade: Bordeaux before 1783. Nowhere in France was the slave trade as important as at Nantes. Taken narrowly, it had only the most modest of influences on French commercial and industrial development. It would be virtually meaningless to speak of a French industrial revolution financed by slaving profits and motivated by the demands of the trade; the English model proposed by Eric Williams simply does not apply.[17] Taken in a much wider sense, the slave trade—meaning the entire colonial plantation economy as well as the trade proper—had further-reaching consequences. The major ports owed a high percentage of their activity to colonial commerce, and French trade with Europe was dependent upon re-exports of tropical commodities. Industry, however, was less affected. Rouen may at first have developed in response to colonial needs, but the Revolution stopped almost all commerce between France and the West Indies. Never again did trade with the Antilles play a major role in French economic life.

Even in Bordeaux, the second most important slaving port of eighteenth-century France, the trade was of little consequence, with the partial exception of the 1783-92 period. During the final decade of the old regime, the trade merely supplemented an increasingly sluggish colonial commerce; slaving did not control the port's economy. Before the American Revolution, Bordeaux experienced such regular and significant growth in colonial commerce that there was little room for the slave trade. Scarcely 200 slavers departed from Bordeaux between 1720 and 1777, and more than half of them left after 1763. Even when most active, the trade was of minimal importance; the pre-1783 peak of 13 departures for Africa (1769) paled in comparison with the more than 150 annual departures for the Antilles from 1763 to 1777. Slaving at Bordeaux was reserved for a few eccentric but powerful merchants occasionally joined by adventurous fortune-seekers.

Direct trade with the colonies dominated the local economy. According to Paul Butel, the Bordelais sent out some 66 ships to the colonies in 1715, but the number increased rapidly as the port emerged as the leader in colonial commerce.[18] By the 1730s, over 100 ships a year left Bordeaux for the Antilles, and following the American Revolution, an average of 250 ships set out annually for the West Indies. This frenetic activity, based on the enviable resources of a rich hinterland, enabled Bordeaux to conquer the colonial market for French goods. Unlike the ships leaving Nantes with minimal cargoes, ships sailing from Bordeaux to the Caribbean were full of merchandise urgently needed in the colonies. At the end of the old regime, Bordeaux was furnishing over 50 percent of Saint Domingue's imports from France,[19] with a typical ship delivering a cargo worth 150,000 livres.[20] As the value of Bordeaux' exports to the Antilles increased steadily during the greater part of the century, local merchants saw little reason to turn to the slave trade. Complementing the growth of Bordeaux' export trade to the islands was a similar increase in the imports of colonial produce at the port, at least during most of the century. Ship arrivals kept pace with departures, increasing from around 140 in 1750 to 225 in the mid-1780s.[21] Until the American Revolution, these ships carried ever-larger and more-valuable cargoes, reflecting the progressive cultivation of Saint Domingue and the growing importance of Bordeaux itself. According to Malvezin, Bordeaux received 20,000,000 pounds of sugar and coffee in 1730, 33,000,000 in 1740, 47,000,000 in 1750, 66,000,000 in 1766, and 100,000,000 in 1776.[22] Only after the American War did this growth subside, as imports averaged 96,000,000 from 1783 to 1787, a fact which undoubtedly encouraged further participation in the slave trade at this time.

With such a volume of colonial imports and exports, Bordeaux became the center of the French re-export trade. During the last decade of the old regime, the city accounted for up to 50 percent of French exports of colonial commodities to Europe, a figure probably approached as early as the 1760s.[23] The establishment of Bordeaux as the major French distributor of tropical produce, as well as the primary supplier of European goods to the French West Indies, offered local merchants great opportunities as entrepreneurs. Whereas the total volume of Nantes' colonial commerce was not enough to enrich more than a few middlemen, so much wealth passed through Bordeaux that the possibilities for an enterprising businessman were endless.[24] Even beyond the borders of France, Bordeaux was famous, renowned as an international commercial center attracting foreign merchants to its gates. Coming from Northern Europe—at first from Holland, then Germany—these merchants formed new companies with close links to Amsterdam, Hamburg, and Danzig. One such newcomer was Henry Romberg, son of a prominent Brussels banker.[25] Arriving in Bordeaux in 1783, he created Henry Romberg, Bapst, and Company, devoted to earning commissions on fitting out ships for Africa and the Antilles and on the sale of colonial commodities.[26] With generous foreign credits, the company prospered until it became hopelessly involved in the colonial economy, at which point it failed, another victim of the troubled pre-Revolutionary maritime economy.

Representing a maximum of 20 percent, and more typically, well under 10 percent, of all capital invested in maritime ventures, the Bordeaux slave trade could not compete against direct trade with the islands. Bordeaux attracted the largest share of colonial exports with its flour, and not with slaves transported from Africa. By sending out enough local products, Bordeaux merchants were able to make respectable profits in the Antilles and then to speculate on colonial commodities. Even though the Bordealais were no wiser than the Nantais and could not normally count on further profit from the sale of the colonial goods in France, the volume of business conducted by the Bordelais in the islands finally earned for the port the privileged position it desired. After the middle of the eighteenth century, the European commodities sold in the Antilles by Bordeaux merchants were worth two or even three times the value of the slaves introduced by Nantes ships. This gave Bordeaux the advantage it needed, and further shipments of colonial goods to Bordeaux inevitably followed. In this manner, Bordeaux became the leading French port in the colonial trade. The slave trade had only a small place in the system.

The Profits of Slaving

Whether the motivating force behind the economy or an occasional diversion, the slave trade attracted merchants for one reason, profits. Of all the investments open regularly to residents of large ports, the slave trade alone had the remote possibility of huge profits. Only the Compagnie des Indes, viewing the trade as merely one part of a much larger structure, remained unimpressed by its potential; the company was apparently more concerned with avoiding losses in its slaving operations. Independent merchants showed no such hesitation: convinced that untold wealth awaited them in Africa and the Antilles, businessmen in ports from Dunkerque to Marseilles participated more and more heavily in slaving. By 1789, about 30,000,000 livres were invested directly in the trade each year, with other millions going to related commerce and industry. Needless to say, the very popularity of slaving made it more difficult to engage in profitably, although merchants discouraged by failure were soon replaced by others eager to seek their fortunes. Predicting gains of up to 100 percent[27] and realizing paper profits of 50 percent,[28] the traders were confident that they had found the true El Dorado. Failure to make commensurate net profits left most of them undaunted and believing that it required only certain modifications to make their most optimistic dreams come true.

A few did despair of ever profiting from the trade, and they began the debate which has lasted into the twentieth century. Was the slave trade profitable? Unsuccessful traders, such as the Chaurands, complained that the trade was a waste of time and money: "We are not disposed to send out any more slavers. The expeditions are too costly[29]"; and "Misfortune seems to attach itself to our expeditions to Guinea. We have not succeeded with a single one. It would be better to yield for a while to circumstances than risk being crushed in fighting misfortune".[30] Complaints such as these were common in late-eighteenth-century France, and they gave rise to what Gaston Martin called the "legend of the unprofitable trade."[31] By Martin's time, the debate had become tinged with ethical overtones: somehow a profitable trade was especially immoral and an unprofitable trade was apparently less objectionable. Martin therefore dismissed the idea of an unprofitable trade, charging that it was incompatible with the obvious wealth of eighteenth-century Nantes. Only recently has the question of trading profits been studied objectively, first by Dieudonné Rinchon[32] and then by Jean Meyer.[33] Although these two historians did not draw any definite conclusions, they did show the real possibility of a losing trade. Meyer, in fact, claimed that slaving sometimes gave poorer results than shipping directly to the Antilles, and that neither was particularly lucrative in late-eighteenth-century Nantes.[34]

A large part of the uncertainty over slaving profits stems from the existing documentation. To begin with, there is a dearth of direct information about the slaving business. The records of most eighteenth-century slaving companies have long since vanished; such papers are so rare that for a time it was commonly assumed that they had been burned by repentant traders or by their embarrassed descendants. Recent discoveries by Rinchon and Meyer have shown that at least some of the documents were merely misplaced and forgotten, not destroyed. In the second place, there has been considerable difficulty in using the available eighteenth-century business papers. Each trader used slightly different accounting methods, which makes comparisons hazardous, although not impossible, for some features were common to all traders' account books. More serious was the normal confusion between slaving and other commerce. Few traders made separate entries in their books for each of their enterprises; there was, instead, a tendency to mix different types of transactions together. If a ship completed a slaving voyage and then returned to the Antilles on a direct voyage from France, most armateurs' ledgers would be unclear as to which expedition certain expenses or receipts related, for example. Thus the intimate ties between the slave and colonial trades carried over into the merchants' books and made it difficult to distinguish one from the other. And finally, there was the unique problem posed by colonial currency. Most transactions in the French islands were expressed in terms of colonial livres, worth two-thirds of French livres.[35] Although colonial pounds were never minted, this non-circulating currency served as the accounting unit for virtually all business conducted in the islands. Since merchants in France also used the colonial livre when referring to colonial business, this intangible money found its way into many slavers' books. Unfortunately, the traders rarely specified which livre they were referring to, and modern historians have confused the two, making mistakes of 33 or 50 percent.[36] The slave traders seemed to like this ambiguity when building a case for the perversity of colonial planters or for the profitability of the trade; by using colonial pounds, they increased their colonial credits and paper profits by half.

Within the limits set by the documents, profits can still be studied. Three groups of factors influenced them, the first related to costs, the second to the purchase and disposal of the slaves, and the third to the acquisition and division of the returns. As Meyer noted, maritime expeditions have expenses before, during, and after a voyage, but the first are far and away the largest.[37] This was true for the eighteenth-century slave trade: before leaving port, a slaver might cost over half a million livres to prepare. These costs, known in French as the *mise-hors,* always included the cargo, the ship and its preparation, advances on the crew's wages, and food. Sometimes an armateur added insurance charges, but insurance was frequently left to the discretion of the investor. Other, smaller, charges might also be included by the armateur, thereby making unqualified comparisons between different armateurs' initial costs potentially misleading, although the differences were never so great as to make all comparisons invalid. Commission, taxes, and the like caused considerable annoyance, but they did not augment the total bill significantly. On the other hand, certain deductions could be large; for example, royal freight or premiums based on slaving tonnage could substantially reduce the outfitting costs.

Cargo was the single most expensive element of a slaving expedition. Most armateurs devoted one-half to four-fifths of the outfitting budget to the purchase of an appropriate cargo, realizing that a successful trade depended on an abundance of attractive merchandise. Expenses relating to the ship usually claimed between a tenth and a third of the outfitting expenditures, with new ships costing the most. Ship depreciation could be treated in two ways: either the ship remained in the possession of the investors, to be used without charge on subsequent voyages, or it could be repurchased by the armateur at a depreciated cost after each expedition and then resold to the investors for the next outing at the new low rate. Although the armateur gained a few livres through commissions earned on the continual repurchasing and reselling of the vessel, there was little real difference between the two methods. Food for the crew and the slaves accounted for about 5 percent of the total cost, while advances to the crew were worth about 2 percent. Insurance normally cost around 5 percent of the expedition's value, although premiums could increase to as much as 50 percent in times of war.

Average outfitting costs rose steadily throughout the eighteenth century, and variations at any one time could be large. Independently owned slaving ships leaving France before the War of the Austrian Succession cost an average of 85,000 livres to fit out and ranged in cost from 18,000 to 144,000 livres;[38] at the same time, Compagnie des Indes' slavers cost more than 200,000 livres each.[39] By the end of the old regime, the mise-hors had increased markedly, with an average expedition costing about 275,000 livres and expensive expeditions more than 500,000 livres.[40] Still, slaving costs never approached the costs of expeditions to China or the East Indies, which might be as high as 2,000,000 livres. Slaving was, however, more costly than direct shipping. Even in Bordeaux, where the direct ship's large outgoing cargoes inflated costs significantly, slaving ships cost nearly twice as much to fit out as direct ones (see table 10.2).

Table 10.2
Slaving Costs

Date	Expeditions	Average Cost	Minimum	Maximum
1713-44 (independents)	11	85,000 livres	18,000	144,000
1749-55	7	168,000	69,000	363,000
1763-69	25	173,000	23,000	421,000
1770-77	24	228,000	36,000	427,000
1783-92	70	275,000	22,000	595,000

Sources: ADG 7B2773; 7B2129 f° 38; ADLA B4497, 11-1-1741; B4498, 20-2-1745; and Meyer, *Armement*, pp. 296, 301-2.

In addition to outfitting costs, slavers incurred expenses during and after expeditions. There were normally two types of expense during the expedition, those in Europe and those in the Antilles. Only rarely did a captain have to make payments in Africa; these would usually be made to other captains in time of dire necessity, such as when the ship was badly damaged. Expenses in Europe resulted from purchases made in France, Spain, or Portugal. These purchases completed the assembly of a cargo which for one reason or another was not completed before leaving the home port. Such purchases could be large, but they were foreseen by the armateur and immediately charged to the investors; they could even be included on the final statement of the mise-hors.[41] We have already mentioned the outlays in the Antilles, costs that were deducted from the slaving debts and not, therefore, charged directly to the investors. Finally, there were the payments necessitated by the ship's arrival, notably the crew's wages and various handling charges. *Désarmement* expenditures could be high, reaching 20 to 25 percent of the initial costs; usually, they were deducted from the money realized through the sale of the returning cargo.

Purchashing, transporting, and selling the slaves were critical elements of the slaving business. The number of slaves bought and sold and the amounts paid and received for them largely determined the profits of the expedition. Like the mise-hors, the prices of slaves rose throughout the century, both in Africa and the Antilles. In fact, there was a close relationship between the African prices and the cost of fitting out the expedition, particularly in the second half of the century. Since slaving ships traded about the same number of slaves per ship in 1789 as in 1750, the armateur's total cost per slave varied directly with the outfitting costs. The armateur paid about 60 percent more to send out his ship towards the end of the century than at the middle, and slaves cost him about 50 percent more. The limited data available reveal that slaves cost the armateur approximately 300 livres each in 1740, 500 livres in 1750, and 750 livres in 1790. These of course, are the total amounts which the armateur in effect paid for the slaves, determined by dividing the mise-hors by the number of slaves traded. Given the barter system prevailing on the coast of Africa, it is virtually impossible to ascertain what the Africans asked for each slave, but it is probable that increased African demands were partly to blame for rising costs per slave.

The sale of the slaves in the Antilles determined the paper profits of the expedition, which were invariably high, even spectacular. According to the Syndics of the Chamber of Commerce of Normandy, French merchants sold some 82,663 slaves for 76,293,330 livres between 1738 and 1744.[42] This meant that the average slave sold for 923 "livres," or since this was certainly in colonial money, some 615 French pounds. At the same time, French slavers were paying about 300 (French) livres per slave in Africa; hence, they earned a profit of over 100 percent on each colonial sale. Similar results obtained later in the century. In the 1780s, for example, slavers bought slaves for approximatly 750 (French) livres each and sold them for about 1,325 (French) livres, an increase of nearly 80 percent. As if these gains were inadequate, the traders increased them by half through the use of colonial livres, thereby realizing average paper profits of 200 or even 300 percent.[43] The trade appeared to be little less than a financial miracle: traders figured that their investment would double or triple in eight months—and still promise further gains from speculation in colonial commodities. The only flaw the traders recognized—except, of course, for colonial intransigence over debt-paying—was slave mortality. The death of each slave on a 300-slave expedition theoretically cut profits by .67 percent, and the average mortality rate of 10 to 15 percent reduced gains by

20 to 30 percent. The financial consequences of a high mortality rate were potentially staggering, and every effort had to be made to keep the slaves alive.

Once he sold his slaves, the trader transferred his attention to the commodities market. Here again, he imagined himself on the threshold of unlimited gains. According to an estimate made at mid-century, a clever trader could easily increase his money by 150 percent:

> The theoretical capital of 600,000 livres [from the sale of slaves] is divided into three equal parts for the purchase of coffee (⅓), sucre brut (⅓), and sucre térré (⅓). At the resale in France, the coffee should bring in 335,000 livres (for a profit of 167 percent); the sucre brut 1,000,000 livres (profit, 500 percent); the sucre terré, 500,000 livres (250 percent). . . . . Deducting various costs (210,595 livres) the net sale price in France is still 1,525,000 livres.[44]

Although the lack of contemporaneous sources makes it impossible to criticize these estimates, later experience shows a less lucrative commerce. Following the Seven Years' War, if not much earlier, it was difficult to make profits on the sale of colonial goods. Primitive communications made it impossible to take advantage of the short-term changes which provided the best opportunities for large profits. By the time a ship returned to France, it was carrying merchandise purchased on the basis of three-month-old conditions. The armateur therefore could count on only modest gains which scarcely covered the freight charges involved. For example, six Chaurand slavers spent 931,000 livres on colonial goods which were sold in Nantes for a total of 1,038,000 livres, or a gross profit of 11 percent, net profits were undoubtedly lower.[45] Given the volume of colonial trade, it would be surprising if profits were ever much higher, except under exceptional circumstances. With up to a thousand ships sailing annually between the French West Indies and Europe, competition was simply too intense to allow major differences between colonial and European prices.[46]

The real problem faced by the slaver after selling his slaves was not making further profits on colonial produce, but getting his money. Having sold his cargo of slaves for hundreds of thousands of livres, he needed most of all to get what was owed him. Anxious armateurs watched with exasperation as their hard-earned gains inexplicably vanished. The Chaurands' ledgers provide an excellent example of this process. Five of their ships sold slaves for a total of 3,546,000 colonial livres—an apparent profit of 167 percent; yet first returns yielded only 709,000 livres, not even half the initial costs.[47] To begin with, one-third of the sale price was artificial as expressed in colonial currency. Then, of the 2,364,000 livres really owing, only 1,085,000 were paid in cash; the rest remained in various notes due in monthly intervals extending over two years. Next, 240,000 livres were lost in diverse expenses, and only 845,000 livres were actually converted into merchandise. Things were hardly better in Nantes. Although the produce sold for 938,000 livres, an increase of 11 percent, further charges reduced this to 709,000 livres.[48] The Chaurands therefore had to wait for the arrival of the 1,305,000 livres still owing, a wait which took several years. Thus the very last step of the triangle was the most difficult to conclude. It was also the most important for the traders.

Given the influence of these factors on the profitability of the slave trade in general, how did specific expeditions fare? Although conditions were generally favorable throughout the eighteenth century, circumstances varied according to time and place. Furthermore, individual expeditions succeeded or failed for particular reasons. Hence, to see the impact of each variable, it is necessary to analyze the results of several voyages fitted out in one port during a limited period of time. Because of the relative abundance of documentation, late-eighteenth-century Nantes provides the most fertile ground for study.[49] Nearly complete information has survived for some twenty-five slaving expeditions fitted out there between 1783 and 1790 (see table 10.3). Although these represent but 8 percent of the expeditions departing from Nantes at this time, they reflect a wide range of experience and are representative. Ten of them made profits, with six gaining more than 19 percent. Six lost money. One expedition was breaking even and eight were in a losing position when payments ceased at the end of 1792; seven of these would have been profitable had even a reasonable percentage of the money owed been remitted. The slave trade produced mixed results in practice, yielding both profits and losses. Both sides in the debate were correct.

Costs (particularly initial costs), the number of slaves delivered, and the sale price of the slaves determined the profitability of the expeditions. The twenty-five voyages cost between 180,000 and 464,000 livres, almost all of which was spent in fitting out the ships. Lower costs meant a higher probability of success: ten of the twelve expeditions costing less than 300,000 livres were, or were likely to be, profitable, while only seven of the thirteen costing more than 300,000 livres made money. The armateurs' ability to keep costs down had a direct impact on profits, but they found it difficult to limit expenditures and always had to struggle against extravagance. Nicolas Arnous, for example, spent between 219,000 and 464,000 livres on his six expeditions, while the Chaurand Brothers spent between 194,000 and 336,000 livres for their nine. Although the temptation to spend too much on the cargo was not particularly dangerous for a trader, expenditures on nonessential items had to be strictly limited. Extra money invested in the cargo usually yielded commensurate returns, but an expensive vessel or unduly high wages brought no such returns and could cripple an expedition economically.

If the armateur made a profitable expedition possible, it was up to the

Table 10.3
Nantes Slaving Profits, 1783-90

Date	Ship	Tons	Armateur	Slaves Sold	Cost of Expedition (000's L)	Net Returns (000's L)	Net Returns (%)	Armateur's Cost per Slave Delivered (L)
1784	*Brune*	418	Chaurands	448	276	432	+57	614
1787	*Aimable Aline*	522	Chaurands	435	286	306	+13*	655
1785	*Jeanne Thérèse*	390	Chaurands	291	194	243	+26	663
1783	*Brune*	418	Chaurands	478	336	401	+19	702
1789	*Phénix*	680	Joubert	460	309			
1790	*Phénix*	680	Favereau, Colleno	500	348			
				960	657	990	+41	731
1785	*Aimable Aline*	522	Chaurands	411	322	352	+ 9	785
1787	*Véronique*	175	Simon, Roques	220	180	(270)	+50	820
1788	*Madame*	390	Delaville, Barthelemi	405	341	235	+10*	842
1785	*Alexandrine*	525	Chaurands	356	307	291	− 3	863
1788	*Sainte Anne*	533	Clanchy, Parran	440	381	452	+19	866
1786	*Sainte Anne*	533	Libault, Parran	380	352	305	+ 5*	927
1783	*Justine*	150	Arnous	256	219			
1785	*Justine*	150	Arnous	334	281			
1788	*Justine*	150	Arnous	216	257			
1789	*Justine*	150	Arnous	296	280			
				1102	1037	978	+10*	948
1783	*Jeanne Thérèse*	390	Chaurands	228	222	228	+ 3	969
1789	*Demoiselle*	356	Portier, Hamelin	270	267	267	+15*	988
1790	*Sainte Anne*	532	Clanchy, Parran	400	401	327	−18	1003
1783	*Prince Noir*	300	Geslin	285	322	272	−15	1132
1786	*Jeanne Thérèse*	390	Chaurands	222	272	211	−22	1225
1784	*Usbeck*	350	Arnous	300	464			
1787	*Usbeck*	350	Arnous	399	408			
				699	872	653	−12*	1252
1787	*Louis*	880	Chaurands	182	261	177	−32	1428
1786	*Aigle*	385	Joubert	260	396	229	−42	1522

Source: Robert Stein, "The Profitability of the Nantes Slave Trade, 1783-1792," *Journal of Economic History* 35 (1975), 786.
*Projected results, assuming half the money owing were paid.

captain to make it a reality. He had to acquire a large number of captives, deliver them alive to the Antilles, and sell them at a good price. Most critical was the purchase of the slaves along the coast: a large number made success most probable, while a meager trade implied losses. Once the captain had purchased the slaves, he had to keep them alive. Although it was unusual, a high mortality rate could turn a potentially profitable voyage into a failure. The captain of the *Alexandrine* bought 517 slaves with his cargo valued at 245,000 livres, but 161 died on the middle passage. Instead of reaping a profit of close to 50 percent, the expedition actually lost 3 percent. Delivering a large cargo of Africans was a virtual guarantee of success; all eight expeditions selling more than 400 slaves in the Antilles were profitable, while only nine of the remaining seventeen made gains. Since there was a loose relationship between the size of the vessel and the number of slaves traded, and therefore usually delivered, the larger the ship, the greater the likelihood of success. All this, of course, was dependent upon controlling costs.

This double consideration was crucial: if the armateur could limit expenses and if the captain could deliver a large number of slaves, profits accrued. The lower the ratio between costs and the number of captives sold, the higher the probability of profits. When Nantes traders during the 1783-90 period paid less than 1,000 livres per delivered slave, they made money; when they paid more, they lost. Furthermore, both profits and losses tended to increase as the divergence from the 1,000-livre level increased. Two expeditions clearly illustrate these points. In 1788, the *Sainte Anne* cost 380,000 livres to fit out. Although this was a relatively expensive mise-hors, it was overcome by an exceptional trade; the ship delivered 440 slaves to the islands. These slaves, which had cost the trader only 866 livres each, sold for an average of 1,550 livres, and the expedition realized a 19 percent profit. On the other hand, the *Aigle,* in 1786, cost 400,000 livres to fit out but sold only 260 slaves in the Antilles. The trader had thus paid over 1,500 livres for a commodity which was selling for far less; he lost 42 percent on the voyage.

The traders did not like to admit their responsibility and tried to blame others for poor results. Ships' captains were often abused for wasting the trader's time and money. Armateurs were particularly sensitive about the stop in the Antilles and severely criticized captains who seemed to tarry in the West Indies. Most armateurs believed that the speed at which the expedition was accomplished directly affected the expedition's profits, and that by delaying the ship's return the captain was diminishing the prospects for success. This judgment was incorrect. A study of the Chaurand Brothers' slavers shows that there was only a superficial relation between time and profits.[50] Shorter expeditions did tend to be more profitable, but their expenses in the islands were no smaller than longer, unprofitable expeditions. The West Indian expenses charged by the Chaurands' slavers bore little relation to the length of the voyages: the second slowest and most unsuccessful of all the Chaurands' expeditions (the *Louis,* seventeen months) cost only half as much in the Antilles as did the quickest and second most profitable (the *Brune*, no. 2, eleven months). Fast voyages were successful, not because they were cheaper, but because they benefitted from good trading conditions in Africa and the colonies.

Slavers reserved their greatest wrath for the colonial planters, whose refusal to pay promptly seemed to jeopardize the entire operation. This fear was justified, but only insofar as prompt payment enabled the traders to reinvest their funds more rapidly. The speed at which remittances were made had little effect upon the results of a particular voyage, although it did influence annual profits. The Chaurands, for example, regularly received most payments within six years of their ship's departure from Nantes, but payments for their most successful ship (*Jeanne Thérèse*, no. 2) were slower than for their least successful (*Louis*). In the first case, it took several years for 75 percent of the debt to be repaid; in the second, the Chaurands received 90 percent of their money within three years. Obviously, even the percentage of the debt ultimately recovered did not have a conclusive effect on the net profits. Those voyages for which the greatest part of the debt was in fact repaid were frequently unprofitable. Annual profits, however, certainly suffered from colonial foot-dragging, as did reinvestment, at least over the short term. This was particularly trying for the smaller trader, who had to wait until most of the returns were in from one voyage before organizing another. Traders with larger capital reserves could afford to finance further expeditions before the original one was amortized. Once a trader had expeditions departing in two or three successive years, his annual profit increased dramatically, because almost all revenue was immedieately re-invested.

Besides delaying payments, colonists were guilty of refusing to honor all of their obligations. By 1783, it had become more or less standard for the planters to withold a small percentage of the money they owed the merchants. For slave sales made by eight of their ships, the Chaurands expected to receive 1,900,000 livres after initial payments. In fact, they were finally credited on December 31, 1792, with a bit more than 1,500,000 livres (gross), about 80 percent of the anticipated return. Counting the initial payments, which were usually worth about 40 percent of the total debt, and assuming that a few more payments would have been forthcoming had it not been for the outbreak of war with England, a total of about 90 percent of the slaving debt was requited; 10 percent was not. This 10 percent was most significant, for it reduced the traders' profits by half, from 30 to 15 percent. An average expedition at this time cost 275,000 livres to fit out and sold some 330 slaves at 1,330 livres each, or 440,000. Planters paid about 40 percent, or 175,000 livres, immediately, of which a third was lost in various expenses, including unloading costs. Hence, the trader received close to 120,000 net for the first installment. Of the 265,000 livres still due, the planter repaid only some 215,000; further expenses reduced the trader's share of this to about 195,000 livres net. Thus, the trader finally received a total of some 315,000 livres, a net profit of about 15 percent. Had the colonists honored all of their engagements, the trader would have pocketed another 45,000 livres.

The colonists' practice of reneging on a part of their debt had important consequences in the mother country. Besides halving slaving profits, it embittered Franco-colonial relations and encouraged a direct participation by the slave traders in the colonial economy. It also created a huge reservoir of rather dubious credit. For example, at the end of the old regime, the colonists owed the Nantais approximately 45,000,000 livres in debts arising from the slave trade during the 1783-92 period alone: 15,000,000 livres for deliveries in progress, 15,000,000 for deliveries made within the preceding three years, and 15,000,000 for earlier deliveries. This total was almost three-fourths of the 63,000,000 livres lost by the Nantes traders as a result of the Haitian Revolution.[51] Hence there was little new investment in the colonies by the Nantais; instead, the traders merely took over the administration or the ownership of financially troubled plantations. Nantes traders, of course, were not alone in this predicament, and those of Bordeaux suffered in a similar fashion.[52]

Once implicated in the colonial economy, the French trader was in a poor position. Not only were profits difficult to obtain from the slave trade, but the financial demands of the newly acquired plantations reduced them even further. The trader was in danger of suffering the fate of the planter. Instead of merely supplying raw materials (slaves) at a profit, he assumed the mantle of consumer as well; instead of simply transporting the finished product (sugar) back to Europe, he was now also a producer. More and more, the trader dominated all the elements of the triangle and not just the most profitable ones. The triangle was therefore far less attractive in practice than it appeared on paper. Much of the credit generated by the trade between France, Africa, and the West Indies was of questionable value, good only for investing in the islands, or at best, for financing further slaving expeditions. The traders were aware of these weaknesses and united to support one another. This happened, for example, in Nantes towards the end of the old regime: "Michel and Ducamp . . . have just been obliged to suspend payments. . . . All the place has come to their aid, and we hope that in a bit they will begin anew."[53] Ties between merchants within each port were so close that the failure of one important company could imply the ruin of several; this could then entail a general collapse. The solvency of the entire community could be placed in doubt all too easily.

The traders had to rely ultimately on the Parisian money market. Although the slavers showed remarkable ingenuity and originality in organizing their resources—and giving in the process the appearance of an exclusively local financing[54]—behind each trader stood a banker, usually in Paris. The relation between the bankers and the merchants was far from clear, but it seemed that money and credit from Paris, Amsterdam, and Geneva supported the slave trade throughout the century. The Parisian capitalists formed their own slaving companies, invested in companies organized in the ports, and supplied credit to merchants residing in the ports. To a large extent, the bankers and financiers set limits to the traders' actions. Within those bounds, the traders were virtually autonomous, free to establish their local organizations and create a slaving community; but few traders were truly independent of the bankers. Towards the end of the old regime in particular, the increased need for capital or credit forced the port merchants to rely more and more on Parisian money-men. The chronic shortage of specie, the weakness of the colonial economy, and the sharp increase in the number of slaving expeditions fitted out by Frenchmen served to reduce the traders to a subservient position vis-a-vis the bankers. Typical was the complaint of one trader: "'The monetary resources which we are all too easily forced to use are crushing us. . . . Credit accorded by Paris bankers is quite expensive.'"[55] Suppliers of credit were clearly in control.

Parisian capitalists either ran or participated in many slaving companies during the eighteenth century. The bankers and financiers formed and controlled several chartered companies, of which the most important was the Compagnie des Indes, or Law's company, founded in 1717.[56] This firm sent out more than one hundred slavers before the War of the Austrian Succession and enjoyed a monopoly over French slaving from 1722 to 1725. As the Compagnie des Indes declined in importance, the Parisians took a more passive role in slaving affairs, preferring investment in the two great companies established at Nantes in 1748, the Société d'Angole and the Société de Guinée.[57] Many financiers like Dupleix de Bacquencourt and Duval du Manoir and bankers like Jean Cottin and Tourton et Baur invested large sums in these companies, which were nonetheless controlled by armateurs in Nantes. Groups of Parisians also held shares in large slaving companies in other ports. Two-thirds of Begouen Demeaux and Company of Le Havre, formed in 1752, belonged to Parisians,[58] while the Honfleur-based Société de la Guadeloupe (1753) and Société pour la Rivière de Sierra Leone (1762) also looked towards Paris for financing.[59]

Later in the century, Parisians were more discreet. The era of the giant slaving companies, whether royally chartered or formed through private initiative, was over, and Parisian bankers no longer pooled their resources so conspicuously. Instead, individual bankers helped support slaving companies established in the ports. The support came in three forms: the bankers or financiers could buy shares in slaving expeditions, they could buy interests in the slaving companies, or they could supply credit to the slave traders. Direct investments in slaving expeditions were fairly common but rarely significant; out-of-town investors usually purchased only small shares in slave ships. Somewhat more important were the instances of participation in the outfitting company itself. Bankers in Paris or elsewhere occasionally held shares in maritime shipping firms; for example, Frederick Romberg and the Walckiers Brothers of Brussels together owned two-thirds of Henry Romberg, Bapst, and Company of Bordeaux.[60]

But the most important slaving activity of the Parisian capitalists was the extension of credit facilities to the slave traders. Virtually every trader relied on one or two Paris—or again, Dutch or Swiss—bankers or financiers to remain liquid.[61] Sometimes these dealings went no further than do modern current accounts: the trader simply used his bankers to handle the technicalities of payment. The respect in which the big capitalists were held meant that notes drawn on them would be honored without difficulty and without substantial discounts. Hence Parisian notes were more reliable and useful than provincial ones: "Payments for sales and purchases of merchandise are made with paper drawn on Paris, and one rarely sees bills circulating which are payable at Nantes.[62] Sometimes, however, the relation between merchant and banker was not one of convenience but of dependence: the trader relied on the capitalist for credit.[63] Bankruptcy papers reveal that the traders were usually heavily in debt to the bankers; in other words, the traders were unable to replace funds advanced by the bankers on their (the traders') behalf. When Corpron Brothers and Son and Company failed in 1787, their biggest debts were to Cottin and Jauge (97,514 livres), Delavau (66,625 livres), and Tourton and Ravel (63,090 livres), all Paris bankers.[64] Some Paris capitalists seemed to specialize in maritime affairs: Tourton and Ravel, Roberjot (*trésorier général des colonies*), and Baudard de Saint-James (*trésorier général de la marine*) had regular dealings with the ports.

Especially when times were bad, therefore, the traders found themselves pressured on two sides. Forced by their own lack of capital reserves and by delays and defaults in colonial debt payments, they had to rely on capitalists in Paris or elsewhere to remain liquid. Merchant credit offered locally was insufficient, and only recourse to the major money markets can explain how companies capitalized at modest amounts could conduct business on a vast scale, particularly when revenues were uncertain. On February 10, 1767, Paul Nairac and Son renewed itself at Bordeaux with a capital of 322,933 livres.[65] During the company's six-year life, it fitted out no fewer than seven slave ships, which together with several ships sent directly to the Antilles must have forced the Nairacs to rely on credit lines established outside of Bordeaux. Much more extreme was the case of Riedy and Thurninger, a Nantes company renewed in 1788 with a capital of 150,000 livres.[66] The company lasted for four years, during which it fitted out nine slavers and invested in at least forty-three others; all told, it spent at least 2,000,000 livres on slaving operations alone.[67] This company almost certainly depended on credit from Switzerland. Both partners were Protestants and were known to have ties with the "Protestant bank."[68] These examples could be multiplied, but the conclusion remains. At the end of the old regime and probably before, bankers and financiers from Paris and other financial centers played an important role in the French slave trade. They supplied traders with the banking and credit facilities which made growth possible. In granting credit, they also set limits to the traders' actions.

11
Armateurs and Investors

Parisian and foreign credit notwithstanding, the slave trade was usually the direct responsibility of merchants living in the ports. Large numbers of businessmen in Nantes, Bordeaux, and other maritime centers devoted their time and effort as well as their fortunes to slaving activities. A few of these men dominated the trade, fitting out most of the ships or investing most of the capital needed at any one time. In each of the major slaving ports, a handful of important merchants possessed the will and the financial resources necessary to participate regularly in the trade. Most lesser figures had to be content with investing small amounts quite occasionally in other merchants' ships; only an exceptionally ambitious entrepreneur could overcome a modest economic position and conduct a major slaving operation. The problem was strictly financial: the slave trade was expensive and risky. Although clever or fortunate traders could make impressive profits, many suffered crippling losses and went bankrupt after two or three expeditions.[1] Only a limited number of rich merchants could afford to continue to invest in the trade after absorbing such losses or while waiting years to realize a profit. Most of the traders did not possess or have access to the appropriate kinds of monetary resources and quickly faded from the slaving scene, to be replaced just as quickly by other fortune seekers. Often the debutant slavers were at the same time new arrivals to the port, lured there by the mirage of huge profits. After the American War in particular, a large number of newcomers with considerable capital participated in the slave trade and went far towards enabling the trade to expand. The most successful of the new arrivals were integrated financially and even socially into the local business community.

151

In spite of their obvious activities, the slave traders remain difficult to identify. Unlike the various artisans, they did not organize themselves into a guild; indeed, they rarely if ever called themselves slave traders, preferring the label *négociant*. A négociant was like a wholesaler, as the Nantes Consulat described it: "The négociants of this town do not allow themselves to sell their merchandise except in bales, cases, or full lots, according to the Edict of 1701. . . . True retail is solely that which is sold to consumers; this business is reserved for *marchands*."[2] Thus, at least in theory, négociants were large-scale wholesalers who were quite different from small retailers or marchands.[3] As far as the négociants were concerned, the fact that most of them had begun as marchands merely emphasized the gap separating the two groups; needless to say, it also reflected their proximity. The bigger négociants, however, went beyond simple wholesaling and approached the world of banking and finance. Besides dealing with commodities on an international scale, the négociant performed various operations of a banking nature, dealing in drafts and bills of exchange as well as sugar, cotton, and coffee. The very name *négociant* stemmed from *négoce*, meaning "trade," often with financial overtones. With a mastery of basic banking techniques, the négociant served as middleman in financial affairs, opening accounts for his colleagues and clients, discounting bills, and extending credit. With business on three continents and with hundreds of thousands of livres invested, the larger slave traders were négociants in every sense of the word.

Slave traders could be armateurs or investors. Although most armateurs invested in the expeditions of at least one colleague, it is more reasonable to treat outfitting and investment separately, at least at first. In the five major slaving ports—Nantes, Bordeaux, La Rochelle, Le Havre, and Saint Malo—members of at least 550 families fitted out 2,800 ships[4] for Africa during the eighteenth century. Hence the average family fitted out only 5 slaving expeditions, very few, considering the period involved—some sixty-five years of peace. This impression is reinforced by other statistics: 487 armateurs (i.e., outfitting families) organized only 1,560 expeditions; in other words, fully 89 percent of the interested merchants were responsible for 56 percent of the voyages, an average of only 3 ships each.[5] Balancing the mass of occasional traders was a small group of specialists who dominated the trade. Eleven percent of the outfitting companies handled 44 percent of the expeditions; that is, some 63 families sent out 1,241 ships, almost 20 each. Some 22 families (4 percent) fitted out more than 20 ships each for a total of 707 (25 percent); of these, only 11 families (2 percent) accounted for 453 ships, or 16 percent (see table 11.1). The national trend merely reflected the situation obtaining in each of the ports. Figures from the five leading ports show that a small number of armateurs

Table 11.1
Major Slaving Families (Armateurs)

Name	Expeditions	Port	Active Years	Year Ennobled
Montaudouin	60	Nantes	1708-1769	1723
Bouteiller	56	Nantes	1739-1789	1751
Michel	52	Nantes	1718-1792[a]	1749
Begouen Demeaux	41	Le Havre	1750-1791	1784
Walsh	40	Nantes	1733-1753	1753
Prémord	39	Honfleur	1763-1792	
Garesché	38	La Rochelle	1741-1791[b]	
Rasteau	38	La Rochelle	1728-1790	
Beaufils	35	Le Havre	1763-1790	
Bertrand	32	Nantes	1727-1765	1731
Meslé[c]	31	Saint Malo	1763-1790	1768
Giraudeau	30	La Rochelle	1735-1786	
Nairac[d]	27	Bordeaux	1740-1792	?
Chauvet	25	Le Havre	1751-1785	
Deluynes	25	Nantes	1709-1775	old nobility
d'Havelooze	24	Nantes	1764-1792	
Feray	23	Le Havre	1750-1792	1775
Delacroix	23	La Rochelle	1732-1755	
Dumoustier	22	La Rochelle	1775-1790	
Magon	22	Saint Malo	1741-1776	1751
Espivent	22	Nantes	1753-1791	old nobility
Portier	21	Nantes	1729-1789	1751
Foache	20	Le Havre	1751-1789	c 1768

[a] Fifty-one ships after 1743.
[b] Thirty-six ships from 1769-91.
[c] Related to Canel, Meslé, and Bernard of Nantes (seven ships, 1783-92).
[d] Related to Nairac of La Rochelle (fourteen ships, 1766-77).

were exceptionally active and in control of the trade in each city. For example, some 71 families sent out nearly 400 slavers from eighteenth-century La Rochelle, but only 13 families (18 percent) were responsible for 259 ships, or 66 percent of the total. The situation was similar in Le Havre, where 8 families (16 percent) accounted for 182 expeditions (60 percent). Even where the trade was the most decentralized, a small group dominated: 10 Bordeaux armateurs sent out 128 slavers (29 percent). The relative democratization apparent at Bordeaux resulted from the sudden massive growth of the trade there following the American War, and not from any fundamental difference in Bordeaux' economic structure. Thus on the local level everywhere a few families clearly took the initiative in slaving. Although the trade was legally open to all merchants and although hundreds of them engaged in it, only a handful managed to fit out slavers on a more or less regular basis.

The active members of these dominant families were slave traders in the fullest sense, especially since most of a family's slaving activity was usually concentrated in a short period and conducted by only one or two men. For example, the most important trading family in eighteenth-century France was the Montaudouin family based in Nantes. Six members of this family sent out some 60 ships to Africa between 1708 and 1769, but Jacques and René Montaudouin alone accounted for 43 in a twenty-one-year period (1708-28). During these periods of intensive slaving, the major armateurs relegated other forms of maritime commerce to secondary positions. For example, slaving specialists at Nantes sent out as many slave ships as ships to the colonies, while occasional slavers fitted out four times as many direct expeditions as triangular ones. Given the much greater expenses involved in slaving, this shows the clear predominance of the trade for the major slaving armateurs.

There were important changes in outfitting patterns during the century, most significantly an apparent shift away from the domination of a few great armateurs. As noted above, this trend, when accompanied by a sharp increase in slaving, gave Bordeaux the most "open" appearance of any French port. Although the other ports were affected by the same process towards the end of the century, they had strong enough foundations to diminish the effects of the change on the century-long statistics. Nonetheless, the final decade of the old regime saw a marked dispersion of outfitting endeavors in all the ports. After 1783, it took more than 20 percent of the armateurs to dispatch half the ships; before, it had taken closer to 10 percent. Obviously, a small group was still preeminent, but not to quite the same degree. This was not so much because of a lack of enterprise among the major armateurs as it was the result of a tremendous increase in the number of slaving departures, an increase made possible by the numbers of men now taking part in the trade. The major traders were as active as ever, averaging one expedition annually, but their impact was lessened. Almost half of the century's 550 slaving armateurs were active during this one decade, but they fitted out only one-third of the century's ships. Thus at the end of the old regime, small businessmen were beginning to "discover" the slave trade. In spite of rising costs, it was still possible after 1783 for a so-called grocer like Clair Ricordel, a man who paid only twelve livres in *capitation* taxes, to mount five slaving expeditions at Nantes. Perhaps it was more possible than ever as a new speculative spirit reigned.

The number of traders active after 1783 underscored the significance of newcomers to the trade. Throughout the century, new traders enabled the trade to grow; this was especially true since few merchant families could afford to remain active in the slave trade over an extended period of time.

In fact, only five families were prominent in fitting out slavers at Nantes during any two of the trade's four major periods (1713-44; 1748-56; 1763-78; 1783-92): the Walshes[6] (1713-44; 1748-56); the Bertrands (1713-14; 1748-56); the Bouteillers (1748-56; 1763-78); the Michels (1748-56; 1783-92); and the d'Haveloozes (1763-78; 1783-92). Needless to say, they were among the richest families in the city.

Outfitting was only the most visible side of slaving: there was also investing. As we have seen, the high cost of operations combined with the long delays in receiving payments to discourage some merchants from fitting out ships and some armateurs from fully financing their own expeditions. At the same time, the would-be armateurs were still interested in the trade, and their interest complemented the need for capital of the practicing armateurs. As a result, there developed the custom of selling shares in slaving ships. At Nantes following the American War, it was standard procedure for an armateur to retain only a 40 percent interest in his ship; the remaining 60 percent was sold to other armateurs (20 percent), local investors (20 percent), non-residents (10 percent), and the captain or crew or both (10 percent). Figures from different ports and different periods are similar and confirm the armateur's dominant though not unchallenged position. There were still many important slave traders who never fitted out a ship.

During the eighteenth century, there was a marked increase in the number of investments made in the slave trade. As the century progressed, businessmen wanted more than ever to participate, but they were also anxious to avoid concentrating too much of their risk capital in any one venture. They therefore purchased numerous ship interests, each of which usually represented only a small fraction of the expedition in question. This served to increase the number of parts for sale and thereby fill the demands of both the armateurs and the investors. The nine largest Nantes armateurs of the pre-1754 period purchased a total of 43 shares in the 175 slave ships whose investors are known; after 1783, they bought 116 shares in 189 expeditions. The nine most active investors—whether armateurs or not—made 98 investments before 1745; they made 296 after 1783. Diversification was a primary consideration in the mind of a prospective investor, and the resulting proliferation of risk capital was a necessary condition for the slave trade's growth.

The increase in the number of investments went hand in hand with the creation of a group of investment specialists. Early in the century, almost all the active investors were also armateurs. Of the nine most prolific investors at Nantes before the Austrian War, eight fitted out slavers, and seven sent out more than one slave ship. By the 1780s this had changed radically: only three of the nine most active investors fitted out more than one Africa-bound ship. Investing was becoming an occupation in itself and not merely a means of expanding an armateur's field of operations. The autonomy of investment complemented the dispersion of outfitting responsibilities. Interest in the trade reached unprecedented heights following the American War, but limited means forced the majority of armateurs to rely heavily on investors for capital. The investors were therefore in a powerful position. They could choose exactly which expeditions they wanted to support, and they could frequently impose conditions before giving that support. Only the richest or best-connected armateurs could dispense with the independent investors. Even some rich armateurs preferred to rely on investors' aid rather than risk everything on a few expeditions. But rather than throw themselves on the mercy of the marketplace, these rich yet conservative armateurs decided to band together to support each other. The groups formed in this manner united the roles of outfitting and investing and became a powerful economic and social force in the community.

With the emergence of a group of investors who specialized in backing slaving expeditions, the term *slave trader* took on a new meaning. No longer was it restricted to the major slaving armateurs, the most visible participants in the trade. Now it included local capitalists whose resources were urgently required by a burgeoning commerce. Frequently, these investors served as a conduit for foreign funds destined for the French trade. We have already seen how the partnership of Riedy and Thurninger channeled Swiss money directly into Nantes outfitting; a similar situation obtained with the investing firm of Pelloutier and Bourcard. In Nantes since 1747, the German Pelloutier formed a partnership in 1756 with the newly arrived Swiss Bourcard (Burkhardt). Both were Protestants, and although neither was particularly active in local shipping before 1783, they were the most important Nantes manufacturers of calicoes used in the slave trade. From 1783 to 1791, they bought shares in 30 slavers. By the end of the nine-year period, they had placed about a million livres in the slave trade, half of it coming in the final two years. Although this increase might have resulted from wise management, it was probably the result of the partnership's foreign ties. The company was involved in international finance and depended on the Basel firm of Christoff Burkhardt and Company for cash and credits.[7] In any case, whether relying on foreign or Parisian financing or upon their own reserves, investors with little interest in fitting out ships were an important force in the second half of the eighteenth century.

A slave trader was therefore a businessman who either fitted out ships to Africa or invested in them on a regular basis. Serious traders not only had an important economic commitment to the trade but also concentrated on it heavily, making the trade central to their business activity. How did such men become slave traders? Although some appeared on the scene with little or no commercial background, most had spent years learning the subtleties of maritime commerce before engaging in the trade, and often two or three generations of toil were needed to produce a slave trader of any significance. Before a family participated heavily in the trade, it might have displaced itself geographically as well as socially and economically. In the history of most trading families, there were recent ancestors who had migrated to the port to work as clerks, captains, or retailers; many of the traders themselves had migrated, to begin their careers on a relatively modest level. Migrants or not, the great majority had at one time been lowly marchands, usually the issue of a long line of ancestors interested in commerce somewhere in France or Europe.

Although conditions varied from port to port, there were some common to all. Traders everywhere in France had similar geographic and social origins. Slave traders usually formed a cosmopolitan group, rejuvenated after each of the century's major wars by new waves of immigration to the ports. The attraction of a Nantes or a Bordeaux was great: these commercial centers were among the richest cities in eighteenth-century France and boasted rapidly growing economies. Although not actually banking centers, they attracted the attention of great European capitalists because of the volume of their colonial commerce. Exporting vast quantities of tropical commodities to Northern Europe, the port cities were well known to distant merchants, many of whom were lured to their gates. Lesser figures, especially from the ports' hinterland, were all the more impressed. With luck, respectable fortunes could still be made in one generation; or, to those who arrived already in possession of ample resources, the ports offered attractive possibilities for investment. Money was forever in demand, and its bearers were always welcome.

Most slave traders came from France, although there was a sizeable foreign contingent, primarily Protestant.[8] About half of the major trading families were long established in their chosen ports by the middle of the eighteenth century. Some had roots in the area extending back to the Middle Ages. For example, the Michels, Espivents, and Bouteillers had been in Nantes since at least the sixteenth century, and most of the important La Rochelle trading families were settled in the port at the time of Henry IV. During the seventeenth century, a large number of trading families arrived in the ports and completed the foundations for the eighteenth-century slaving communities. In Nantes, many of the newcomers were Dutch Protestants, but they were soon converted to Catholicism and naturalized as Frenchmen, becoming for all practical purposes Nantais.[9] These families did not form a lasting ethnic or religious community, and they did not revert to Protestantism when religious toleration was finally introduced. Their assimilation was complete, and by the eighteenth century they enjoyed the same advantages as other long-established families. They had time to develop close social relationships with local merchants, and they could depend on the goodwill of the community. Although there was always room for a wealthy newcomer, it took time to supplement the initial economic rapport with a more binding social one.

Immigration to the ports continued unabated throughout the eighteenth century and reached a peak with the conclusion of the American War. About a quarter of the trading families active at Nantes in 1789 arrived after 1750; they included major figures like Riedy, Thurninger, Aubry de la Fosse, and Plumard. Several important traders in other ports also arrived during the eighteenth century: Begouen Demeaux in Le Havre, Nairac in Bordeaux and La Rochelle, Chateaubriand in Saint Malo. Many of the newcomers were foreign, coming from Ireland (Walsh, to Nantes by way of Saint Malo), Belgium (Romberg, to Bordeaux), Germany (Roques, to Nantes), and Switzerland (Weis, to La Rochelle). The foreigners were generally rich, often noble, and, with the exception of the Irish, invariably Protestant. Most of the newcomers, however, were still French, coming from the hinterland and following ancient trade routes. Nantes, for example, attracted merchants from Rennes and from cities up the Loire River, while Bordeaux drew upon the Protestant strongholds in Aquitaine. There was also considerable movement between the major ports, as merchants moved either permanently to begin anew or temporarily to establish a subsidiary. Younger sons or brothers were especially mobile and useful in creating branch companies. Jean Baptiste Nairac left his older brothers in Bordeaux to establish a major outfitting house in La Rochelle, while Jean Jacques Urbain Meslé extended the family business by moving from Saint Malo to Nantes. Relocations like these helped create a vital network between slave traders in different ports.

The traders' socio-economic origins were far less diverse—the majority came from commercially active families. Most of the major traders began fairly well off, although there was usually a marchand, or even a whole series of marchands somewhere in the recent family history. Important traders were usually sons of prominent négociants, for a healthy paternal legacy was a virtual necessity for founding a large-scale commercial operation. The aristocratic Espivent family of Nantes, for example, maintained an ever-increasing interest in the slave trade through three generations, with each generation building on the foundations laid by its predecessor. By the end of the old regime, the Espivents were among the most important businessmen in the port and served as hosts to Arthur Young.[10] Lesser figures were more often the children of marchands, but in these cases the rather ambuiguous line dividing marchands from négociants was more obscure than ever. Some small traders remained marchands themselves; Belloc of Nantes identified himself as a *marchand droguiste* in the 1780s.

Two other professions accounted for almost all the rest of the slave traders: ship's captain and clerk. About a quarter of the slavers had been ship's captains or were the sons of captains. Most of the captains-turned-traders had little impact on the slave trade; there was simply not enough time for one man to amass a small fortune as a captain and then transform it into a large one as a slave trader. The few major traders who had begun as captains were important more for the number of ships they fitted out than for the sums they invested. Sons of ship's captains, however, had a better chance of becoming important slavers. Captain René Drouin's son Louis became the "second richest man in Nantes."[11] Using at least part of his father's fortune of 80,000 livres,[12] Louis Drouin built a commercial empire centered on the slave trade and worth some 5,000,000 livres in 1789.[13] Several slave traders began as clerks (*commis*) for armateurs. This usually thankless job[14] occasionally served as the springboard to fortune, especially if the clerk were fortunate enough to be brought into partnership with his employer. A *commis* might rise to the rank of an *associé* when a merchant needed a responsible working partner and not just a simple clerk. And Nicolas Arnous of Nantes was the son of a ship builder, while Henry Roques was the son of a German pastor. The trade attracted the adventurous and ambitious from many walks of life.

A final element in the slave traders' background was religion. Although France was officially a Catholic country after the Revocation of the Edict of Nantes in 1685, small numbers of non-Catholics were tolerated. These minorities, when present in commercial centers, tended to assume an importance out of all proportion to their size, and they inevitably influenced the slave trade. With one exception, the minorities were Protestant. The exception was at Bordeaux, where a handful of Jewish merchants also participated in the slave trade. This participation was on a small scale and had slight impact.[15] Only two Jewish families, Gradis and Mendez, fitted out more than one slave ship each during the entire eighteenth century: both families were of Portuguese origin, and both managed to overcome local hostility to achieve prominence in the Bordeaux commercial community. So successful were the Gradis' that they were ennobled in 1751, an event of extreme rarity in the old regime.[16] Although the Gradis' had a fairly active interest in the slave trade, they were more deeply involved in other branches of French colonial commerce. During the Seven Years' War, they supplied New France with food and other necessities, and following the war they had a monopoly over French commerce at Gorée.[17]

The Protestant involvement was much more significant. Although Protestant merchants never equalled Catholics in fitting out slaving expeditions, they were responsible for a large percentage of slaving activity overall and were exceptionally powerful in two major ports. Protestant armateurs accounted for about 20 percent of all slaving expeditions leaving France during the eighteenth century, a percentage which rose slightly towards the end of the old regime, when a wave of Protestant immigration struck the French ports. In spite of the newcomers, it was still the long-established Protestants in La Rochelle and Bordeaux who had the greatest impact on the trade. A Protestant stronghold since the Reformation, La Rochelle was still kind to Protestant merchants in the eighteenth century. Protestants were only a small percentage of the population, but they dominated maritime commerce in general and the slave trade in particular.[18] Protestant armateurs sent out more than 50 percent of all La Rochelle slavers during the century, and most of the major traders in the port were Protestant. The situation was similar in Bordeaux, where the majority of important traders were Protestant; here, however, they accounted for about 30 percent of the slaving expeditions. Working closely together and capitalizing on their natural international ties, they succeeded in overcoming a numerical disadvantage to play an important role in the French slave trade. The few Protestants who did engage in the trade invariably became major traders.

Notwithstanding the obvious Protestant contribution, the slave trade was primarily a Catholic business. Members of the Church fitted out more than three-quarters of all expeditions. Although hundreds of Catholics had only a trivial interest in the trade, there were still many important Catholic slavers: more than fifteen of the twenty-two largest armateurs (table 11.1) were Catholic. Nantes was almost exclusively Catholic, and the city's great slaving dynasties all embraced the national religion. To only a slightly lesser degree, the same held true for Le Havre and Saint Malo. Even Bordeaux was heavily Catholic, in spite of the unchallenged preeminence of a few Protestant traders. Only in La Rochelle were the Catholics reduced to a secondary position, but that was because of the unique history of that port. If the Catholics lacked Protestant cohesion and could not claim international banking assistance almost as a birthright, they developed their own networks based on family groupings. Several families worked together to promote the ventures of each. The groups usually had strong social ties; intermarriage between member families was common. In this way Catholic families managed to pool their resources and undertake large-scale operations.

Thus the typical French slave trader was a Catholic whose father or grandfather had migrated to the port and amassed a small fortune through commerce. The trader himself learned his profession in one of several ways. If he had been a ship's captain or had worked in the office of an active slaver, the metamorphosis was simple: as soon as he saved enough capital to begin his own business, the captain or clerk became a slave trader. A former merchant would have to learn elsewhere. If he came from a rich family his father would undoubtedly bring him into the family business, just as Guillaume Bouteiller of Nantes formed a partnership with his sons Charles and Henry. But if he was a man of more modest means, he would probably go to the islands as an intermediary between the French traders and the island planters. This was a well-travelled and potentially lucrative route. Middlemen in the colonies made money on almost all transactions and risked little of their own capital, except when investing, perhaps not always voluntarily, in French shipping.[19] Frequently, when a merchant had accumulated sufficient capital in the Antilles, he would return to France to begin slaving. Becoming a slave trader could thereby entail a long apprenticeship.

12
Slave Traders in Public

Virtually all aspects of a slave trader's life reflected his business. There were no clear distinctions between his private and public lives: economic considerations so closely paralleled social ones that he was not an individual, alone, but was also a member of a community whose chief objective was making money. Even the most personal affairs in a trader's life were often related to that objective. In many cases, his very being in the port city was the result of a conscious decision to attempt to improve financially. Similarly, his choice of a marriage partner was frequently dictated by the current state of business. Marriages could be useful in cementing financial ties between business partners or among members of an informal trading group. In a community dominated by the use of credit, personal relationships were all the more significant, and they even extended far beyond the gates of the port. But although the traders' world may have included many cities on three continents, within each town it was largely confined to a small collection of like-minded merchants whose interest was making profits from the slave trade or from the commerce in colonial commodities.

For such people, politics were clearly secondary to business. From the government, the slave traders wanted commercial freedom and certain guarantees of support. These political demands, however, did not stem from ideology; they were merely the most obvious means of encouraging the best possible trading conditions for the merchant. There is no reason to assume an inherent conflict between the monarchy, however absolute, and the French merchants during the eighteenth century: as long as the voice of commerce was heard and was rewarded with low duties or other incentives, the slave traders were satisfied with the political structure of old regime France. If they supported certain phases of the Revolution, it was primarily because those phases proved favorable to commerce and not because of any abstract philosophical considerations. Similarly, the attitude of the traders towards their slaves was strictly businesslike, although the traders sincerely believed that their actions were bringing glory to France and to their respective ports. Slaves were but one commodity among many, and since it paid to treat them well, they were given adequate living conditions. The traders, even those who also owned plantations and slaves, lived thousands of miles from their slaves and did not have an emotional commitment to their workers' well-being.

Of course, even for hard-headed businessmen money was not the exclusive goal, especially in a society like that of eighteenth-century France. Money was a means as well as an end, in this case yielding the possibility of social distinction through ennoblement. With sufficient resources, a man could buy into the nobility or if he were more fortunate and conspicuous, he could have nobility bestowed upon him in recognition of services rendered the state. Most of the important slave traders, and a few of the lesser ones, reached noble rank during the eighteenth century. Although the economic privileges of this social advance were limited, nobility was an honor much sought after by the slave traders. But whether the ennobled merchants felt truly noble in 1789 is a difficult question to which no simple answer can be given. It is much easier to say that from a business point of view, ennoblement made no difference whatsoever; newly ennobled traders continued in their chosen profession as before, oblivious of the possibility of disapproval on the part of their new peers. Several merchants did not begin to trade slaves until they had become nobles, in fact.

Nowhere was the union between private and public life more apparent than in religious and family matters. Protestants, in particular, exploited their religious affiliation for business purposes.[1] This was especially true in ports where they were a small minority and could not always rely on each other for financial support. In these cases of local weakness, ties with the European Protestant community were more immediate and hence more important. Such was the situation in Nantes at the end of the old regime, where virtually every major Protestant trader had close ties with bankers in Basel. Where Protestants were in the majority (in other words in La Rochelle) and a local organization evolved to fulfill most of the basic needs of the merchants, the international affiliations were less direct. La Rochelle Protestants still relied ultimately on their international contacts, but only to guarantee local commitments. In this respect, the Protestants of La Rochelle were like the Catholics in the other French ports. Being members of the one official church in France, Catholic slave traders could make no special claims based on religion but instead had to rely on other unifying devices to consolidate their financial position. Since business in the old regime was intensely individualistic, they depended on personal relationships to reaffirm business connections. In effect, the Catholics used the family where the Protestants used religion, and for the same reasons. The expenses involved in slaving forced participating merchants to rely on one another for investments (regardless of who ultimately provided the credits behind the investments), and complete trust resulted only from intimate social bonds. The rare joint-stock companies established for slaving were Parisian in orientation and were never popular in the ports, where direct involvement was the norm. More than three-quarters of all slaving investments originated in the ports, and most were made by friends and relatives of the armateur. In this sense, the trade's financial structure was truly a "closed vase," as described by Meyer.[2]

The slave traders looked to each other for financial support. Although most of the smallest as well as some of the very largest were self-sufficient or quite random in their relations with their colleagues, the typical medium or large-scale armateur had to ally himself with a few peers for two reasons. First, he had to assure adequate financing for his own expeditions; second, he had to be able to diversify his own investments. By associating regularly with a small group of similarly situated merchants, the trader managed to combine the roles of armateur and investor: he sacrificed some control over his own expeditions in order to spread his risk capital. The resulting small investment groups were informal and based largely on economic factors; this meant mutual investments and, occasionally, the use of colonial houses run by members of the group. At the same time, most groups originated or were reinforced with marriges. Other factors, such as geographic or social origin or even the length of time in the port, influenced the creation of groups but were clearly secondary to the need for capital and security. The group in no way restrained its members from investing beyond the immediate circle, but most participants confined the majority of their investments to their own group.

Tightly knit groups developed in response to the growth of the slave trade. Although investment by parts had been a feature of the trade from the earliest times, it was only with the increase in slaving traffic and costs that such investment followed clear patterns. Rudimentary groups which began to appear even before the Austrian War became more sophisticated after the Seven Years' War and reached their peak after the American War. This development was most complete at Nantes. Excluding a rather ambiguous Protestant association—the Protestants were too limited numerically to create a full-scale group—six investment groups were functioning in Nantes from 1783 to 1792.[3] The thirty members of these associations fitted out 190 slave ships; they also made 335 investments in the trade, of which 196 were in the expeditions of their fellow members. Twenty-one of the twenty-eight investing participants (two only fitted out ships and did not make investments) purchased more than half of their slaving shares from members of their respective groups. Each group had a particular character. For example, one was dominated by merchants originally from Saint Malo who were related to one another by marriage. Another was composed primarily of former ship's captains and had three recent marriages between the six participating families. A third was formed by newcomers to Nantes with no apparent connection to each other.

The most remarkable group centered on the Portier family of Nantes. This group combined slaving investments with marriages and even with ennoblement, and managed to survive with ever-changing membership for almost eighty years. Two pairs of marriages contracted early in the eighteenth century formed the basis for the group, marriages linking the Rozées to the Portiers and to the Trochons, and the Budans to the Drouins and to the Le Jeunes. Business ties followed, the most important being the establishment of the company Veuve Rozée (*née* Trochon) et Portier. Besides supporting at least one of Charles Trochon's slaving expeditions during the 1708-22 era, Rozée and Portier strengthened the links with the Budan-Drouin-Le Jeune alliance by buying a share in an early Budan slaver.[4] Trochon also bought a share in that ship and was able to sell interests in one of his own slavers to Budan and to Le Jeune the following year.[5] In this way, the initial, tentative contacts between the two trios—which had apparently been made in 1717 when Trochon, Le Jeune, and Budan each acquired shares in Poleau's *Intrepide*[6]—developed into a more regular association. In the meantime, Drouin and Le Jeune had been buying interests in Budan's slavers, and their brother-in-law reciprocated by investing in Drouin's *Salomon* in 1722.[7]

Until the Austrian War, the group remained relatively stable and increasingly active. Members regularly purchased shares in each other's slave ships and occasionally joined forces to support an outsider's expeditions. It was only during the 1748-55 period that major changes occurred in the group's composition. Taking the places of the Budan and Drouin families were the Chaurands, the Foucaults, and the Libaults. Each of the new families was related by recent marriage to the Portiers, and in the 1750s the newcomers joined the Portiers in the nobility.[8] From then on ennobled members always outnumbered commoners. With a solid core, the group expanded after the Seven Years' War and enjoyed an era of great activity. Twelve families now participated, making sixty-seven of their ninety-nine slaving investments in their colleagues' thirty-eight ships. After the American War, however, the group shrank considerably as members died, allied themselves with other

Table 12.1
Participation in the Portier Group, 1708-92

Name	1708-22	1726-35	1736-44	1748-55	1763-77	1783-92
Portier*	x	x	x	x	x	x
Rozée	x	x	x	x	x	
Le Jeune	x	x	x	x		
Trochon	x	x	x	x		
Budan*	x	x			x	
Drouin*	x				x	
Chaurand*				x	x	x
Foucault*				x	x	
Libault*				x	x	
Deurbroucq*					x	x
Gerbier					x	x
Dulac					x	
Jogues					x	
Menard					x	
Aubry*						x

* Ennobled.

groups, or followed no apparent pattern in their investments. Nonetheless there was still great strength in the association: of the six families who quit it but remained active in slaving, only one—the Foucaults—had marital ties with a family from the core of the group. From 1783 to 1792, the five remaining members fitted out twenty-nine ships, of which the investors in twenty-one are known (11 percent of the Nantes total of 189); forty-seven of their hundred and one investments (47 percent) were made within the group.

The longevity of the Portier group was unique to Nantes, and it illustrated well the importance of social relationships in organizing and financing the slave trade. Working together, members increased their capacity to send out slaving expeditions. At least ninety-nine slavers were fitted out by the fifteen families during their periods of participation in the group. In the short run, each slaver could count on finding ready capital for his ships in the hands of his group colleagues, and he could be sure of having a convenient and probably reliable place to invest his own money. Over the long run, only marriages ensured the stability of the association. Merchants participating in a group without a marriage link to one of its members were only too ready to leave it when something better arose. Relatives alone could be trusted to retain their allegiance.

The union of public and private was also evident in the creation of the slaving communities. Virtually all the traders, regardless of importance, participated in local communities based on a common interest in the slave trade. The basis of each community was economic. The practice of selling shares in slave ships encouraged close relationships between merchants, particularly at the end of the old regime, when the number of slaving shares multiplied rapidly. With thousands of financial bonds linking them, the traders had to work closely together for the common good. But economics alone did not unite them: if financial interactions were the building blocks of the slaving community, social ties were the cement. In Nantes and La Rochelle, the two ports where the trade took precedence over other forms of commerce, the traders developed a dense social network as well as a financial one.[9] The slaving communities of the 1780s were the products of nearly a century of development, and by the end of the old regime most families interested in the slave trade were related to each other by marriage. Given the length of time and the number of marriages contracted, this should not be particularly surprising; it is still significant that these family relationships did in fact exist and could support or reinforce the financial connections. Not only were slave traders usually dealing with their business colleagues, but also they were as often as not dealing with relatives, perhaps distant but nevertheless relatives.

The situation in the core of each slaving community was even more dramatic. The major slave traders tended to form an exceptionally close social group. Since they were usually among the wealthiest men in their ports, they preferred to form alliances with their financial peers, who most often were slave traders themselves. For example, the Rasteaus of La Rochelle managed to contract marriages with most of the major trading families in the city. Fitting out some thirty-eight slavers during the eighteenth century, they intermarried with the Giraudeaus (armateurs of thirty slavers), the Belins (eighteen slavers), the Viviers (fifteen), and the Carayons (eleven). The Belins' alliances were equally impressive, including matches with the Nairacs (fourteen ships), the Carayons, the Weis's (ten), and the Hoogwerfs (nine), besides the Rasteaus. The Carayons married with the Gareschés (forty ships), Rasteaus, Belins, Hoogwerfs, and Amyraults (five).

In some ways, the slaving communities transcended local boundaries to form a national slaving interest. Simple business ties formed the basis of this nationwide community, since a slave trader was obliged to have contacts in every major port in order to deal with any eventuality. Sometimes it was merely a guestion of exchanging information: Daniel Garesché of La Rochelle, for example, learned about Captain van Alstein from the Montaudouins of Nantes.[10] Usually it involved the purchase or sale of various goods: sugar belonging to a Le Havre merchant might be shipped to Bordeaux; a slave ship leaving from Saint Malo might require repairs in La Rochelle; an Honfleur trader might need to buy calicoes in Nantes. Occasionally, bigger transactions were conducted: it was not at all unusual for a ship owner in one port to arrange to have his ship fitted out elsewhere by a friendly merchant. In its early days, the Compagnie des Indes used to have armateurs working for it in various ports, a practice followed by some large companies later in the century; Brillantais Marion of Saint Malo, for example, engaged armateurs in Nantes, La Rochelle, and Bordeaux to fit out his ships.

As he did in choosing a colonial agent, the slave trader took pains to select good correspondents in each port. The ideal choice, of course, was a relative, and major traders often had family representatives in several ports. There were Amyraults in La Rochelle and Nantes, Nairacs in Bordeaux and La Rochelle, Meslés in Nantes and Saint Malo, and Thurningers in Le Havre and Nantes. If relatives were lacking, old family friends would do. Although apparently unrelated, the Chateaubriands of Saint Malo and the Espivents of Nantes relied heavily on one another. These two families of the old nobility had probably known and respected each other for centuries, a circumstance which encouraged close commercial relations when both turned to the slave trade in the eighteenth century. The Espivents invested in several Chateaubriand slavers,[11] while Chateaubriand fitted out at least one Espivent ship.[12] Acquaintanceship based on common geographic origin was another common feature of interport relationships. Marion of Saint Malo had dealings with two Nantes companies established by recent emigrants from Saint Malo—Canel, Meslé, and Bernard, and Millet and Caillaud.[13] Whenever possible, a merchant preferred to deal with someone he knew personally.

The national slaving interest was a delicate construction comprising a series of local communities, each of which was in turn based on a common economic interest and reinforced with close social ties. Working for the extension of the slave trade and all its auxiliary commerces, the national interest occasionally acted as a political force. Although dissension amongst the ports usually prevented any cohesive action, the traders never abandoned their efforts to achieve a united front capable of influencing or determining governmental policy. The problem was that there was no official voice reserved for the traders. The slave traders had different powers in each port, depending on the importance of the trade locally. In Nantes, the trade was of capital importance and the traders therefore dominated local political and commercial bodies. In Marseilles, on the other hand, the trade counted for little, and the traders' demands were likely to go unnoticed. Although all major ports had merchants interested in slaving, the majority of merchants in most ports had little to do with it. Hence other questions usually received more attention, and the traders' interests were subordinated to different priorities. This made concerted political action between the ports almost impossible. In spite of the hundreds of letters written from chamber of commerce to chamber of commerce, unanimous agreements were rare, and the ports never gained much influence nationally.[14]

Only in Nantes were the slave traders truly dominant, having a large say in municipal government and effectively controlling commercial administration. The main representative body for Nantes merchants was the Consulat, a traditional organization much like a chamber of commerce.[15] Composed normally of one *juge* serving for a year and four *consuls* serving for two years and retiring annually by pairs, the Consulat had certain juridical powers over local business practice. It was also responsible for informing the central government of the feelings of Nantes merchants on important issues. This could be done by letter or petition or by an appeal to a lobbyist stationed in Versailles. The Consulat also wrote letters to the chambers of commerce in other major cities, usually in an effort to organize a concerted campaign to affect government policy. Slave traders were generally a majority on the Nantes Consulat;[16] as the richest members of the merchant community, it was only natural that they should have a preponderant representation in commercial administration. During the 1783-90 period, when the colonial and slave trades were of exceptional interest nationally, four of the seven men who served as juges in the Nantes Consulat fitted out ships to Africa. Similarly, of the sixteen men serving as consuls during that period, twelve were involved in the trade, nine of them deeply; most of the five non-traders were either closely related to slaving families or were from former slaving families themselves. Obviously, it can be assumed that the Consulat looked out for the interests of the slave traders.

The slave traders were concerned almost exclusively with economic problems. Even in the *cahier de doléances* drawn up by the third estate of the Nantes region, the emphasis was on economic concerns, with about one-fourth of all demands related directly to colonial trade.[17] In the Consulat papers, the preoccupation with commerce was almost complete, as the Nantes merchants tried to force their viewpoint on Versailles. In so doing, they claimed to have only the best interests of the kingdom at heart. In a letter to the Marquis du Chillon, the "Commerce of Nantes" declared itself ready to help win the fight against the "general conspiracy to deliver the wealth of France to foreign countries and to its natural enemies."[18] According to the Nantais, political superiority could arise only as a result of commercial superiority—in fact, all wars were fought only because of commercial rivalry. If France desired to keep up with its "eternal rival," it must adopt English methods and do all it could to encourage trade; otherwise, it must inevitably lose its "external consideration."

It was to achieve these national goals that the traders continually appealed to the government. The Nantais had two basic obstacles, the central government and the colonists. It was the duty of Versailles to keep the whole system running smoothly. The government was responsible for the general condition of commerce because of its power to declare war, protect the rights of traders, control the colonies, and encourage trade in general. Wise policy makers in Versailles or Paris could ensure prosperous conditions in the ports and consequently—or so the merchants thought—throughout the kingdom. From the colonies, the Nantais wanted money and obedience, but received instead worthless promises and obstruction. By 1789, French traders and Antillean planters scarcely bothered to give the appearance of a common interest.

The traders loved to complain, especially at the end of the old regime. The spirit of optimism following the American War quickly dissipated, leaving the Nantes merchants with little good to say. The Chaurands wrote in 1783 that "never have we seen so much misery."[19] Five years later, the Consulat claimed that all French shipping was on the decline, that foreigners were taking over Saint Domingue, and that the colonists were making fortunes at the expense of French merchants.[20] In a similar vein, the Nantais compained in 1789: "In effect, the State is without money, the Minister without authority; the Americans think of their own interests; finally, the National Assembly allows itself to foresee the abolition of the trade of blacks and the liberty of our colonies. So many subjects of fear should alarm French merchants and make them expect a total subversion of maritime commerce."[21] A bleaker picture could scarcely be imagined, if it were all true. Needless to say, these outbursts tended to be something between gross exaggerations and outright lies: French shipping was booming in almost all respects, abolition had hardly been mentioned by 1789 and independence even less, and the colonial planters were rarely in a favorable position vis-a-vis the traders. Only with respect to foreign incursion into the islands were the complaints fairly well founded, but the foreigners still had a long way to go before dominating the French Antilles.[22] In short, the merchants were exaggerating their troubles, probably as a result of frustration arising from an apparent failure of the entire colonial system to work efficiently and return maximum profits to France.

Ultimately, the traders held the government responsible for this failure. From their point of view, they made reasonable demands on Versailles; indeed, they desired only two things, liberty and protection. That these two basic demands may have been in conflict with each other under certain circumstances did not bother them; neither did it worry them that there were numerous manners of defining and instituting such principles. To the Nantes merchants, it was all quite clear: "Commerce needs only liberty and protection."[23] Naturally, the Nantais were more than willing to give the government their interpretation of these key ideas; hundreds of letters from the Consulat explained what they should not mean in practice, and a few gave an idea of what they should mean. Of course, the traders were not philosophers and were little concerned with establishing perfectly logical definitions of the key ideas; instead, they used the words almost as *leitmotivs,* letting them be heard whenever certain sentiments were to be evoked. The convenient and easily identified lables often concealed a mass of complex and even self-contradictory schemes, all meant to be beneficial to the Kingdom of France as well as to the traders' pocketbooks.

For the traders, "liberty" meant that the trade should be open to all Frenchmen equally. Perhaps their greatest pre-Revolutionary fear was that there would be a return to the old system of *privilège,* which restricted certain commercial practices to special groups.[24] Although there were no attempts by the government to subordinate the entire slaving triangle to a general monopoly, there were several particular privileges granted in the 1780s; all were met with stiff resistance by the Nantes traders. For example, the Compagnie de la Guyane, which had had exclusive trading rights along part of the Senegal coast since 1777, sought in 1783 to extend its domain to the whole of Senegal. The Nantais were quick to react: "This news has spread the most active fears among the merchants of this city. . . . Exclusive privileges are contrary to healthy politics, to His Majesty's justice, and to liberty. They upset the competition and the equality which should reign among all faithful subjects."[25] Even when the privileges were granted specifically to encourage French trade with newly "developing" areas, the traders were suspicious and usually opposed; if the new regions should become lucrative, the Nantais did not want to be barred from them.[26] Besides worrying about closed markets, the traders feared unfair competition from the priveleged companies. The Compagnie de la Guyane, for example, was supposed to ship its inexpensive slaves only to the French colony at Cayenne, but it once introduced some illegally to Saint Domingue and could, as the traders claimed, do so again.[27] For the nonprivileged traders, the monopoly represented a real threat, even though most of the privileged companies ended in failure.

Underlying the belief in an open slave trade was the assured legality of slavery and of slave trading. During the old regime, the position of the trade was virtually unquestioned; nobody in a prominent political position raised the question of abolition, at least not loudly enough to provoke a reaction from the traders. With the compilation of the cahiers de doléances and the calling of the Estates-General, however, abolition became a more important issue.[28] The traders reacted predictably to the birth of a potent abolition movement. The first significant statement on the matter was made in mid-May 1789 by the Nantes Consulat: "If the trade is prohibited, as is proposed by the English Parliament, then it would be necessary to give up sugar, coffee, indigo, cotton, navigation and maritime commerce. This project, born of exalted minds, would be more humane than politic."[29] The inital reaction to an as yet distant threat contained the two basic points which the traders would constantly reiterate in the lengthy debates which followed: economics and European tastes demanded the extension of an admittedly inhumane system. On a more personal level, the traders were deeply shocked at the sudden and probably unforeseen increase in demands for abolition. Calls for the end of slavery and the slave trade alarmed ''not only the owners of plantations resident in France, but also the merchants of maritime ports who have the better part of their fortunes in these establishments.''[30]

In supporting the continuation of the trade, the merchants naturally claimed to have only the best interests of the nation at heart: ''Abandoning the trade, the colonies, and the marine would strike blows against France which would be infinitely more cruel than was the Revocation of the Edict of Nantes. For all the people attached to maritime commerce would emigrate and would begin anew wherever they found refuge.''[31] As usual, this new source of foreign competition, which would undoubtedly be actively supported by the host governments, would be too strong for the French merchants and would lead to the ruin of the empire. From the traders' point of view, there was almost always an identity between their needs and the better interests of the state as a whole. Insofar as the traders could rationalize their own greed, they were highly patriotic indeed.

The liberty sought by the traders was basically the freedom to make money at their chosen occupation. It had little to do with eighteenth-century civil liberty or nineteenth-century economic liberty, because the traders demanded protection at the same time. They meant by this everything from the presence of the French marine along the African coast to the institution of economic incentives for encouraging the trade. In their insistance upon protection, they actually gave narrow limits to their liberty, but this paradox was of secondary importance. All that mattered was the creation of favorable conditions for maritime commerce. The traders expected the government to interfere in commercial affairs to shield the merchants from the ill effects of a truly free trade.

At its most literal, ''protection'' meant guaranteeing the safety of French shipping. This could even imply war, but few merchants supported such a policy. Although many believed that France was sometimes justified in initiating hostilities, they stopped short of advocating a policy of war.[32] Traders did, however, demand that the government send ships to Africa to defend the rights of French slavers to trade along those sections of the African coast historically considered open. When, towards the end of 1783, rumors reached Nantes of a Portuguese closure of Cabinda in West Africa, a place where French ships had hitherto been allowed to trade, the Nantais immediately complained to the French government.[33] In spite of the government's quick denial of any knowledge of the attack,[34] the traders claimed to have proof that it had happened, and they requested some action, even military.[35] Although the episode ended quietly when Portugal denied everything,[36] the traders had already displayed their feelings towards their government. They considered it quite reasonable for France to commit its marine to fight thousands of miles from home to protect private commercial rights. The traders had a high estimation of their value to the realm.

To the traders, "protection" usually meant economic assistance. It was the government's responsibility to ensure favorable trading conditions such as resulted from a sound monetary policy; it was also for the government to control colonial trade in a manner advantageous to French merchants. That these two problems were related was a fact not unnoticed by the traders, who urged the government to consider the effects of the one upon the other. Versailles, however, could not always act with only the interests of the slavers in mind. International politics, the feelings of the colonists, and the finances of the crown all had to be considered before the ministers could make their decisions. The complexity of the matter escaped the traders, and they often ended gaping in amazement at what they took to be the stupidity of the French lawmakers. It was all very simple for the traders who demanded nothing short of complete economic protection: they wanted the government to subsidize the slave trade, close the French islands to foreign merchants, and force the colonists to pay all debts immediately.

If the government rarely complied with their extreme demands, the merchants were not overly distressed. Regardless of official policy, the trade grew throughout the eighteenth century, and clever merchants were capable of realizing profits from it any time during the century. In short, once the traders received permission to trade, politics were of limited importance to them. Correspondingly, the traders occupied a most ineffectual position in the old regime. They were distant from the decision-making centers and almost always were presented with *faits accomplis;* rarely, if ever, was their advice asked by the government. Even the most important governmental action, the Decree of August 30, 1784, allowing foreigners to trade in the French colonies, came as a complete surprise to the traders, who then attempted to mount a campaign for its repeal.[37] The government did not ask the traders for their opinion, nor did it launch a trial balloon to solicit public reaction to the proposed legislation. Virtually the only advance knowledge the traders received came in the form of rumors, frequently unfounded; reliable information usually came too late for anything but rear-guard action. Of course, other groups were also left in the dark about government policy. The 1786 treaty with Great Britain, laden with consequences for French trade and industry, came as a surprise to most of the interested parties in France.

In order to avoid repetition of the unwelcome surprise of the August 30 decree and in order to gain a more effective voice in government, the traders came to favor changes in the political structure of the state. Demands for such changes were made only in the cahiers de doléances, which were compiled at the request of the crown. Although not written exclusively by slave traders, the cahier for the third estate of the city of Nantes reflected the tenor of thought among the rich, commercially active men of Nantes, who certainly counted the traders among their number.[38] Since the trade was so important to the city as a whole, the commercial demands of the cahier reiterated the traders' views. For example, there were denunciations of the August 30 decree and the special privileges granted to various companies; there were also requests for premiums to encourage trade with northern Europe, Tobago, and Cayenne.[39] Protection for French ships along the African coast was demanded, as were greater controls on the introduction of foreign goods into the colonies.[40] The colonists were asked to pay their debts.[41] The basic consistency between the cahier and the traders' traditional position was clear.

To implement these programs, the traders suggested changes in the French constitution. The Bourbons were to retain power, but the "nation" was also to have definite rights. Every three years, the nation would meet to deliberate and vote—by head—on all laws proposed by the crown.[42] To make sure that these laws adequately reflected the needs of commerce, a ministry was to be established, along with a general council of commerce, in which the deputies from various towns would have a voice.[43] Civil liberties were also considered: individual citizens were to be assured certain legal rights, property was to be guaranteed, and the press was to be free (except when to allow such freedom was judged unwise).[44] The crown may have conceded some of its prerogatives, but the real losers were the representatives of the old social order, the nobility and the clergy. Almost all feudal rights were to be abolished, while many of the church's temporal powers were to be assumed by the state.[45] Significantly, it stated that "all citizens without distinction will be placed under the same laws and punishments."[46]

The cahier gives the best indication of the traders' political ideology during the old regime. With hindsight, one can find in the lists of grievances the origins of the Girondins, the Thermidoreans, the Imperialists, and the Monarchists; from the positions adopted in 1789, almost anything could have developed logically. This is because the traders were not political philosophers; they were businessmen who sought in politics an aid to better and more secure profits. Almost all their dealings with government had to do with economic matters and were invariably concerned with improving commerce between France and Saint Domingue. Non-economic matters were of scant interest. The events leading to the calling of the

Estates-General and to the Revolution itself went virtually unnoticed by the traders except insofar as national economic and political policies were undermining local trade. What the traders expected in 1789 was an improved economic position, and not a general restructuring of French political life.

The demands for reform found in the cahier of the Nantes third estate were uninspired. They were not the products of a conservative, a liberal, or a radical mind, but reflected the eminent practicality and economic self-interest of the merchants. The old regime had obviously been good to the traders, providing the opportunity to establish respectable fortunes and to rise to positions of considerable local importance. If the traders did not have direct political power on a national level, they were certainly strong economically, and even the social position of the most important among them was quite honorable, despite the taint of buying into the nobility. They had little cause to complain about the general political situation, and indeed, there is little evidence that they took more than a passing interest in the great events of the day. In the thousands of letters written by the Chaurands, only a few paragraphs were devoted to current political affairs, and most of the time the Chaurands were content to give concise, objective reports. There were no indications of dissatisfaction with the regime as a whole and not a hint of a desire for a thoroughgoing reform program based on certain abstract principles. At most, it could be said that in 1789 the traders adopted notions which were in the air[47] and which could enable commerce to have a more effective voice in national government.

13
The Slave Traders at Work

The traders limited their political activity in part because they simply did not have the time to spare: each of the major traders spent most of his waking hours at work. This preoccupation ultimately led the trader to interpret the world in terms of business exigencies. Politics, like friendship, religion, and even family, became for him a mere extension of business practice. In this way, his sociability was forced, the consequence of economic imperatives. The most natural attitude of a merchant engaged in extensive slave-trading bordered on isolation: alone, or with a handful of clerks all but devoid of independent existence, he passed most of his adult life in his office trying to make his fortune. Although a trader could be aided by generally prosperous times or by rich relatives, the amassing of each fortune was a private affair enveloped in a cloud of secrecy. Slave traders prided themselves on their independence and were loath to expose their business dealings to public scrutiny. Armateurs, for example, never announced the contents of their ships. Members of the Nantes Consulat declared, "We are absolutely ignorant of the objects which go out in each ship for the islands. That is the armateur's secret, and he could not divulge it without exposing himself to a ruinous competition."[1] Ironically, such secrecy often led to precisely the competition the armateurs were seeking to avoid, leading the Nantais to complain, "French and neutral ships are continually arriving with considerable shipments of merchandise which is without price or demand and with which one scarcely knows what to do."[2] But this was a small price to pay for the maintenance of strict security. Like Guillaume Bouteiller of Nantes, the typical trader was "opposed to giving out any information about his affairs."[3]

The major slave trader, like other important merchants in the French ports, was in his office from dawn to dusk six days a week.[4] There were, of course, exceptions, for not even the most obsessed merchant could face such a dreary existence. Every day before noon the trader went to the market (*bourse*) to take the pulse of the economy; there he bought and sold colonial commodities and bills of exchange from all over Europe.[5] He would leave his office on official business, also, to sign various declarations required by the Admiralty, although a clerk with limited powers of attorney was often sent to sign for him. Traders also called on notaries (*notaires*) with great regularity, since virtually all transactions of any significance had to be conducted in their presence; indeed, before the eighteenth century, even bills of exchange had had to be notarized. Here, too, the trader sent a clerk to represent him whenever possible. If the trader occupied an administrative position, he had to spend several hours a week at meetings. The Nantes Consulat, for example, met on Wednesdays and Saturdays, and when important matters were discussed there were large turnouts. And finally, the trader might leave his office for extended periods during certain seasons, particularly during the grape harvest.[6]

In spite of these excursions, the trader was usually in his office, which was more often than not merely a room in his house. In the case of a partnership, one of the associates would provide the office space in return for a modest allowance; Riedy, for example, received 5,000 livres annually for providing offices, warehouses, and upkeep for the firm of Riedy and Thurninger.[7] The allowance for the use of the office was small, because the room rented was far from impressive and contained only the barest necessities. The traders did everything in their power to reduce their overhead, and they eschewed luxury in their offices. All was strictly functional; a table or two, a pair of chairs or benches, and the odd cabinet were adequate to conduct business. When Pierre Feydieu of Bordeaux died on December 2, 1764, his office, one of ten rooms in his house, contained "one wooden cabinet, a large table, two wood benches, two letter holders," and a bag containing 1,072 livres in cash.[8] The frugal surroundings of the office complemented the minimal salaries drawn by the partners and paid to the employees. Since the only real concern was making the business grow, the traders could not afford to spend money unnecessarily.

The office had its public side, serving as a communications center for the trader's dealings with merchants in town and throughout the Atlantic world. Much of the contact was in person: the trader met his colleagues, clients, and employees in the office.[9] Prospective investors had to be convinced of the wisdom of a given venture, while armateurs came in search of investments for their expeditions; merchants specializing in the re-export trade wanted to discuss colonial commodities, while representatives of foreign houses offered help in obtaining merchandise for the trade; ship's captains came for interviews and, once hired, awaited detailed instructions. In addition to these direct encounters, the trader communicated by letter with merchants from Europe and the Antilles. This correspondence was of the utmost importance, as it served to link the trader with the world. Letters from abroad "immediately informed the merchant both about the general trend and about the workings of his own ventures."[10] So vast was this correspondence that it had to be filed geographically; the Chaurands, for example, kept registers of letters to the Antilles, to France, and to Europe.[11] All told, some twenty-five volumes of the Chaurands' correspondence have been discovered, representing about a third of their extant business papers. Needless to say, letters were almost exclusively devoted to business; the traders discussed prices, shipments, and all other aspects of maritime commerce in detail. Given the primitive state of eighteenth-century communication, traders and their correspondents had to serve as financial news services for each other, supplying vital information not readily available elsewhere.

The trader also looked after day-to-day business in his office. This was primarily a question of accounting, of keeping a close eye on incomes and expenses. To do this, he needed help in the form of specialized laborers and books. By the eighteenth century, accounting methods in the French ports had become sophisticated enough to require trained accountants; double-entry accounting had become the rule for important merchants engaged in international trade.[12] The merchants themselves often had only a rudimentary notion of the art, and had to confide their ledgers to their skilled employees. Of course the sons of rich merchants usually learned the sophisticated techniques by working in large commercial houses, often in Amsterdam or Hamburg, but this education was meant to enable them to control their own clerks better.[13] Since keeping the books was a full-time occupation, a merchant, no matter how well educated, could not afford to do it himself.

Each trader had a score of account books to keep track of all the transactions he conducted. The books formed the heart of the business, and their loss spelled ruin for the merchant. For example, when Baignoux' house in Bordeaux burned down on November 10, 1790, it was considered the worst possible disaster that could befall the poor merchant, and he even received letters expressing sympathy over the destruction of his commercial papers.[14] Every trader had several account books, all subordinate to the *grand livre,* a massive register weighing up to fifty pounds and occupying up to five cubic feet.[15] It was the ledger in which were recorded all revenues and expeditures. Entries were made at least twice, and each entry had a reference to the other. There were numerous headings, classifying transactions by name of client, name of ship, type of business conducted, and monies received or paid. Although the grand livre contained a record of virtually all the merchant's affairs, by itself it was nearly incomprehensible, for it rarely described in detail the nature of the transactions it recorded. To understand the grand livre, an index was necessary, and this was provided by the *journal*. Cross-referenced with the grand livre, it gave a short description of the dealings so tersely entered in the ledger. For example, the journal described why a payment was being made and under what terms. It also itemized transactions: where the grand livre might simply credit a ship with 50,000 livres, the journal would explain that 200 barrels of sugar arrived in payment for a slaving expedition conducted three years ago, and that on gross sales of 60,000 livres, the net proceeds were 50,000 livres. When the merchant kept his books conscientiously, most of his business can be reconstructed from the journal and grand livre alone.

Other books were for more specialized purposes. Particularly important for slave-trading armateurs was the book of ships, containing detailed records of the various ships fitted out by the merchant and including complete information on costs involved, slaves sold, and net returns. Yet other books kept equally comprehensive records of purchases and sales of colonial commodities which the merchant transacted either for his own account or on behalf of a colonial planter. Finally, a trader with landed interests might also keep a special book relating to his properties. Of course, not all traders were so well organized, and poorer traders in particular did not keep such detailed accounts. In this vein, Paul Butel concluded that it was the French armateur (as opposed to the European middleman) who kept the least faithful books.[16] In any event, money and education obviously were reflected in the economic and aesthetic appreciation of accounting practices.

Long hours of painstaking work characterized a trader's day as he devoted his life to making a fortune. In this the slavers realized a certain success, although it would be rash to conclude that all were extremely wealthy. Indeed, the hierarchical structures implicit in outfitting and in investment practices were also apparent in the slavers' fortunes. Among the established traders in each port, there was usually a relation between personal wealth and involvement in the slave trade, with almost all the major traders in possession of larger fortunes than the minor traders. The slave trade was truly an affair of the rich, although it is impossible to say with certainty whether the trade made the traders rich or whether rich merchants turned to slaving. The evidence from individual family histories is not conclusive; it appears that it worked both ways. What is clear is that the more active traders were generally wealthier than their less active colleagues, that the rich traders' assets were heavily tied up in the trade, and that the largest slaving fortunes were often insecure.

The relative wealth of the traders can be quickly established from the tax rolls (*rôles de la capitation*). The *capitation* theoretically reflected an estimate of a man's total wealth: an assessor had to guess what each taxpayer was worth and then assign him an appropriate imposition.[17] Hence, the tax paid represented the value of a man's assets and not his current income. The major slave traders invariably paid the highest taxes in their cities. In Bordeaux, for example, the leading slaver, Paul Nairac, paid 600 livres capitation in 1777, the largest single imposition for a merchant that year.[18] It was the same in Saint Malo, where Pierre Meslé paid 780 livres in taxes in 1787, the highest tax in the port.[19] Even in smaller towns, the slavers were heavily taxed: Nicolas Lacoudrais, the most active trader in Honfleur following the American War, paid 40 livres capitation in 1785, one of the city's largest impositions.[20] Obviously, the major slave traders were considered to be among the richest men in each port, and they carried an important share of the municipal tax burden. Saint Malo residents had to pay 32,807 livres capitation in 1787, of which a few major trading families paid more than 20 percent; members of the five most active families alone paid well over 2,000 livres. In Nantes, the slave traders, comprising perhaps 1 percent of the population, paid 17 percent of the city's taxes in 1789 (17,000 livres out of 100,000 livres).[21]

Although traders were the wealthiest group in most ports, and although the biggest traders paid some of the highest taxes, there were wide disparities in their wealth. At Nantes in 1789, some one hundred slave traders paid about 17,000 livres in capitation. This meant that the average imposition was more than 150 livres, about fifteen to twenty times more than the average Nantes resident was taxed. Payments by the slavers varied sharply, ranging from Joseph La Lande's 3 livres to the Bouteillers' 1,450. In general, however, the richest slave traders were the most active and the most active traders were the richest. In Nantes, fifteen of the thirty largest traders paid more than 100 livres in capitation in 1789.[22]

It is difficult to establish the exact size of the slavers' fortunes. In certain cases, the tax assessment can be multiplied by a constant to reveal the total value of a given trader's assets, but such a method has too many shortcomings to be generalized. For the very richest Nantes merchants at the end of the old regime, Jean Meyer concluded that taxes represented about 1/3500 of net worth, a figure which seemed appropriate for the Bouteillers.[23] More modest traders were probably taxed at higher rates of from 1 in 1,500 to 1 in 500. In 1790, for example, Pierre Morin declared his assets to exceed his liabilities by 100,000 livres; since he had paid 70 livres in taxes the previous year, he had been assessed at about 1 in

1,400.[24] Similarly, the estate of Aubry de la Fosse, who personally had a 90-livre tax bill in 1789, was valued at 50,000 livres in 1794, for a 1 to 550 ratio.[25] Using a 1 to 1,000 ratio, most of the Nantes slavers at the end of the old regime were worth about 50,000 to 75,000 livres. The entire community possessed some 50,000,000 livres, divided unevenly: 5 traders had 4,000,000 livres each, 8 had 2,000,000 each, 23 had 500,000, and 110 had 50,000. Here, too, the domination of a few wealthy figures was clear.

A large portion of the traders' assets came from the islands, but it is almost impossible to know to what extent these colonial holdings were considered when the capitation was imposed. The traders held both credits and plantations in the Antilles, with values probably equal to or even exceeding their wealth in France. A document in the files of the Nantes Chamber of Commerce listed the assumed value of the plantations as well as monies owing the Nantais. This paper, entitled "Losses Suffered by the Commerce of Nantes as a Result of the Revolution in Saint Domingue" (see table 13.1),[26] mentioned the colonial assets of seventy-six Nantes firms, fifty-two of which were active in the slave trade from 1783 to 1792. As far as can be seen, the anonymous author was very well informed and accurate. For example, he evaluated the colonial fortunes of the Chaurands and the Deluynes at 4,500,000 livres and 3,000,000 livres, respectively; working independently, Rinchon and Meyer carefully assessed these fortunes at similar values.[27] All told, Nantes merchants were credited with 78,000,000 livres' worth of assets in Saint Domingue, with the traders holding over 80 percent of that (63,000,000 livres). Again, a handful of established, large traders were preeminent; five families had 34,000,000 livres: the Bouteillers, Drouins, Arnous, Chaurands, and Mosnerons.[28]

The significance of these assets is debatable, depending on the interpretation given capitation figures. On the one hand, it was possible that, as Meyer proposed, the capitation reflected only "French" wealth,[29] in which case the 63,000,000 livres owing the Nantes slavers by the colonists was supplementary. Even here, however, the colonial holdings could not be entirely separated from the French ones, because plantations, at least, may well have been mortgaged on the security of landed interests in France. The two types of property can still be compared in terms of value, with all colonial assets being somewhat more valuable than French ones. Thus, even under this system, the larger part of the traders' fortunes would have been inextricably tied to the colonial economy. On the other hand, it was possible that the capitation did take into account colonial assets. It seems clear that on certain occasions, at least, colonial credits or landed interests or both were considered by the assessor when evaluating a slave trader's fortune. This happened to the Chaurands in 1788-89. Worth an estimated

Table 13.1

Losses Suffered by the Commerce of Nantes as a Result of the
Revolution in Saint Domingue (millions L)

Bouteiller	12.0	La Brosse	0.3
Louis Drouin	7.0	Portier	0.2
Nicolas Arnous	5.0	Portier Lantimo	0.3
Chaurand	4.5	Sarrebourse*	0.4
Deluynes*	2.0	Perrotin*	0.7
Montaudouin*	2.0	Lincoln	0.3
Guillon	2.5	Prébois*	0.2
Geslin	1.8	Darreche*	0.1
Gerbier	1.2	Plumard	0.2
Chanceaulme	0.8	Millet	0.5
Michel	1.6	Edelin*	0.6
Le Roux	1.4	Fruchard	0.4
Paimparay, etc.	1.3	Gaudais and Trottier	0.3
Mosneron Dupin, etc.	5.5	Plombard and Le Gris	0.4
Lieutaud*	1.2	Lantimo and Hamelin	0.4
Le Ray and Charet	1.0	Lory*	0.3
Heirs of Nicolas Charet	0.8	Le Masne aîné	0.2
Langevin	2.0	Vve. Le Masne and Praud	0.6
Riedy and Thurninger	1.0	Tourgouilhet and Rousseau	0.4
Jogues and Dufou	0.9	Struckman and Minyer	0.3
d'Havelooze and Dumaine	0.9	A. Marcorelles	0.6
Canel, Meslé, Bernard	0.7	Simon and Roques	0.4
Bernard aîné	0.3	Heirs of Taillefer*	1.0
Doré and Aubry	0.7	Boittard and Antoine	0.4
Espivent	0.7	Foucault and Pitteu	0.3
Desclos Lepelley	0.3	A. Menard	0.1
Froust and Guinebaud	0.5	Tiby	0.2
Corpron	0.6	Orry*	0.4
Ducoudray Bourgault	0.4	Lamaignère aîné and heirs	0.2
Doucet and Prins and		Simon and Lavigne	0.2
their uncle, Poisson	0.3	Vilmain*	0.1
Deguer*	0.7	Thebaudières*	0.2
Laville	0.4	Pouele*	0.4
Ricordel	0.4	Jollier*	0.7
Odiette	0.5	Lebourg*	0.3
Rucher*	0.2	Peletier	0.1
Clanchy and Parran	0.5	Panneton*	0.1
Libault	0.4	Morin and Vallin	0.1
		Dacosta*	0.1

Source: ADLA 6JJ30. "It is beyond doubt that the old houses of Grou, Michel, Rozée, Perissel, de Senne, Deurbroucq, Budan, Richard, and others should find a place in this table. I leave their evaluations to cleverer hands than mine" (note of the eighteenth-century author).

*Having either no or a very limited interest in the slave trade during the 1783-92 period.

4,000,000 livres, on which they quite typically paid slightly over 1,000 livres in taxes, the Chaurands had about 1,500,000 livres in colonial credits and about 3,000,000 livres in plantations on the islands.[30] Although their company was worth perhaps 500,000 livres, they seemed to have had few other possessions in the mother country.[31] Their tax payment made sense only if it included at least some of their colonial assets. This seems to have been true in the majority of cases. In Nantes, at the end of the old regime, most merchants were taxed on varying parts of their wealth in the colonies as well as on all of their assets in France.

Based to a large extent on dubious colonial credits, the slaving fortune was usually smaller in reality than on paper.[32] The spectacular growth of family fortunes reflected peculiar accounting methods as much as real wealth. Typical was the case of the Drouins, considered one of the richest families in Nantes at the end of the old regime and closely related to the Bouteillers, the richest family. The Drouins had a comfortable fortune in 1725 of 130,000 livres, including 80,000 livres for René and 50,000 livres for his brother François.[33] Both brothers were involved in maritime commerce, with René having worked as a ship's captain. The two branches of the family were close, and in 1742 François' only son Christophe married one of René's daughters, the two dowries totalling about 50,000 livres.[34] René had seven other children, of whom two apparently died young, two became nuns, and three married. Two of the marriages took place within a four-month period in 1739-40: first Jeanne Drouin married Augustin Seign (a future partner of Louis Drouin), and then Jean Baptiste Guillaume Drouin married Marie Moreau. Both Drouin newlyweds received about 20,000 livres.[35]

At some time in the 1740s, Louis Drouin, the sole surviving son of René, must have left for the islands, leaving Christophe as the family's only male representative in Nantes. Although Christophe seemed to bide his time (his taxes went from 40 livres to 50 livres between 1750 and 1764), Louis fared well in the colonies. Associating with different merchants, he earned a fair amount before returning to Nantes around 1763 (?), the year of his marriage to his cousin Marie Françoise Budan and the year before his name first appeared on the tax roles. His marriage portion was nearly 80,000 livres,[36] while his tax assessment was 120 livres. It was at this time that Louis Drouin began his career in earnest as a ship outfitter. Alone, or with various partners, he sent out twenty ships to the colonies and two to Africa in the 1760s, thirty-four to the colonies and seven to Africa in the 1770s, and thirty-nine to the colonies and four to Africa from 1780 to 1791. He also invested about 1,000,000 livres in the slave trade from 1783 to 1792 alone.

This intense activity produced commensurate financial harvests. By

1777, when he was ennobled, Louis was worth 580,000 livres;[37] in 1789, when he was taxed 900 livres personally, he was probably worth more than 5,000,000 livres.[38] Although much of this apparent success must have been the result of wise slave trading, a lot of it can be explained by a rather special system of accounting. The 1778 fortune (580,000 livres) seems eminently honest, at least in terms of real wealth based in France. Most of it was spent, or at least pledged, over the next decade as dowries for his only three children, all daughters: each child was endowed with 200,000 livres, to be paid at the rate of 10,000 annually for twenty years. His maritime operations could have been carried on for an initial capital of as little as 300,000 livres, with the rest of the business built on credit.[39] The 1789 evaluation was quite optimistic and bore little relation to Drouin's real wealth. Unfortunately, Drouin had no inventory after his death so that his landed possessions are not known, but it is quite possible that they were meager.[40] Only if the 7,000,000 livres in colonial assets attributed to him were even partly considered by the tax collector was the Drouin fortune explicable.[41] Drouin's plantations were probably counted for capitation purposes, although money owing from Saint Domingue was probably discounted sharply.

The Arnous family fortune also relied heavily on colonial assets. Like the Drouins the Arnous' amassed a small fortune before turning to the slave trade. Descended from a line of master carpenters and shipbuilders, the family first appeared on the Nantes tax roles in 1750, with an imposition of 170 livres for Nicolas, a "shipbuilder," and 50 livres for his brother Joseph, a "wood merchant." Four years later, Nicolas was charged 190 livres and his son—undoubtedly Nicolas (II), born in 1719—40 livres; Joseph paid 60 livres. Thus the family was probably worth around 300,000 to 400,000 livres at this time. It was then that the family's interest in maritime commerce began. "Nicolas Arnous, Father and Son" originally comprising Nicolas (I) and his son Pierre, a ship's captain, fitted out their first ship in 1751; by the end of the old regime, the company, under changing management, sent out more than one hundred ships to the colonies, at least eleven of which went via Africa. Growth was slow at first, however, and when Nicolas (II) married Marie Millet in 1753, he received a small dowry of around 20,000 livres.[42]

By the 1760s, the fortunes were up. In 1762, the family was taxed some 426 livres, divided between Nicolas Father and Son (300 livres), Joseph (90 livres), and his son Joseph (II) Arnous-Rivière, also a wood seller (36 livres); apparently the war years had been kind to these merchants still involved in ship building. Two years later, however, the main Arnous company was back down to 198 livres in taxes, while the other members remained unchanged. The cause of the sudden decline was not clear but was probably the death of the elder partner and the subsequent reorganization of the company. Unfortunately, the date of Nicolas' (I) death is not known, but since his younger brother died in 1769 at the age of seventy-five it is very possible that Nicolas also died in the 1760s. In any event, the next tax register (1788-89) had the Arnous' at 716 livres: 636 from Nicolas (II) and 80 from his rather distant cousin Jean Joseph, son of Joseph (II). This represented a fortune of about 2,500,000 livres, easily double the 1764 amount. The great fortune was earned in the 1770s and 1780s. After having fitted out about forty ships between 1751 and 1769,[43] the company sent out forty-one ships from 1770 to 1778, and twenty-four, including nine slavers, from 1783 to 1791. By 1778, they were very rich indeed. In that year Marie Suzanne, daughter of Nicolas (II), married Gabriel Augustin Michel, a match which marked the social "arrival" of the family. The bride was endowed with 120,000 livres, the sum that her sisters would receive when marrying nobly a few years later.[44] Also indicative of the social ascendancy of the Arnous' was the purchase by Nicolas (II) of the ennobling office of *secrétaire du roi* in 1774.[45] By the end of the old regime, the family was considered to be one of the wealthiest in Nantes.

But how solid were the Arnous' fortunes? Ironically, Jean Joseph's smaller holdings were more firmly established than his cousin's. Worth 150,000 livres plus one-fifth of Nicolas Arnous Father and Son when married in 1787, Jean Joseph was taxed 80 livres in 1788-89 on an assumed evaluation of about 200,000 to 300,000 livres. Most of this was put to good use in 1791 when he bought extensive lands near Orléans, where he finally moved.[46] Nicolas' wealth was more chimerical: his estate was valued at only 9,333 francs in 1807, plus the value of a large house in Nantes and more than one plantation in the Antilles.[47] Although it would be easy to blame the Revolution for this apparent decline, it was not the cause. The presumed fortune of 1788-89 was based half on credits or speculative investments. His real assets included his house, purchased for 200,000 livres,[48] the capital of his company, of which his share probably did not exceed 600,000 livres,[49] and his daughters' dowries, worth 360,000 livres if the sum were in fact paid. The rest of the fortune was "in the colonies," and particularly in the plantations which Nicolas purchased in 1763 and 1783.[50] Altogether Arnous supposedly had 5,000,000 livres due him from the colonies, and the tax collector obviously considered a large part of this when computing Arnous' assessment. Thus the Arnous fortune, which could have been estimated at up to 7,000,000 livres, was actually about 1,000,000 livres. Only a spiraling system of credit, ultimately founded on an ailing colonial economy, gave illusions of much greater success.

Even the celebrated Gradis family fortune had its weaknesses.[51] The Gradis' started as simple merchants at the end of the seventeenth century, but had become one of the richest families in Bordeaux by the end of the old regime. The company founded by Diego Gradis and run by his son David was worth 5,000 livres in 1695. By 1728, after a decade of fitting out ships for the colonies, the company had a capital of 162,000 livres. When David died in 1751, his estate was worth 400,000 livres, and by 1788, the family fortune passed the 4,000,000-livre mark. Although the Gradis' were changing their orientation from commercial to landed interests, they still remained deeply involved in the colonial economy and had more than 2,000,000-livres' worth of holdings on Saint Domingue and Martinique on the eve of the Revolution.

The Begouen Demeaux' of Le Havre followed a similar pattern.[52] Arriving in Le Havre in the 1720s, Jacques François Begouen Demeaux quickly learned about commerce and made a small fortune. By the end of the Austrian War, he was ready to participate heavily in the slave trade, and he did so with uncommon wisdom. To avoid risks, he limited himself to a one-third share in his slavers, but to maintain his freedom of action, he sold the other two-thirds to out-of-town investors. Business was good, and after the Seven Years' War, Begouen Demeaux was one of the most active slave traders in the kingdom. Having worked closely with his brother-in-law Stanislas Foache, who operated one of the largest houses on Saint Domingue, Begouen Demeaux was worth some 3,000,000 livres when he died in 1779. Much of this, however, existed only on paper in the form of colonial credits, and it was only during the Revolution that the family fortune was consolidated in France. Although Begouen Demeaux had bought a 257,000-livre home in the 1770s, the family became important landowners only in 1791-92, when they bought 1,000,000 livres' worth of nationalized lands.

These family histories display many features typical of successful slaving careers. Most striking is the volatile nature of their fortunes. Merchants arrived in a port with modest assets and within a generation or two were considered millionaires. Almost everything involved in slavers' finances was touched with an aura of exaggeration, especially the size of their fortunes and the speed at which they were made. It is difficult to establish the true size of a slaver's fortune. Contemporaries apparently counted colonial assets as well as French ones, perhaps believing that the former were as well founded as the latter. This, however, was a mistake, especially toward the end of the old regime, when direct investment in the island economies frequently represented weakness and not strength. There was little new investment in the colonies following the American War, and most of the increased participation resulted from foreclosures and the involuntary extension of credit.[53] But changed management or ownership could not begin to remedy the ills afflicting the colonial economies: restricted to commerce with France and kept without specie, the colonists were unable to create a viable economy.

The effects of colonial weaknesses should not be overestimated. In spite of the difficulties in repatriating their money, the major French traders succeeded in amassing respectable fortunes. If the fortunes were not as large in reality as they appeared on paper, they were nonetheless of sufficient importance to enable their possessors to purchase ennobling offices, *hôtels* in the city, and modest estates in the countryside. The undeniable success of the great slavers encouraged numerous other merchants to participate in the trade. There were few other enterprises which offered the possibility of such vast riches, and slaving fortunes showed amazing growth rates on paper, particularly in the second half of the eighteenth century: the Arnous' paid 324 livres in taxes in 1764 and 716 livres in 1788; over the same period, the Drouins' assessments grew from 170 livres to over 900 livres; and from 1751 to 1780, the Gradis fortune went from 400,000 livres to 4,000,000 livres.[54] Colonial problems notwithstanding, the major slave traders were among the most active and most prosperous merchants in eighteenth-century France.

14
A Slaving Civilization

When asked in the 1780s to serve as a director of the newly created Bordeaux Museum, Charles Lemesle replied, "I am infinitely flattered by the invitation with which you have honored me, and I would accept with the greatest pleasure if my manifold but much less agreeable occupations allowed me the time to cultivate letters."[1] Lemesle did not refuse because he was a boor; in fact, he himself had heartily welcomed the foundation of the museum in 1783. "Anything which can contribute to increasing knowledge and to inspiring a taste for the sciences, letters, and the arts," he wrote, "can only be infinitely useful in a big city where fortune provides all the means to cultivate them."[2] Instead, his refusal to accept the directorship reflected an attitude common among eighteenth-century French merchants: non-business matters were laudable only if they did not interfere with what was truly important. Once again, business considerations took priority, and the slaver returned quietly to his office.

Incidents like this underline the fact that the slave traders did not quite fit into old regime society. On the one hand, the major traders were among the richest people in the realm; even setting aside their colonial wealth, they were a match for all but the wealthiest of men not dependent directly on the court for their riches. If the traders' fortunes never equalled those of the great financiers, they nonetheless far exceeded the often hopelessly diminished holdings of a good part of the old nobility. On the other hand, the slavers did not have a rung on the social ladder accurately reflecting their particular economic interests: many rich traders became nobles while poorer ones remained commoners. Although they made efforts to become aristocrats with an interest in maritime commerce, they remained true businessmen in their thoughts and actions and were inhibited from creating much of a distinct culture beyond their businesses. They were proud to be merchants, confident that they were bringing glory to France,[3] yet they also sought eagerly to accommodate themselves to the traditional organization of society by buying offices or receiving letters of nobility. This incongruity between social and economic status deeply bothered many successful traders.

The traders aspired to the nobility.[4] They knew that noble standing was a necessary condition for joining the established elites of society, and they were determined to occupy this valued station. Very few slaving families were of the old nobility: the Chateaubriands of Saint Malo, and the Deluynes and Espivents of Nantes, were the only truly noble families who played significant roles in the trade. The Chateaubriands are too well known to warrant further discussion. The Deluynes originated in Orléans and moved to Nantes near the beginning of the eighteenth century. From 1709 to 1774, members of the family took an active interest in the slave trade and fitted out a total of twenty-five ships for Africa. The Espivents had been noble since medieval times, and members of the family participated heavily in maritime commerce throughout the eighteenth century. The Espivents were proud of their heritage and tried to contract marriages with other established noble families only. And only once in the eighteenth century did an Espivent deign to take even an ennobled spouse: in 1750, Pierre Antoine Espivent de la Villeboisnet married Elisabeth Montaudouin, daughter of an *anobli* from the richest family in Nantes. Although an Espivent did not refuse the position of *juge-consul*,[5] and although the family offered hospitality to Arthur Young in 1788,[6] the Espivents kept the Nantes commercial world at a distance. They rarely invested in other merchants' ships,[7] and they almost never accepted investments in their own expeditions.[8] Apparently, the Espivents felt that they could behave like merchants without really becoming merchants.

In practice, this nonchalance was the social goal of many French slave traders. Although they may well have desired an end to the entire system of ennoblement,[9] they wanted a preferred position in it for as long as it lasted. In every major port in France except for Protestant-dominated La Rochelle, the biggest slave traders acquired noble status during the eighteenth century (table 11.1). Outside of La Rochelle, successful Protestant and even Jewish traders were ennobled: Feray in Le Havre; Nairac, Gradis, and Laffon in Bordeaux. Most of the ennobled were, of course, Catholics, to whom this came almost naturally. A major Catholic slave trader could legitimately expect ennoblement because of the harmony between government policy and the merchants' wishes. The government was prepared to offer noble status as an encouragement to maritime commerce, while merchants clearly desired to be honored with nobility. The only question was whether the traders, once ennobled, would continue in their chosen occupation, given the traditional aristocratic hostility towards business. Indeed, it was precisely the reluctance of established noble families to enter maritime commerce which had originally forced the government to adopt the policy of ennobling successful merchants.[10] In spite of government encouragement, members of the old aristocratic families for the most part refused to participate in a traditionally demeaning endeavor like commerce; as we have seen, only three truly noble families engaged in the slave trade. It seemed at first that the new nobles were going to follow the example of the old. According to Guy Richard, it was common early in the eighteenth century for merchants to abandon commerce upon ennoblement;[11] like Jean Pellet of Bordeaux, these men made every effort, however farcical, to live nobly.[12] Later in the century, however, the ennobled merchants valued their businesses more highly than they feared the wrath of their new peers, and continued to participate in commerce.

After 1750, the anoblis dominated the slave trade. In Le Havre, Begouen Demeaux, Feray, and Foache entered the nobility between 1768 and 1784, but their improved status obviously did not affect their slaving careers adversely. Between the American and French revolutions, these three men together fitted out thirty-five slave ships, or more than 20 percent of the local total. In Bordeaux, anoblis Nairac, Laffon, Gradis, Castaing, Testart, and Journu sent out thirty-seven slavers following the American War, a seventh of the Bordeaux total. But it was at Nantes where the anoblis were most active: members of fourteen ennobled families participated in companies fitting out eighty-six slave ships (22 percent of the Nantes total) from 1783 to 1792. Many of the new Nantes aristocrats even banded together in informal investment groups to expand their commercial operations. Aubry, Chaurand, and Deurbroucq participated in one such group with the less-active interest of Libault, Foucault, and Portier, while Drouin, Arnous, and Michel were the pillars of another group; all were ennobled. In the ports, the traders found that the esteem bestowed on commerce outweighed the traditional social pressure against it; they therefore continued not only to engage in the slave trade but also to participate in local government and in the administration of commercial affairs.[13] The conflict between the local (and old peer) appreciation of business and the noble disparagement of it was decisively resolved in favor of the former; even the sons of ennobled traders generally continued in commerce.

Ennoblement had somewhat more effect on social relations. The investment groups formed by Nantes anoblis reflected marital ties between the newly honored families. For example, the Chaurands married with the Portiers, the Deurbroucqs, and the Libaults; the Libaults with the Deurbroucqs, the Foucaults, and the Portiers; and the Portiers with the Foucaults (twice). Children of anoblis not marrying other anoblis often sought alliances with the older nobility. The most successful of these at Nantes were the daughters of Gabriel Michel: one married the *haut et puissant* Marquis de Maboeuf, the other the *très haut et très puissant* Marquis de Levis. For the most part, however, the anoblis preferred to choose spouses from similarly situated families, a practice which had the extra advantage of keeping more money in the commercial realm. If there were many children, marriages with prominent non-noble merchants were usually concluded. Thus of the spouses of the nine marrying children of Dominique Deurbroucq of Nantes, four were from common commercial families, four from newly ennobled families, and one from an old aristocratic family. Ennoblement, therefore, worked almost as a form of self-flattery which made little difference to the ennobled trader himself and only slightly more to his family. It was like joining an exclusive club which suddenly and briefly opens its doors to a large group of new members who, although anxious to assimilate into the old crowd, remain closer friends than ever before. Because of the anoblis' continued involvement in maritime commerce, social divisions within the slaving community rarely presented any problems, especially since money could overcome all barriers between merchants. Children of rich commoners could find ennobled spouses, and partnerships between ennobled and common merchants were not at all unusual.

Thus in spite of their aspirations toward nobility, the traders remained merchants at heart and maintained a system of values far removed from the aristocratic one. Honor for them meant primarily being a good credit risk—in striking contrast to the celebrated noble attitude toward debt paying. Even in the smallest matters, it was important for the trader to appear scrupulously honest, as one wrote to complaining colleagues:

> I enclose, sirs, the ten sous which you have requested. I do not owe them to you; I can attest and prove that your parcel did not come in the bag. . . . It's a petty sum which I little regret, but I owe it to the public, whose esteem is dear to me, and I know that a *little-known man* can easily . . . give an *unfavorable twist to the most innocent things*. . . . You must not speak of this to anyone without showing my letter.[14]

The traders saw themselves as participants in the most advanced movement in the world: commerce was the key to the future and the new foundation for French glory. Merchants were anxious to establish and maintain a good public image, and they did not hesitate to sing their own praises. For example, when the trader Baignoux' house burned down in Bordeaux, local merchants helped him through the difficult period. This generosity was much lauded by the Saint Domingue merchants Plombard and LeGris, who wrote, "Such actions are well made to pass into posterity."[15] Having a good image also meant giving the impression of wealth. As a Nantes trader noted, "One knows how much it matters to a merchant to admit that his fortune is lower than the public estimation of it."[16] Money was at the center of a slaver's world.

At times, concern over money reached obsessive proportions, revealing a streak of miserliness in the traders which was far removed from the generosity supposedly characteristic of the aristocrat.[17] Even in the smallest matters, traders were careful of their financial interests. They complained when they felt their taxes were too high, one of them going so far as to protest formally against what he considered to be a four-livre overcharge.[18] The slave traders rarely gave the impression of generosity. Their domestics were not well paid, nor were the servants particularly well cared for upon their master's death. Considering the amounts of money handled by them, they were stingy when it came to charitable works. For example, upon founding a new company with a capital of 150,000 livres, Riedy and Thurninger donated 100 livres per year to the local poor.[19] Although local legend saw the Nantes traders as selfless benefactors of the city's less-fortunate residents,[20] there is little to suggest that they ever gave away more than a negligible fraction of their worth; they certainly contributed a far smaller percentage than demanded by modern governments in taxes. There were, of course, some notable exceptions to this rule of frugality, but the exceptions were usually inspired by unique circumstances. Abraham Gradis, for example, donated 61,000 livres in 1777 to improve the Bordeaux synagogue, and willed thousands of livres to the poor of Jerusalem and Bordeaux; these generous gestures were undoubtedly motivated by the precarious legal position of the Jewish residents of Bordeaux.[21]

Monetary considerations imposed limits on the trader's way of life. Thoroughly imbued with the commercial spirit, he was not anxious to squander his hard-earned fortune by living far beyond his means; this was true at least during the second half of the eighteenth century. Although successful traders did not refrain from buying *folies* and country houses,[22] the city remained their true home. Indeed, Bordeaux merchants bought country estates primarily to produce wines for export.[23] The city house was often large but simply appointed. The interior of the hôtel Grou in Nantes, for example, was so disappointing that revolutionary authorities returned more than once to search for objects of value that might have been overlooked.[24] The traders lived comfortably but not extravagantly, preferring to reinvest all revenues in their businesses rather than spend too much on home furnishings.[25]

Business was clearly preeminent in the slaver's perception of the world. Traders thought in financial terms, and their view of themselves, local society, and France was highly colored by economic considerations. Slaving merchants prided themselves on their realism and their ability to interpret events in the "proper" manner. Of course, even this capacity for considered judgment and articulation was related to the business of a merchant: all the slave traders were literate because literacy was essential to international trade. In fact, if any trait was particularly characteristic of the traders, it was their great interest in the written word. Whether in the form of business letters or books, writing formed the link between them and the world. As we have seen, their business forced the traders to carry an extensive correspondence around the Atlantic world. More significantly, they kept large libraries filled with practical books of every description. Always active, they had tremendous curiosity about the world, which they relied on books to satisfy. Their libraries were heavily biased towards nonfiction, particularly geography, history, and languages. Religious works occupied but a small corner, and the classics were poorly represented.[26] The traders consumed journals and newspapers as voraciously as they did books. Financial papers from Paris, England, and Holland circulated in the ports and were even sent by the French merchants to their friends in the West Indies.[27] Arthur Young noted that "the Nantes *chambre de lecture,* or what we should call a book-club . . . is particularly flourishing."[28]

Given their practical orientation, the traders could be expected to have only one attitude towards the slaves they transported and frequently owned. As far as they were concerned, slaves were simply a perishable commodity[29] to be handled with a certain care to prevent damage. In the ledgers, dead slaves were treated as irreparably ruined goods whose loss was regretted only insofar as it meant a loss of revenue. Indeed, had the traders any emotional reaction to the slaves' fate, they could not have been slave traders. It was for the church and the philosophers, and not for the traders, to debate the spiritual advantages of a Christian upbringing under bondage. The traders were content merely to accept Jacques Savary's pronouncement on the subject:

> This commerce appears inhuman to those who do not know that these poor men are idolators or Moslems, and that the Christian merchants, in buying them from their enemies, save them from a cruel slavery and place them on the islands where they encounter not only a sweeter servitude but also the knowledge of the true God and the path of salvation by the good instruction given them by priests and religious people who take care to make them Christian; and there is reason to believe that without these considerations, this commerce would not be allowed.[30]

The slavers stopped trading only when it was no longer profitable to continue.

As slave owners, the traders showed greater concern for the slaves, although this attitude was again purely practical. It was, however, to the traders' credit that they did not overtly espouse the murder of nonproductive laborers in a final attempt to keep costs down. Although some plantation owners in the Antilles thought that the cheapest method might have been to work a slave to death in a few years and then replace him with a new one,[31] the French slave traders never consciously adopted such a policy, preferring to breed slaves in the colonies. The Chaurands often warned their agents against overworking slaves:

> We are strongly of your opinion that the greatest care should be taken of the Negroes, feeding and clothing them well, displaying attachment and friendship, and not overburdening them with work.[32]

> One cannot be too tender to the Negroes and especially to the new ones. We prefer to have a few too many on the plantation than to overwork them.[33]

> We learn with pleasure . . . that you have had a hospital constructed as needed to treat with care and zeal our poor Negroes. . . . our interests are involved in it, for it seems impossible that with fifty Negroes on this plantation, only twenty-two to twenty-five are able to go to work.[34]

The tenderness, however, was limited. The Chaurands, like most traders, believed that the Africans did not like to work hard; according to them, "the black without a master will never work except to fulfill his own needs."[35] Hence, it was necessary to subject the slave to a harsh regime: "You express the greatest kindness to the Negroes in never punishing them with the cane, but with the whip instead—and so that they will always remember their errors."[36] The result, in spite of exhortations to moderation, was a brutal system. In practice, the colonial foremen, under constant prodding from their absentee landlords, could not avoid overworking the slaves, and the mortality rate on the plantations was appalling.[37] The owner always had to expect reports of increased capital expenditure necessitated by slave deaths.

The owner-traders may have been unmoved by the fate of their blacks on the islands, but they were more concerned with the slaves they possessed in France itself. During the eighteenth century, it was common for ship's captains, returning colonists, and merchants to own slaves in the ports and even in Paris. Although the practice was widespread throughout Western Europe, it was of dubious legality in most places. England, for example, rid itself of slavery in 1772, but France was less decisive. As early as 1571, the Parlement of Bordeaux had declared that there could be no slavery in France,[38] but subsequent practice contradicted the ruling in several ways, most importantly by not denying the right of colonists visiting France to keep their slaves. Although fear of an expanding black population encouraged the government to prohibit each visitor from introducing more than one slave,[39] the principle of possession was reaffirmed, and slave-owning merchants and captains, as well as the colonists, managed to circumvent the official restriction. There were thus many slaves in the ports, usually serving their masters as domestics.[40] The parish registers listed the vital statistics of the black community under a special heading, with no qualms about referring to the Africans as slaves, even when recording a baptism: "On July 7, 1787, was baptized . . . Clement Pierre, aged nineteen years, native of Gavinque, Angola . . . Negro belonging to M. Clement Duchesne, ship's captain currently on voyage."[41] The lot of the slaves in France was obviously better than in the Antilles, and the problems of ownership—financial, moral, and legal—frequently led to the slave's emancipation. The notarial papers have several "acts of liberty" which bear witness to the "humanity" of the traders when confronted personally with an incongruous situation.[42] Slaves outside the colonial plantation system made little sense to the merchant and were interesting only as diversions. The slave trader, like the trade itself, was motivated by economics, not hatred.[43]

Conclusion

The slave trade is absolutely necessary.
Vicomte de Mirabeau

Blessed with great riches, the French slave traders of the eighteenth century presented a striking contrast to the slaves they traded. In the traders' minds, particularly, there was an abyss between the two types of humanity. The traders and their supporters had a negative view of the black slave:

> This degraded species of humanity lacks the energy of the northern savage, either from natural injustice, which witholds from some what it offers in abundance to others, or from failing to be perfected by civilization; the Negro's intelligence is infinitely restricted. . . . Carelessness, laziness, and an aversion to work are natural for the inhabitants of Africa. Born in irons, born for slavery, they do not know liberty; and the Negroes sold to Europeans merely change their chains. They miss their country; they do not miss a freedom they have never known.[1]

Opposed to this was the traders' favorable image of themselves. They took pride in their hard work and intelligence, and they had faith in the values of their civilization. Typical was the example of Jacques François Begouen Demeaux, who made a tremendous fortune from the slave trade and who used his money to raise his nephew properly.[2] He sent him on a grand tour of England, Holland, and Germany, had him instructed in law, languages, and philosophy, and gave him a dowry of 600,000 livres. Slavery and the slave trade divided humanity into two camps and then connected them in a brutal fashion. The misery of more than a million Africans made large fortunes for a few merchants and enabled wealthy Europeans to purchase some luxury goods at slightly lower prices.

A few commercial fortunes and cheaper sugar and coffee could not by themselves justify the entire operation. People believed that something fundamental was at stake, namely, the economic well-being of the nation: "If we changed the established order, several million Frenchmen would fall into poverty; and if humanity tells us to improve the lot of the Negroes, reason orders us to confirm their enslavement."[3] The eighteenth-century French slave trade was intimately related to the institution of slavery in the French colonies, itself merely the necessary condition for the commerce in colonial commodities. What really mattered was the re-export trade in

196

sugar and coffee. During the eighteenth century, these tropical products formed the cornerstone of France's foreign trade and provided the country with respectable surpluses. From 1784 to 1788, for example, France exported an average of 350,000,000 livres' worth of goods to Europe, of which nearly half represented tropical produce; at the same time, French imports from Europe averaged only 300,000,000 livres. Although the precision of these statistics is open to question today, in the eighteenth century it was not, and men in responsible positions could draw only one conclusion from them: the colonial plantation economies had to be encouraged and not just tolerated. If the plantations required slave labor, then slavery had to be accepted. If the slaves could not reproduce quickly enough to fulfill the labor demands naturally, then the slave trade had to be encouraged. The entire program stemmed from considerations of "national interest," and individual plantation owners or slave traders could decide only the fine points of its implementation.

If the eighteenth-century French slave trade depended ultimately on larger questions of international commerce for its existence, it nonetheless functioned as a semi-autonomous branch of commerce. Once legalized by the government, it grew in response to market conditions in the French West Indies. As the colonies expanded in the first half of the century, so did the slave trade, which benefitted from a legal monopoly in the French Antilles. During the third quarter of the century, however, there was a marked disparity between the growth of the colonial and slave trades, as the planters relied more and more on cheaper British slaves. Finally, after the American War, the French regained the colonial slave market, and the French trade grew enormously to match colonial needs. The slaving triangle also reflected the trade's partial autonomy. The triangle had as its purpose the realization of profits through the purchase and sale of African captives. French slave traders tried to maintain a distance between the slave and colonial commodities' trades and complained bitterly when forced to participate directly in the colonial economy. They would have preferred to receive cash for their slaves in the Antilles and then decide whether to speculate on colonial produce, but the structure of the colonial system argued against a completely independent trade. Lacking the specie to pay for the slaves, the planters forced the traders to become involved in colonial commerce.

It took more than one revolution to destroy this system. The French Revolution of 1789 temporarily wiped the slate clean, abolishing slavery and the slave trade. Although both had been eliminated *de facto* before the official decrees, the *de jure* interdictions were considered radical moves without parallel. Next, the Haitian Revolution made a mockery of Napoleon's attempts to restore the old colonial system in its entirely. Although

Napoleon did reimpose slavery and legalize the trade, the loss of Saint Domingue reduced the French Caribbean trade to a trivial position: no longer could France dominate the European market for sugar and coffee. The early days of the industrial revolution then reaffirmed the secondary place that the commerce in colonial commodities had in the French economy; manufacturing began to take precedence over the re-export of tropical produce. And finally, the revolutionary government of 1848 put an end to slavery on French soil. With the stroke of a pen, Victor Schoelcher rid the French territories of slaves thenceforward.

The crumbling of the French colonial system did not end the French slave trade as much as modify it. Technically, the trade was outlawed in 1814-15, but in reality it continued until the second half of the nineteenth century. This illegal trade was radically different from the legal trade of the eighteenth century. The slave trade no longer found its justification in the re-export trade; it became a completely independent form of commerce. Traders were finally able to engage in the trade without risking participation in ailing colonial economies. This was because the French slave trade of the nineteenth century had little to do with the remaining French colonies of Martinique, Guadeloupe, Guiana, and Reunion; other, foreign, destinations awaited French slaving ships. Thus prohibiting the slave trade in the nineteenth century was vastly different from prohibiting it in the eighteenth. Now the prohibition of slaving merely reflected the weakness of the French colonies, rather than leading to such weakness. The truncated French empire of the early nineteenth century was similar in many respects to the troubled British empire of the late eighteenth century. Without accepting the Williams theses in their entirety,[4] it can still be seen that the rapid decline in production in the French West Indies made the slave trade, and perhaps slavery, less necessary than ever before. As the re-export trade vanished, France could afford to adopt more humane policies which, as cynics might suggest, cost less than maintaining slavery. Nineteenth-century French slave traders performed no vital services for the nation; their more or less clandestine operations had little impact on the national economy.

Even Nantes did not benefit greatly from the nineteenth-century trade. Although Nantes' slaving during the Restoration compared favorably with prerevolutionary levels, the port was in obvious decline. Restoration Nantes lost its position of international significance and became merely another provincial port. In spite of Libaudière's claim that in 1830 Nantes was on the verge of a "new era of prosperity,"[5] official figures show only stagnation. According to the Nantes Chamber of Commerce (established as such by Napoleon), imports of sugar in 1835 were at half the pre-Revolutionary levels, while coffee was down by three-quarters.[6] The decline was dramatic, especially since no other commodities filled the gap. The commerce in *bois d'ébène*[7] did not provide the same general prosperity as before the Revolution. Even the small complex of commercial and industrial activities which had developed towards the end of the eighteenth century to nourish the slave trade was largely abandoned.

A quarter-century of warfare followed by an official ban on trading forced the old regime slave traders to re-evaluate their commercial practices. Almost to a man, the pre-Revolutionary traders permanently abandoned transatlantic commerce after 1792, and terminated their association with the slave trade even more decisively. Other economic ventures attracted them, particularly heavy investment in land, and to a lesser degree, in new commercial enterprises often centering on maritime activity. This latter field included the fitting out of *corsaires,* and the execution of certain municipal commissions such as locating, purchasing, and delivering adequate supplies of grain. Needless to say, these operations could be lucrative, and it would be misleading to assume that the lack of colonial commerce during the Revolution necessarily spelled the financial ruin of all the slave traders. Although most of them left behind piles of worthless colonial credits and very little hard currency, the traders who died during the Revolutionary period also usually bequeathed important landed interests to their heirs.

Land had great appeal for the traders. Some managed to consolidate their fortunes by speculating on nationalized properties (*biens nationaux*). Begouen Demeaux, for example, purchased immense properties for virtually worthless *assignats,* the Revolutionary paper money which suffered from a devastating rate of inflation.[8] Other traders did not rely on nationalized lands but simply took advantage of the chaotic times to make wise purchases of privately owned land. The Revolution provided ideal conditions for land speculation, and many traders whose fortunes were shaky before 1789 succeeded in converting their wealth into real estate during the Revolution. This was particularly true of the new traders of the 1783-89 period. These *nouveaux riches* wanted to achieve through land purchases the financial security which the slave trade had denied them.

Complementing the traders' interest in real estate was an enduring association with maritime enterprise. During the early years of the Revolution in particular, this meant fitting out corsaires or performing duties for the government. By far the most popular activity was privateering, and hundreds of voyages were made by the quasi-warships during the two decades of war. Even before war broke out, the crown was encouraging an aggressive attitude on the part of the French armateurs. In 1787 the practice of selling *commissions en guerre* began; by paying 15,000 livres to the government, the captain was authorized to take and keep ''all that he could conquer.''[9] About twenty ships per year were granted this license in Nantes alone, and almost all of them were slavers, for which the *commissions* also gave a guarantee of free trade in Africa. When war finally came, the French were quick to respond to the English threat with corsaires. Privateering increased rapidly until there were hundreds of corsaires on the seas. This dangerous activity could yield spectacular results: one Nantes armateur supposedly received some 8,500,000 francs in prizes of war over a three-year period.[10]

With the disappearance of the slave trade and the increased interest in other branches of maritime commerce or in real estate, the old slaving communities lost their reason for being and simply vanished. In Nantes, for example, it would have been difficult to discern a distinctive slaving community after 1792: the traders no longer formed a special group within the Nantes commercial world. Of course, many of the most important old regime traders continued to dominate the local economy, but just as many lost their positions of prominence through death, departure from Nantes, or economic misfortune. To fill this vacuum, several less-important figures arose. Traders, some of whom had only modest resources at the end of the old regime, now combined with rich new arrivals to construct a new elite in the Nantes business world.

The most significant change in the old slaving community was the withdrawal of the anoblis. After 1792, most of them simply ceased to engage in commerce. This economic phenomenon was matched by a social one, as they tended, after 1792, to close ranks and exclude all but the very richest of commoners. The anoblis had achieved an honored status in the old regime, a status they were anxious to maintain. In the nineteenth century, they were less willing to accept common spouses than before. Even in forming companies, the anoblis who remained in business displayed an exclusiveness which they could ill afford under the old regime. Money no longer bridged the gap between noble and commoner as easily as it had in the late eighteenth century; whereas seven ennobled Nantes traders had gone into partnerships with commoners between 1783 and 1792, none did so in Revolutionary times. Decreased needs for capital after 1792 also discouraged *anobli-roturier* partnerships. For example, Armand François Delaville no longer needed a Barthelemi to help meet the costs of fitting out slaving expeditions; he could now finance Delaville and Son himself.

The virtual disintegration of the slave-trading interest group did not result solely from the abolition of the legal trade and the long years of warfare; the very nature of the group itself militated against its survival. In spite of its size, the French slave trade lacked a solid financial foundation in the ports. Merchants interested in the trade never succeeded in developing a business organization which functioned on its own. The traders could not overcome their attachment to the old forms of partnership and to the practice of investment by parts. Each slaver wanted to be personally involved in the trade, a fact which made for inefficiency and instability, since almost every expedition had to be organized entirely independently. Each time a merchant wanted to fit out a slaving ship, he had to start almost from scratch. Although informal investment groups developed to supply armateurs with investment capital, they, by their very informality, only limited the problem and did not solve it. Nothing prevented a participating merchant from suddenly and inexplicably quitting the group, just as nothing forced him to buy a share in a colleague's expedition. Investment by parts enabled tradition-minded merchants to conduct the slave trade but kept them from rationalizing the trade's financing. Only the creation of large joint-stock corporations could have eliminated the difficulties and overcome the debilitating effects of an all-too-intense competition. The agreement made by the Guinea and Angola companies to divide the Senegal trade was a first step in this direction, but support for the experiment was lacking in the ports.

In part, social pressures discouraged the traders from appreciating the benefits of larger, more impersonal business structures. The family was of paramount importance, and advancing the family's position through wise matches or ennoblement was a primary goal. The anonymity of a larger corporation was alien to this goal. With very few exceptions, slave traders were self-made men seeking to transform modest paternal legacies into vast fortunes that would qualify them for the nobility and enable their children to marry well. Working for a large corporation would probably have yielded neither of these results. Furthermore, big business implied a confidence in strangers which the traders were incapable of expressing. Eighteenth-century French businessmen could not rely on institutions: they had to rely on men. There were no modern banks, only bankers who usually doubled as merchants. There was no official paper money, only notes issued by merchants or officials. There was scarcely a true bureaucracy, as administrators owned their offices and confused private with public business. Under such circumstances, the merchants could depend only on relatives or other people whom they knew well.[11] The capitalism of eighteenth-century France was a capitalism lacking in trust, and the prevailing air of suspicion helped prevent its development.

Institutions and attitudes thus tied the trader firmly to the past and made them a true part of the old regime. Their interest in making a profit through business may have marked them as a modern element in eighteenth-century France, but their deep attachment to traditional forms of business organization, their striving for status, and their apparent apathy in noneconomic political matters, placed them in the tradition of medieval merchants more than of modern industrial capitalists. Risking everything on one or two expeditions, they hoped to make large gains through the purchase and sale of exotic merchandise on three continents. Although modern enough to remain in their home ports and hire others to do the actual traveling and trading, the slavers nonetheless retained the other characteristics of medieval businessmen. Even the central object of trade reflected an ancient set of values, one which enabled them to seek riches from an ignoble and abhorrent commerce.

REFERENCE MATTER

Appendix: The Statistical Study of the French Slave Trade

Sources

Primary. Documents relating to the French slave trade abound in both Paris and the ports, and many of them contain statistical data. Unfortunately, there are several problems with the documents, making their use difficult. Some are incomplete or stand in contradiction to others. For example a manuscript which lists, in theory, "all" slaving departures from a particular port may miss nearly a quarter of the departures listed on another so-called comprehensive list. Many documents are so vague on certain points that they are useless: trying to determine the African or even Caribbean destinations of slaving ships is almost impossible because of the uncertain meaning of terms like "the African coast" or "the islands." Many eighteenth-century documents are simply inaccurate as far as numbers are concerned; it is not at all uncommon to see different values for the same measurement, or obvious errors in arithmetic. In spite of these problems, however, the documents are obviously valuable and if used carefully can yield results which probably have a moderate resemblance to the truth. Nothing more should be claimed.

Virtually all the statistical information on the French slave trade comes from the Admiralty papers in each of the ports. As holdings vary widely, it is necessary to give a port-by-port description of the extant documentation:

1. Nantes. Documents in ADLA. Fortunately, the premier slaving port has the best collection of documents available, in spite of the destruction of most Chamber of Commerce papers during World War II. Three series are of particular interest: the *rôles d'armement et de désarmement* (1700–1800; *fonds marine*); the *rapports des capitaines* (1714–78; B4577-4596); and the *actes de propriété* (1693–1791; B4477-4511). At Nantes, the rôles d'armement list the captain's and armateur's names, the destination of the expedition, and information about the crew (size, rank, salary, often age) and the ship (name, size, cannons). The property acts list the investors in the expedition, together with the size of their investment (usually expressed as a fraction of the whole). The captains' reports provide detailed information about the expedition: dates of arrival and departure for each stop, numbers of slaves traded and delivered, number and dates of crew deaths, and accounts of unusual occurences. Some captains' reports at Nantes fill several folio-sized pages.

2. Bordeaux. Documents in ADG. The holdings for Bordeaux are much poorer, with only one major series, the *soumissions* (1715–92; 6B85-115). These list the names and sizes of the ships, their armateurs, and their proposed destinations.

3. La Rochelle. Documents in ACM. These are also poor, with one series, the *congés* (1727–92; B247-259bis). These provide the ship's name, capacity, armateur, and proposed destination; some also give the date of return. In addition,

205

there are property acts from 1783 to 1789 (B5782-5798), listing the investors with their investment, again expressed as a fraction of the whole.

4. Le Havre. Documents in ADSM. There are two important series, the rôles d'armement (1764–92; 6P7/4-6P7/7) and the similar *rôles d'équipage* (1750–93; 6P6/1-6P6/20). Together they provide for each ship, the name, capacity, captain, armateur, size of crew, and crew salaries. Many also provide dates of arrival and departure for each stop along the route, the number of slaves traded and delivered, and the name of the colonial agent handling the sale. There are a few property acts for Le Havre (1765–67; B216BP9). Also, AMLH has a register, HH 69-70, listing departures for the slave trade.

Papers for other ports include:

5. Saint Malo. ADI-V 1F1934-1935 (1698-1792), rôles d'équipage (compiled by Leon Vignols); 9B168-176 (1702-92), *actes de société des navires;* and 9B480-514 (1710-92), rapports des capitaines.

6. Lorient. APL 1P2 *repertoire générale;* 1P256B *journal des certificats.*

7. Honfleur. AMHonfleur, II516-537 (1681-1737; 1751-91), actes de propriété.

Secondary. Besides the archival documents, there is much published material relating to the statistical study of the slave trade. Indeed, each major slaving port has at least one history giving useful data. These include:

1. Nantes. Dieudonné Rinchon, *Le trafic négrier* (Brussels, 1938). Jean Meyer, *L'armement nantais dans la deuxième moitié du XVIIIᵉ siècle* (Paris, 1969). Gaston Martin, *Nantes au XVIIIᵉ siècle: L'ére des négriers (1714-1774)* (Paris, 1931).

2. Bordeaux. Théophile Malvezin, *Histoire du commerce de Bordeaux,* vol. 3 (Bordeaux, 1898). Paul Butel, *La croissance commerciale bordelaise dans la seconde moitié du XVIIIᵉ siècle* (Poitiers, 1973).

3. La Rochelle. Henri Robert, *Trafics coloniaux du port de la Rochelle au XVIIIᵉ siècle* (Paris, 1960).

4. Le Havre. Pierre Dardel, *Commerce, industrie, et navigation à Rouen et au Havre au XVIIIᵉ siècle* (Rouen, 1966), and *Navires et marchandises dans les ports de Rouen et du Havre au XVIIᵉ siècle* (Paris, 1963).

5. Honfleur. Jean Mettas, ''Honfleur et la traite des noirs au XVIIIᵉ siècle,'' *Revue française d'histoire d'outre-mer* 60 (1973), 5-26.

6. Marseilles. Gaston Rambert, *Histoire du commerce de Marseille,* vol. 6 (Paris, 1959). Charles Carrière, *Négociants marseillais au XVIIIᵉ siècle* (Marseilles, 1973).

Tables

The following tables have been made by using the data in the primary and secondary sources.

Table A.1 is a continuous table in seven parts. Cumulative totals appear as they fall in the sequence of years and are printed in boldface type.

Table A1
Slaving Departures from French Ports, 1700-1793

Port	pre-'13*	'13	'14	'15	'16	'17	'18	'19	'20	'21	'22	'23	'24	'25
Nantes	25	15	19	8	7	7	18	13	18	27	16	1	1	2
Bordeaux									1			1	1	
La Rochelle							1							
Le Havre			1	2	1	1					2		2	1
Saint Malo	5						1	3	5	5		3		
Lorient		1							4	1	4	6	11	12
Honfleur				2	3	2								
Marseilles	3		1											
other		2		1		1					1		1	1
Total	**33**	**18**	**21**	**13**	**11**	**11**	**20**	**16**	**28**	**34**	**22**	**11**	**16**	**16**

Table A1, *cont'd.*

Port	'26	'27	'28	'29	'30	'31	'32	'33	'34	'35	'36	'37	'38	'39
Nantes	17	4	14	16	19	12	7	6	10	8	14	17	22	34
Bordeaux			1		2	1			1	1	1	2	3	2
La Rochelle		1	3	5		3	3	5	3	7	5	11	10	15
Le Havre		1		1			1			1			1	
Saint Malo	6	3	3	3	2	1			1			1		
Lorient	4	2	5	8	6	5	3	3	4	6	3	5	3	3
Honfleur														
Marseilles			1	1	1						3	2		
other					1									
Total	**27**	**11**	**26**	**35**	**31**	**22**	**14**	**14**	**19**	**26**	**25**	**35**	**40**	**54**

Table A1, *cont'd.*

Port	'40	'41	'42	'43	'44	'45	1700-45 total	'46	'47	'48	'49	'50	'51
Nantes	33	30	18	34	14	1	**507**	2	1	10	42	24	18
Bordeaux	4	9	7	8			**45**			6	10	5	2
La Rochelle	23	14	11	12	1		**133**			9	12	7	2
Le Havre	1			1			**17**				6	1	4
Saint Malo	1	2	3	7			**56**		2	6	2	3	11
Lorient	7	5	3	2			**115**				2	1	
Honfleur				1			**8**					1	
Marseilles		1					**13**						
other		2	2	4			**16**					3	
Total	**69**	**63**	**44**	**69**	**15**	**1**	**910**	**2**	**3**	**31**	**77**	**42**	**37**

Table A1, *cont'd.*

Port	'52	'53	'54	'55	'56	'57	'58	'59	'60	1746-60 total	'61	'62	'63
Nantes	37	33	31	19	1					**218**			34
Bordeaux	10	2	9	2						**46**		1	4
La Rochelle	6	3	10	5						**54**			1
Le Havre	3	3	5	9						**31**			8
Saint Malo	4	9	3	2						**42**			8
Lorient						1				**4**			
Honfleur				1						**2**			3
Marseilles			1							**1**		3	1
other	1	1					1			**6**	1		8
Total	**61**	**51**	**59**	**38**	**2**	**1**				**404**	**1**	**4**	**67**

Table A1, *cont'd.*

Port	'64	'65	'66	'67	'68	'69	'70	'71	'72	'73	'74	'75	'76	'77
Nantes	34	30	26	22	21	24	20	23	16	27	19	17	22	18
Bordeaux	5	3	8	8	10	13	4	12	6	6	12	10	11	3
La Rochelle	2	5	4	1	4	6	6	12	5	4	13	8	9	13
Le Havre	6	10	7	8	7	4	4	5	5	16	10	12	12	12
Saint Malo	5	6	6	8	7	7	7	3	4	3	5	3	2	1
Lorient														
Honfleur	4	3	7	5	2	5		1	1	1	4	2	3	2
Marseilles	1	4	1	1	1		1		1	2	1	1		
other	4	2	2		2			1	1		1	1		1
Total	**61**	**63**	**61**	**53**	**54**	**59**	**42**	**57**	**39**	**59**	**65**	**54**	**59**	**50**

Table A1, *cont'd.*

Port	'78	'79	1761-79 total	'80	'81	'82	'83	'84	'85	'86	'87	'88	'89
Nantes	5	1	**359**	3	4	3	41	20	36	45	36	35	46
Bordeaux	1		**117**				14	7	17	31	23	32	43
La Rochelle	3		**96**			1	17	18	16	24	12	9	9
Le Havre	3	1	**130**				13	15	18	20	20	23	20
Saint Malo			**75**				1	2	3	1	3	3	4
Lorient							4	1	1	6		4	1
Honfleur	1		**44**				5	4	7	7	7	9	4
Marseilles			**18**				2	5	6	9	10	12	10
other	1		**25**				3						
Total	**14**	**2**	**864**	**3**	**4**	**4**	**100**	**72**	**104**	**143**	**111**	**127**	**137**

Table A1, *cont'd.*

Port	'90	'91	'92/3	1781-92/93 total	1700-92/93 total
Nantes	49	44	35	397	1481
Bordeaux	23	33	30	253	461
La Rochelle	13	5	1	125	408
Le Havre	16	15	7	167	345
Saint Malo	2	3	3	25	198
Lorient	2			19	138
Honfleur	9	14	6	72	126
Marseilles	10	10	7	81	113
other	1			4	51
Total	**125**	**124**	**89**	**1143**	**3321**

*Ships belonging to independent armateurs.

Key to columns in Tables A2-A9

a   all ships
b   privately owned ships
c   ships owned by chartered companies

Table A2
Slaves Mortality Rates (%)

	a	b	c
1713-15	21	21	
1716-22	16	16	
1722-25	13		13
1726-36	13	15	6
1737-43	14	15	10
1749-54	15	15	
1763-77	12	12	

Table A3
Slaves Traded per Ship

	a	b	c
1713-15	306	306	
1716-22	261	261	
1722-25	367		367
1726-36	339	333	362
1737-43	345	335	464
1749-54	319	319	
1763-77	364	364	

Table A4
Slaves Delivered per Ship

	a	b	c
1713-15	242	242	
1716-22	219	219	
1722-25	320		320
1726-36	294	282	340
1737-43	296	286	416
1749-54	270	270	
1763-77	322	322	

Table A5
Ship Size (*tonneaux*)

	a	b	c
1713-15	184	184	
1716-22	138	136	228
1722-25	323		323
1726-36	170	145	271
1737-43	159	142	361
1749-54	179	179	
1763-77	179	179	

Table A6
Slaves Traded per Ton

	a	b	c
1713-15	1.7	1.7	
1716-22	1.9	1.9	
1722-25	1.1		1.1
1726-36	2.0	2.3	1.3
1737-43	2.2	2.4	1.3
1749-54	1.8	1.8	
1763-77	2.0	2.0	

Table A7
Slaves Delivered per Ton

	a	b	c
1713-15	1.3	1.3	
1716-22	1.6	1.6	
1722-25	1.0		1.0
1726-36	1.7	1.9	1.3
1737-43	1.9	2.0	1.2
1749-54	1.5	1.5	
1763-77	1.8	1.8	

Table A8
Slaves Traded per Year

	a	b	c
1713-15	5206		
1716-22	5536	5335	201
1722-25	4489		4489
1726-36	7702	6090	1612
1737-43	18433	16578	1855
1749-54	17385	17385	
1763-77	20452	20452	
1783-92	41000	41000	

Table A9
Slaves Delivered per Year

	a	b	c
1713-15	4110	4110	
1716-22	4658	4490	168
1722-25	3909		3909
1726-36	6676	5159	1517
1737-43	15828	14152	1676
1749-54	14708	14708	
1763-77	18104	18104	
1783-92	37000	37000	

Table A10
Total French Slave Trade

	Ships	Slaves Traded	Slaves Delivered
1700-45	910	300,000	255,000
1746-60	404	130,000	110,000
1761-79	864	310,000	280,000
1780-92	1143	410,000	370,000
Total	**3321**	**1,150,000**	**1,015,000**

Notes

Abbreviations Used in the Notes

AD	Archives Départementales
BP	Pyrénées-Atlantiques (Pau)
BR	Bouches-du-Rhône (Marseilles)
CM	Charente-Maritime (La Rochelle)
G	Gironde (Bordeaux)
Guad	Guadeloupe (Basse-Terre)
I-V	Ille-et-Vilaine (Rennes)
LA	Loire-Atlantique (Nantes)
Morb	Morbihan (Vannes)
SM	Seine-Maritime (Rouen)
ACCLR	Archives de la Chambre de Commerce de la Rochelle
ACN	Archives Communales de Nantes
AMBx	Archives Municipales de Bordeaux
AMHonf	Archives Municipales de Honfleur
AMLH	Archives Municipales du Havre
APL	Archives du Port de Lorient
BMBx	Bibliothèque Municipale de Bordeaux
BMN	Bibliothèque Municipale de Nantes

Epigraphs to both the Introduction and Conclusion have been taken from an undelivered speech by the Vicomte de Mirabeau, 8-3-1790, *Archives parliamentaires de 1787 à 1860, première série (1787 à 1799)* (Liechtenstein, 1969, and Paris, 1966–71), vol. 12, p. 77.

Introduction

1 Eric Williams, *British Historians and the West Indies* (London, 1966), p. 233.
2 The latest major work on the British trade, Roger Anstey's *The Atlantic Slave Trade and British Abolition* (London, 1975), also concentrates on abolition.
3 See Serge Daget, *La France et l'abolition de la traite des noirs de 1814 à 1831* (Paris, 1969).

4 *Nantes au XVIIIe siècle: L'ère des négriers (1714-1774)* (Paris, 1931). This is condensed in the same author's *Histoire de l'esclavage dans les colonies françaises* (Paris, 1948).

5 *Le trafic négrier d'après les livres de commerce du capitaine gantois Pierre-Ignace-Liévin van Alstein* (Brussels, 1938).

6 *Les armements négriers au XVIIIe siècle* (Brussels, 1956).

7 *Pierre-Ignace-Liévin van Alstein, capitaine négrier* (Dakar, 1964).

8 *L'armement nantais dans la deuxième moitié du XVIIIe siècle* (Paris, 1969).

9 Other authors have followed in Meyer's footsteps, for example, Paul Butel, *La croissance commerciale bordelaise dans la seconde moitié du XVIIIe siècle* (thesis, Paris, 1973), condensed as *Les négociants bordelais, l'Europe et les îles au XVIIIe siècle* (Paris, 1974), and Charles Carrière, *Négociants marseillais au XVIIIe siècle* (Marseilles, 1973).

10 See Alfred Cobban, *In Search of Humanity* (London, 1960). I am indebted to Professor J. F. Bosher for this idea.

Chapter 1
Origins of the Trade

1 Arthur Percival Newton, *The European Nations in the West Indies, 1493-1688* (London, 1933), p. 47.

2 Charles Frostin, *Histoire de l'autonomisme colon de la partie française de Saint Domingue aux XVIIe et XVIIIe siècles* (Paris, 1972), p. 9. For the best eighteenth-century description of Saint Domingue, see Moreau de Saint-Méry, *Déscription topographique, physique, civile, politique, et historique de la partie française de l'isle de Saint Domingue*, 3 vols. (1797; Paris, 1958).

3 For the differences between the pirates and hunters, see Frostin, *Histoire*, p. 12.

4 Newton, *European Nations*, pp. 199-200.

5 Letter from the Chamber of Commerce of Guienne to the Minister of the Marine, 25-11-1775, quoted in Pierre Dardel, *Commerce, industrie et navigation à Rouen et au Havre au XVIIIe siècle* (Rouen, 1966). p. 290.

6 Dieudonné Rinchon, *Le trafic négrier* (Brussels, 1938), p. 17.

7 Annic Le Corre, "Le grand commerce malouin," *Annales de Bretagne* 65, no. 3 (1958), 324; also Jean Delumeau, "Les relations de Saint Malo et de Nantes avec les îles à la fin du XVIIe siècle," *An es des Antilles* 10 (1962), 9; and Henri Robert, *Trafics coloniaux du port de la Rochelle au XVIIIe siècle* (Paris, 1960), p. 3.

8 On Colbert's distrust of individual merchants, see Guy Chaussinand-Nogaret, *Les financiers de Languedoc au XVIIIe siècle* (Paris, 1970), p. 20.

9 Gaston Martin, *Nantes au XVIIIe siècle: L'ère des négriers (1714-1774)* (Paris, 1931), pp. 195-99, 378.

10 Paul Butel, "Le trafic colonial de Bordeaux, de la guerre d'Amérique à la Révolution," *Annales du Midi* 79 (1967), 304-6; Jean Meyer, *L'armement nantais dans la deuxième moitié du XVIIIe siècle* (Paris, 1969), pp. 220ff.

11 This was realized in the eighteenth century; see G. T. Raynal, *Histoire philosophique et politique des établissements et du commerce des Européens dans les deux indes*, 6 vols. (Geneva, 1775), vol. 2, p. 356.

12 Guy Lasserre, *La Guadeloupe, étude géographique* (Bordeaux, 1961), p. 339.
13 Ibid.; also Frostin, *Histoire,* pp. 14-15, etc.
14 Noel Deerr, *The History of Sugar* (London, 1949); W. R. Aykroyd, *Sweet Malefactor* (London, 1967).
15 Frostin, p. 16; Newton, p. 21.
16 As this developed on Saint Domingue, see Frostin, p. 16, and on Guadeloupe, see Lasserre, p. 341.
17 J. H. Parry and Philip Sherlock, *A Short History of the West Indies,* 3rd ed. (New York, 1971), p. 63.
18 Lasserre, pp. 340-42; Dieudonné Rinchon, *Pierre-Ignace-Liévin van Alstein, capitaine négrier* (Dakar, 1969), pp. 227-28; F. R. Augier et al., *The Making of the West Indies* (London, 1960), pp. 79-89. The classic description is in P. R. Labat, *Nouveau voyage aux isles de l'Amérique,* 6 vols. (1742; Fort de France, 1972), vol. 2, pp. 155-280.
19 C. A. Banbuck, *Histoire politique, économique, et sociale de la Martinique sous l'ancien régime (1635-1789)* (Paris, 1935), p. 239, says that some refining occurred on Martinique until late in the seventeenth century.
20 Tobacco was also the favorite crop of early American pioneers; Ray Billington, *Westward Expansion,* 3rd ed. (New York, 1967), pp. 40-44.
21 Frostin, pp. 248-58; Lasserre, pp. 340-50.
22 Labat, summarized by Lasserre, pp. 354-55.
23 On the owner's house, see Gabriel Debien, "Les grand' cases des plantations à Saint Domingue aux XVIIe et XVIIIe siècles," *Annales des Antilles* 15 (1970), 1-39.
24 See Gabriel Debien, "Les vivres sur une caféière de Saint Domingue (1786-1791)," *Enquêtes et documents* (Centre des recherches sur l'histoire de la France atlantique, Nantes), vol. 1, pp. 137-49.
25 Lasserre, p. 275.
26 Newton, pp. 18-19.
27 On the *engagés,* see Gabriel Debien, *Les engagés pour les Antilles (1634-1715)* (Paris, 1952).
28 Leon Vignols, "Le travail manuel des blancs et des esclaves aux Antilles," *Revue historique* 175 (1935), 308-15. The typical eighteenth-century attitude was captured by Raynal, *Histoire philosophique,* vol. 2, p. 646: "The French islands . . . can only be cultivated by blacks."
29 After the development of the slave trade, slaves could be found in ports throughout Europe. See Dieudonné Rinchon, *Les armements négriers au XVIIIe siècle* (Brussels, 1956), p. 31; see also Philip Curtin, *The Atlantic Slave Trade: A Census* (Wisconsin, 1969), pp. 17-21, for information about slavery in Iberia.
30 See Newton, pp. 3-21; Curtin, *Census,* pp. 17-21.
31 Lasserre, p. 275.
32 Gaston Martin, *Histoire de l'esclavage dans les colonies françaises* (Paris, 1948), p. 18.
33 Newton, pp. 62-63.
34 Curtin, pp. 119-21.
35 Ibid., pp. 170, 216.
36 Chaussinand-Nogaret, *Les financiers,* p. 111.

37 Pierre Dardel, *Navires et marchandises dans les ports de Rouen et du Havre au XVIIIe siècle* (Paris, 1963), p. 129. On the Compagnie du Sénégal, see Aboulaye Ly, *La Compagnie du Sénégal* (Paris, 1958).

38 Herbert Lüthy, *La banque protestante en France de la révocation de l'Edit de Nantes à la Révolution*, 2 vols. (Paris, 1959-61), vol. 1, p. 299; also Simone Berbain, *Le comptoir français de Juda (Ouidah) au XVIIIe siècle* (Paris, 1942), p. 35.

39 Chaussinand-Nogaret, p. 110.

40 Lüthy, *Banque protestante*, vol. 1, p. 298; Chaussinand-Nogaret, pp. 110-12.

41 The system was universally accepted and rarely questioned; see, for example, ADG C4381, 2-5-1765.

Chapter 2
The Slave Trade from 1713 to 1744

1 On the statistical study of the French slave trade, see the appendix. I have footnoted only extraordinary figures. See also Philip Curtin, *The Atlantic Slave Trade: A Census* (Wisconsin, 1969); J. E. Inikori, "Measuring the Atlantic Slave Trade," *Journal of African History* 17 (1976), 197-223; and Philip Curtin and J. E. Inikori, "Measuring the Atlantic Slave Trade Once Again," *Journal of African History* 17 (1976), 595-627.

2 Found in ADBP B supp. no. 11.

3 I.e., *gomme*, used in making medicines and setting dies. André Delcourt, *La France et les établissements françaises au Sénégal entre 1713 et 1763* (Dakar, 1952), p. 44.

4 Jean Tarrade, *Le commerce colonial de la France à la fin de l'ancien régime* (Paris, 1972), p. 93.

5 Pierre Dardel, *Navires et marchandises dans les ports de Rouen et du Havre au XVIIIe siècle* (Paris, 1963), p. 392.

6 From the preamble; ADG C1621.

7 Dardel, *Navires*, p. 736, and tables, pp. 61-62.

8 For a complete list, see Tarrade, *Commerce coloniale*, p. 88.

9 Charles Carrière, *Négociants marseillais au XVIIIe sia'2ecle* (Marseilles, 1973), pp. 80ff.

10 ADG C4382.

11 Jean Meyer, *L'armement nantais dans la deuxième moitié du XVIIIe siècle* (Paris, 1969), p. 60; this summary account relies heavily on that work, pp. 53-72.

12 ADLA C607, 10-12-1785, letter from the Nantes Consulat.

13 See Jean Delumeau, "Les relations de Saint Malo et de Nantes avec les îles à la fin du XVIIe siècle," *Annales des Antilles* 10 (1962), 18.

14 Pierre H. Boulle, "Slave Trade, Commercial Organization and Industrial Growth in Eighteenth-Century Nantes," *Revue française d'histoire d'outre-mer* 59 (1972), 78.

15 Paul Jeulin, *L'évolution du port de Nantes, organisation et trafic depuis ses origines* (Paris, 1929), p. 256.

16 Guy Chaussinand-Nogaret, *Les financiers de Languedoc au XVIIIe siècle* (Paris, 1970), pt. 2, ch. 2.

17 Herbert Lüthy, *La banque protestante en France de la révocation de l'Edit de Nantes à la Révolution*, 2 vols. (Paris, 1959-61), vol. 1, pp. 298-300; Delcourt, *Établissements françaises*, pp. 63-65.

18 Dardel, *Navires*, pp. 136-37.

19 Lüthy, *Banque protestante*, vol. 1, p. 416.

20 ADG C4266, 17-5-1721, from the Chamber of Commerce of Guienne.

21 During this three and one-half year period, a few private slavers did manage to leave France, including three from Saint Malo and two from Bordeaux. It is possible that they were fitted out by local representatives of the company.

22 Lüthy, vol. 1, p. 299; Dardel, p. 130.

23 Based on sixteen ships from 1724 to 1725; APL 1P241 1.6J.

24 ADG 7B2773.

25 ADG 7B2179.

26 ADLA B4497, 7-10-1741.

27 APL 1P305 no. 70, 22-5-1723, and 28-6-1724.

28 ADLA C741, "Observations. . . ."

29 For French outposts, see Delcourt, and Simone Berbain, *Le comptoir français de Juda (Ouidah) au XVIIIe siècle* (Paris, 1942).

30 Théophile Malvezin, *Histoire du commerce de Bordeaux*, 4 vols. (Bordeaux, 1892), vol. 3, p. 308; Jeulin, *Nantes*, p. 238. Bordeaux and Nantes together accounted for 60 to 70 percent of the French colonial trade.

31 Jeulin, pp. 238, 272; Malvezin, *Histoire*, vol. 3, pp. 303, 308.

32 ADG C4404.

33 Jeulin, pp. 238, 272; Malvezin, vol. 3, pp. 303, 308.

34 ADG C4404; Jeulin, pp. 238, 272; Malvezin, vol. 3, pp. 303, 308.

35 Gaston Rambert, *Histoire du commerce de Marseille*, 7 vols. (Paris, 1959), vol. 6, p. 159.

36 Charles Frostin, *Histoire de l'autonomisme colon de la partie française de Saint Domingue aux XVIIe et XVIIIe siècles* (Paris, 1972), p. 507.

37 Based on 47 examples; 29 went to Cap Français.

Chapter 3
The Slave Trade from 1744 to 1778

1 Théophile Malvezin, *Histoire du commerce de Bordeaux*, 4 vols. (Bordeaux, 1892), vol. 3, pp. 302-5; Paul Jeulin, *L'évolution du port de Nantes, organisation et trafic depuis ses origines* (Paris, 1929), pp. 238-39; Pierre Dardel, *Navires et marchandises dans les ports de Rouen et du Havre au XVIIIe siècle* (Paris, 1963), pp. 60-61; Hector Valladier, *Histoire de la raffinerie de Nantes*, 3 vols. (typed ms, 1940, in ADLA), vol. 1, pp. 58-60; Claude Fernand Laveau, *Le monde rochellais de l'ancien régime au consulat 1774-1800* (unsubmitted thesis in ADCM), pp. 303-6; ADLA C706, 716, 717; ACCMx I29.

2 Jean Tarrade, *Le commerce colonial de la France à la fin de l'ancien régime* (Paris, 1972), p. 28; see also fn. 1, above.

3 Philip Curtin, *The Atlantic Slave Trade: A Census* (Wisconsin, 1969), pp. 75-84.

4 Ibid., pp. 211, 216.

5 From 1741 to 1760, I have 57 percent (162,000 of 298,000).

6 Curtin, *Census*, pp. 211, 216.

7 Tarrade, *Commerce colonial*, pp. 95-110.

8 Charles Frostin, *Histoire de l'autonomisme colon de la partie française de Saint Domingue aux XVIIe et XVIIIe siècles* (Paris, 1972), p. 526.

9 Alan Burns, *History of the British West Indies* (London, 1965), p. 484.

10 For example, see ADLA C607, 20-4-1786, letter from the Nantes Consulat to the Maréchal de Castries.

11 André Delcourt, *La France et les établissements françaises au Sénégal entre 1713 et 1763* (Dakar, 1952), pp. 72-79; Herbert Lüthy, *La banque protestante en France de la révocation de l'Edit de Nantes à la Révolution,* 2 vols. (Paris, 1959-61) vol. 2, pp. 168-71; Gaston Martin, *Nantes au XVIIIe siècle: L'ère des négriers (1714-1774)* (Paris, 1931), pp. 240-47.

12 ADLA B4489, 5-6-1728; B4491, 5-6-1730.

13 *Banque protestante,* vol. 2, p. 170.

14 The other went to Saint Domingue.

15 Martin, *Nantes*, p. 236. Pierre H. Boulle, "Slave Trade, Commercial Organization and Industrial Growth in Eighteenth-Century Nantes," *Revue française d'histoire d'outre-mer* 59 (1972) 70–112, seems to believe this, too.

16 Jean Meyer, *L'armement nantais dans la deuxième moitié du XVIIIe siècle* (Paris, 1969), pp. 81-82.

17 ACCLR carton XVII nos. 5905 and 5907.

18 Burns, *British West Indies*, pp. 485-89.

19 Tarrade, p. 13.

20 Both left from Bayonne. F. Jaupart, *L'activité maritime du port de Bayonne au XVIIIe siècle* (Bayonne, 1969), pp. 520-21.

21 Jeulin, *L'évolution*, pp. 238-39.

22 ADG C4381, 2-5-1765, "Memoire sur l'étendue et les bornes des loix prohibitives du commerce étranger dans nos colonies" (by a Martiniquais).

23 Frostin, *Histoire*, pp. 575-648.

24 Boulle claims this for Nantes.

25 Meyer, *Armement*, p. 82.

26 This is somewhat higher than Curtin, p. 211. More ships participated in the French slave trade at this time than Curtin believed.

27 Curtin, pp. 211, 216, assuming a 12 percent death rate.

28 Ibid. The British exported 468,000 slaves and imported 421,000, an almost perfect balance, assuming a 12 percent death rate. Re-exports from Jamaica were, however, probable, and could have accounted for the French imports not resulting from the French trade.

29 Tarrade, pp. 93, 305*n63*.

30 ADG C1639 no. 32.

31 See Tarrade, pp. 224-328.

Chapter 4
The Slave Trade After 1778

1 Théophile Malvezin, *Histoire du commerce de Bordeaux*, 4 vols. (Bordeaux, 1892), vol. 3, p. 323.

2 Jean Meyer, *L'armement nantais dans la deuxième moitié du XVIIIe siècle* (Paris, 1969), pp. 83-84.

3 Most of these were from Nantes, but a few came from Le Havre.

4 George F. G. Stanley, *New France: The Last Phase, 1744-1760* (Toronto, 1968), p. 196.

5 ADLA 1JJ26.

6 Philip Curtin, *The Atlantic Slave Trade: A Census* (Wisconsin, 1969), p. 211.

7 ADLA 1JJ1, 21-12-1782, letter from the Chaurands to de Jussi.

8 Jean Tarrade, *Le commerce colonial de la France à la fin de l'ancien régime* (Paris, 1972), pp. 488-89.

9 See Curtin's figures, *Census,* pp. 211, 216.

10 See Tarrade, *Commerce coloniale,* pp. 433-34, 421; also Pierre Dardel, *Navires et marchandises dans les ports de Rouen et du Havre au XVIIIe siècle* (Paris, 1963), pp. 134, 137.

11 Tarrade, p. 759; in 1787, 30,839 of 31,193.

12 See, for example, ADG C4266, 28-5-1785.

13 ADG 6B18, 27-5-1786.

14 Found in ADG C4383, no. 32.

15 Guy Chaussinand-Nogaret, *Les financiers de Languedoc au XVIIIe siècle,* (Paris, 1970) pp. 245-48; Herbert Lüthy, *La banque protestante en France de la révocation de l'Edit de Nantes à la Révolution,* 2 vols. (Paris, 1959-61), vol. 2, pp. 689, 700; and Denise Ozanam, *Claude Baudard de Saint-James* (Geneva, 1969), pp. 93-97.

16 If half were sucre brut taxed at 2.5 livres and half were sucre terré taxed at 8 livres, the average tax would be 5.25 livres; half would be 2.625 livres, which multiplied by 15,000 equals about 40,000 livres.

17 In ADG 6B17, 26-10-1784.

18 ADCM B259 and B259bis.

19 ADCM B259, 23-8-1783; B259bis, 5-8-1786.

20 Public Record Office (London), HCA, 32-772-1.

21 ADLA 1JJ3, 3-4-1787.

22 See Claude Fernand Laveau, *Le monde rochellais de l'ancien régime au consulat, 1774-1800* (unsubmitted thesis in ADCM), pp. 157-63.

23 For example, ADLA C607, 3-1-1788.

24 Robert Lacombe, *Histoire monétaire de Saint Domingue et de la République d'Haiti jusqu'en 1874* (Paris, 1958), p. 33.

25 See below, p. 269.

26 Tarrade, p. 747, for quantities of sugar and coffee.

27 Ibid., pp. 771-72, for prices of colonial goods.

28 See the speech by the Vicomte de Mirabeau, 8-3-1790, in *Archives parlementaires de 1787 à 1860, première série (1787 à 1799)* (Liechtenstein, 1969, and Paris, 1966-71), vol. 12, p. 77.

29 *Archives parlementaires de 1787 à 1860,* vol. 12, p. 72.

30 Ibid., 15-5-1791, vol. 26, p. 97.

31 ADLA C608, 10-5-1791; letter from the Consulat to de Gouy.

32 *Archives parlementaires,* vol. 25, pp. 635-768, and vol. 26, pp. 1-97.

33 Ibid., 25-8-1791, vol. 29, p. 706.

34 So the Chaurands described it in a letter to Hamon, ADLA 1JJ7, 27-7-1791.

35 *Archives parlementaires,* 28-3-1792, vol. 40, pp. 575-76.

36 The premiums were suspended on 27-7-1793.

37 Hubert Deschamps, *Histoire de la traite des noirs de l'antiquité à nos jours* (Paris, 1971), p. 177.

38 ADLA C608.

39 ADLA 1JJ8, letter from the Chaurands to Hamon, 11-12-1791.

40 *Recueil des lois relatives à la marine et aux colonies,* 17 vols. (Paris, 1797-1808), vol. 12, pp. 260-61, 30 Floréal X, Article 3.

41 23-2-1815. England had abolished it on 23-2-1807; see Deschamps, *Histoire,* p. 179, and Harold Nicolson, *Congress of Vienna* (London, 1945), pp. 209-14.

42 See ADLA 1M2260, 16-2-1818, letter from the Minister of the Interior to the Prefect of the Loire-Inférieure, which discussed the various acts prohibiting the French trade.

43 On the enforcement, see Serge Daget, *La France et l'abolition de la traite des noirs, 1814-1831* (Paris, 1969).

Chapter 5
The Triangle

1 Trade between the major European nations and the Far East was always controlled by large companies; thus, goods going from Asia to West Africa had to go via Europe. French merchants had to buy many of these goods in Amsterdam. ADI-V 9B509, 31-8-1767.

2 Most notably the Royal African Company. See Kenneth G. Davies, *The Royal African Company* (London, 1957).

Chapter 6
In France

1 *Travels in France,* ed. Jeffrey Kaplow (New York: Anchor, 1965), p. 97.

2 Ibid., p. 96.

3 Ibid., p. 57.

4 Jean Mettas, "Honfleur et la traite des noirs au XVIIIe siècle," *Revue française d'histoire d'outre-mer* 60 (1973), 10.

5 Gaston Rambert, *Histoire du commerce de Marseille,* 7 vols. (Paris, 1959), vol. 6, pp. 144-76, has 54 ships from 1783 to 1792; Charles Carrière, *Négociants marseillais au XVIIIe siècle* (Marseilles, 1973), pp. 346-50, has 80.

6 See, for example, the reaction of merchants from outside of Saint Malo to the

trade monopoly granted Marion Brillantais, in Denise Ozanam, *Claude Baudard de Saint-James* (Geneva, 1969), p. 97.

7 ADLA 1JJ2, 27-2-1785, letter from the Chaurands to Ramville.

8 The best known were at Nantes during the 1750s, the Société d'Angole and the Société de Guinée. See ADLA C738, "Association du commerce maritime" (1767). There were probably others; one at least was contemplated.

9 AMBx, Fonds Nairac, no. 2 (société Paul Nairac et fils aîné), 10-2-1767.

10 For example, ADLA C738, "Association. . . ."

11 See, for example, Maurice Begouen Demeaux, *Mémorial d'une famille du Havre,* 2 vols. (Le Havre, 1948), vol. 1, p. 81. This was a four-year company established to send out three slavers; Begouen Demeaux had two-thirds of the capital. See also the acte de société of the Société d'Angole, in Gaston Martin, *Nantes au XVIIIe siècle: L'ère des négriers (1714-1774)* (Paris, 1931), pp. 249-57.

12 Jean Meyer, *L'armement nantais dans la deuxième moitié du XVIIIe siècle* (Paris, 1969), p. 99.

13 AMBx, Fonds Nairac, no. 2, 10-2-1767. This company was started when Mme. Nairac quit the preceding company; most likely her husband had been associated with the firm earlier and had then died.

14 The Loyson family served as intermediary here.

15 See Herbert Lüthy, *La banque protestante en France de la révocation de l'Edit de Nantes à la Révolution,* 2 vols. (Paris, 1959-61), vol. 1, p. 339, vol. 2, pp. 215-16, 695n, etc.

16 On this company, see Françoise Thésée, *Négociants bordelais et colons de Saint Domingue* (Paris, 1972).

17 Lüthy, *Banque protestante* vol. 2, p. 305. For Michel, see ADLA E1046 and B4478.

18 ADLA 1Q1573, 9 Thermidor X.

19 ADLA, *notaire* Girard, 14-12-1787, marriage contract.

20 For example, ADLA B4507, 23-7-1784: Antoine Marcorelles agreed to invest 24,000 livres in Boittard's *Mafouque* provided that the slaves be consigned to Fourneau and Co.

21 ADI-V 9B168-176 (*actes de sociétés des navires*).

22 ADLA B4477-4511.

23 This according to the rule of October 24, 1681, as is mentioned in every entry in the property acts.

24 Found as far away as Basel, Switzerland (Schweizerischer Wirtschaftarchiv, Handschriften 420, N 1-4).

25 See AMBx, Fonds Delpit, no. 156, "Projet," and ADG 7B3041.

26 AMBx, Fonds Delpit, no. 156, "Projet."

27 BMBx, Br. 306.

28 ADLA, B4510.

29 ADG 7B1589, nos. 98, 103, 108.

30 ADLA B4510, 6-3-1789.

31 ADLA B4510, 14-6-1790.

32 ADLA B4510, 12-7-1788 and 16-7-1790, *notaire* Briand du Marais, which has different values for "equal" parts, depending on cash or merchandise payments.

33 See the description in Raoul Ottenhof, "La course et les prises à Nantes pendant la

guerre de la ligue d'Augsburg (1688-97),'' (typed D.E.S., Rennes, 1961), pp. 85-91.

34 Information in ADG 7B2179, Journal d'Elie Thomas (1742-47), f⁰ 38.

35 For a biography of a slaving captain, see Dieudonné Rinchon, *Pierre-Ignace-Liévinn Alstein, capitaine négrier* (Dakar, 1964), upon which this section is largely based. Pp. 227-32 deal with the officers and crew.

36 See APL 1P305 no. 70, 22-5-1723, 28-6-1724.

37 ADSM 6P6/4 to 6P6/17.

38 Rinchon, *Alstein,* p. 33.

39 For health, see Marie-Claire Chiche, *Hygiène et santé à bord les navires négriers au XVIIIᵉ siècle* (Paris, 1957).

40 *Remèdes et médicaments,* ADG 6B389.

41 APL 1P306/37/3.

42 Ibid.

43 See, for example, ADG 6B389.

44 ADG 6B2053, 10-12-1790.

45 ADG 6B2053, 12-10-1790.

46 ADG 6B2052, 24-12-1768.

47 AMBx, Fonds Delpit, no. 156.

48 On the ships, see Rinchon, *Alstein,* p. 44, and J. M. Filliot, *"La traite des esclaves vers les mascareignes au XVIIIᵉ siècle"* (thesis, Paris, 1970), pp. 90-96,

49 Filliot, p. 90.

50 This was the *Comte de Forcalquier,* belonging to Daniel Garesché of La Rochelle and sailing in 1787 and 1790. Since these dates followed the 1784 decree regarding premiums, they are suspect.

51 Filliot, p. 95.

52 This is reproduced in many places; for example, Jehan Mousnier, *Journal de la traite des noirs* (Paris, 1957), pp. 200-1.

53 AMBx, Fonds Delpit, no. 156.

54 See Rinchon, *Alstein,* pp. 103-6, for this section.

55 See, for example, ADG 7B3041, ''Avitaillement du navire *La Vigilence* . . . ,'' 22-3-1783.

56 See the memoire on biscuits, ADG C4392, no. 2.

57 ADG C4263, 28-4-1753, letter from the Chamber of Commerce of Guienne to Castaing.

58 Meyer, *Armement,* p. 148, says that all ships were insured, but ADLA 1JJ2, 15-2-1785, seems to contradict this. Insurance was a notoriously complicated subject, and whole registers of test cases exist; for example, ADG C4270-80.

59 ADG 7B2179. Thomas bought insurance for the *Amiral* two days after the ship departed.

Chapter 7
In Africa

1 ADLA B4592, 9-1-1755. See also Pierre Dardel, *Navires et marchandises dans les ports de Rouen et du Havre au XVIIIᵉ siècle* (Paris, 1963), p. 128.

2 G. T. Raynal, *Histoire philosophique et politique des établissements et du commerce des Européens dans les deux indes*, 6 vols. (Geneva, 1775), vol. 2, p. 393.
3 These exist here and there in the archives. See, for example, APL 1P305, 9-6-1725.
4 Dieudonné Rinchon, *Pierre-Ignace-Liévin van Alstein, capitaine négrier* (Dakar, 1964), p. 82.
5 ADSM 6P7/6, 30-4-1790.
6 ADI-V 9B505, 23-3-1752.
7 AMBx, Fonds Delpit, no. 142, *Utile*, 3-2-1785.
8 *Alstein*, p. 28.
9 See, for example, Kwame Yeboa Daaku, *Trade and Politics on the Gold Coast, 1600-1720* (Oxford, 1970), pp. 73ff.
10 ADLA C738, 27-4-1775.
11 Moreau de Saint-Méry, *Déscription topographique, physique, civile, politique, et historique de la partie française de l'isle de Saint Domingue* (1797; Paris, 1958), p. 47.
12 Ibid., p. 45.
13 Ibid., p. 53.
14 Jean Mettas, "Honfleur et la traite des noirs au XVIIIe siècle," *Revue française d'histoire d'outre-mer* 60 (1973), 10.
15 For a first-hand account of this procedure, see the letter written by Captain Gamont, 27-9-1773, ADSM Fonds Begouen Demeaux, liasse 48.
16 In locating the exact slaving sites, only the most detailed sources (such as the captain's reports) are of value, but these rarely give the number of slaves traded at each site.
17 Gaston Rambert, *Histoire du commerce de Marseille*, 7 vols. (Paris, 1959), vol. 6, p. 149.
18 On Senegal, see André Delcourt, *La France et les établissements françaises au Sénégal entre 1713 et 1763* (Dakar, 1952); also, Dardel, *Navires*, pp. 128-37; Marie-Hélène Knight-Baylac, "La vie à Gorée de 1677 à 1789," *Revue française d'histoire d'outre-mer* 57 (1970), 377-420; and Philip Curtin, *Economic Change in Precolonial Africa* (Wisconsin, 1975).
19 Except from 11-1-1784 to 10-11-1786, on which date the Compagnie de Guyane became the Compagnie de Sénégal.
20 On Ouidah, see Simone Berbain, *Le comptoir français de Juda (Ouidah) au XVIIIe siècle* (Paris, 1942). Also Karl Polanyi, *Dahomey and the Slave Trade* (University of Washington, 1966).
21 Berbain, p. 49; also the appropriate captain's reports.
22 ADLA C738, various mémoires on Cabinda; also see the letters from the Nantes Consulat in ADLA C607, 20-12-1783, 17-1-1784, 14-2-1784, and 8-5-1785.
23 APL 1P305, no. 8, 9-6-1725.
24 APL 1P305, no. 70, 7-12-1725.
25 Mettas, pp. 14-19.
26 ADLA B4593, 21-9-1765.
27 ADLA B4595, 16-4-1775.
28 ADLA B4577, 29-8-1715.

29 Journal of the *Africain,* in Jehan Mousnier, *Journal de la traite des noirs* (Paris, 1957), pp. 96-97.

30 See Walter Rodney, *A History of the Guinea Coast (1545-1800)* (Oxford, 1970), chs. 7 and 10, especially pp. 194-99. On the nature of trade between Europeans and Africans, see Curtin, *Economic Change,* ch. 6, especially pp. 233-37.

31 ADLA B4577, 29-8-1715.

32 Mousnier, p. 97.

33 Rinchon, *Alstein,* p. 161. Also, Polanyi, *Dahomey,* p. 128. This description of the trade is a synthesis and is typical of conditions prevailing in different places and different times. It should be noted, however, that regional and temporal variations could be significant.

34 Raynal, vol. 2, p. 378.

35 ADLA B4577, 7-9-1715.

36 Curtin, *Economic Change,* pp. 59-91; also Daaku, *Trade,* pp. 23-24. For a discussion of the complex delivery systems, see Paul E. Lovejoy and J. S. Hogendorn, "Slave Marketing in West Africa," to be published in H. Gemery and J. S. Hogendorn, eds., *The Uncommon Market: The Economics of the Trans-Atlantic Slave Trade* (New York, 1979). I am indebted to Professor Lovejoy for allowing me to see a copy of this manuscript.

37 Curtin, *Economic Change,* p. 155; Daaku, *Trade,* p. 28.

38 See, for example, Rodney, p. 253; and Kwame Yeboa Daaku, "Trade and Trading Patterns of the Akan in the Seventeenth and Eighteenth Centuries," in Claude Meillassoux, ed., *The Development of Indigenous Trade and Markets in West Africa* (London, 1971), pp. 170-75.

39 Martin A. Klein and Paul E. Lovejoy, "Slavery in West Africa," to be published in Gemery and Hogendorn, eds., *The Uncommon Market.* I am indebted to Professors Lovejoy and Klein for allowing me to see a copy of this manuscript.

40 See especially Suzanne Miers and Igor Kopytoff, "African Slavery as an Institution of Marginality," in Miers and Kopytoff, eds., *Slavery in Africa* (Wisconsin, 1977), pp. 3-81; also Curtin, *Economic Change,* pp. 29-37.

41 Klein and Lovejoy, "Slavery"; also Martin A. Klein, "The Study of Slavery in Africa," *Journal of African History* 19 (1978), 601-2, 608-9.

42 Curtin, *Economic Change,* p. 154.

43 Daaku, *Trade,* p. 30. This is similar to the argument first proposed by Raynal in the eighteenth century, vol. 2, p. 383.

44 This is a generalized account of the trading process; conditions varied from site to site throughout the century.

45 This description follows Rinchon, *Alstein,* pp. 162-63, closely.

46 On the near impossibility of estimating accurate values for eighteenth-century slave prices in Africa, see Curtin, *Economic Change, Supplement,* p. 87.

47 On the trade at Ouidah, see Berbain; Rinchon, *Alstein,* pp. 342-44; and Polanyi, especially ch. 10.

48 On "assorment bargaining," see Curtin, *Economic Change,* pp. 247-53.

49 ADI-V 4Fg42, *Compte de la traitte des noirs,* February, 1768.

50 Mousnier, p. 80.
51 ADLA B4592, 24-9-1755.
52 ADLA B4593, 21-9-1765.
53 ADLA C738, 21-10-1762.
54 ADSM 6P7/5 and 6P6/17, 16-10-1788.
55 ADLA B4594, 15-2-1769.
56 ADI-V, 4Fg42, *Compte.* . . .
57 ADLA B4591, 14-2-1752.
58 ADLA B4596, 23-8-1777; B4596, 8-7-1776.
59 ADLA B4594, 6-7-1768.
60 Mousnier, pp. 156-57.
61 ADLA B4595, 18-4-1771.
62 Mousnier, pp. 192-93.
63 Ibid., p. 78.
64 ADLA B4594, 7-7-1770.
65 ADLA B4596, 5-11-1777. See also BMBx Br 305 and Br 306, for stories of British help against the Africans.
66 ADLA B4594, 6-7-1768.
67 ADLA B4591, 12-8-1751.
68 ADLA B4594, 5-5-1769.
69 For example, the purchase of an anchor, ADLA B4594, 7-7-1770.
70 One mutiny occurred on the *Hazard,* ADLA B4592, 28-6-1755.
71 ADLA B4596, 28-7-1777.
72 APL 1P305. Even the armateurs could be guilty of fraudulently introducing pacotilles; see ADLA B5548, 10-12-1791.
73 Polanyi, p. 127. This view of the strength of the Dahomey kings has been challenged by Robin Law, "Royal Monopoly and Private Enterprise in the Atlantic Trade: The Case of Dahomey," *Journal of African History* 18 (1977), 555-77.
74 ADLA B4577, 29-8-1715.
75 ADLA B4596, 1-2-1777.
76 ADLA B4577, 29-8-1715; also ADLA B4591, 14-2-1752.
77 ADG C4383 no. 1, 23-9-1737, and C4262, 19-11-1748, 20-12-1749, and 27-12-1749, for complaints about the British.
78 Occasionally foreigners, and particularly the Portuguese, seized French ships trading in "neutral" waters. See the celebrated case of the *Saint Jean Baptiste* in ADLA B4596, 8-7-1776, and C738, 27-4-1775 (mémoire); also, various notes in ADI-V 4Fg42.
79 ADLA B4595, 18-4-1771, 21-4-1771, and 27-4-1771.
80 For a similar event, see ADLA B4594, 3-6-1768.
81 BMBx Br 305.
82 For a similar event, see BMBx Br 306.
83 ADLA C608, 13-11-1790, letter from the Consulat to Mosneron.
84 Jacques Savary, *Le parfait négociant* 4th ed. (Lyon, 1697), pt. 2, p. 206.
85 Mousnier, pp. 105-6, describes slaves expecting death.
86 Savary, pt. 2, p. 206.

Chapter 8
Completing the Triangle

1 Quoted in Dieudonné Rinchon, *Pierre-Ignace-Liévin van Alstein, captaine négrier* (Dakar, 1964), p. 80.
2 Ibid., p. 264.
3 Ibid.
4 ADLA B4595, 6-4-1775. See also Marie-Claire Chiche, *Hygiène et santé à bord les navires négriers au XVIIIe siècle* (Paris, 1957), p. 32.
5 See AMBx, Fonds Delpit, no. 156, "Projet. . . ."
6 APL 1P305, no. 70, 22-5-1723. The company gave the captain six livres per slave for less than 5 percent mortality; three livres for less than 10 percent; two livres for less than 15 percent; and one livre for less than 20 percent.
7 J. M. Filliot, *La traite des esclaves vers les mascareignes au XVIIIe siècle* (thesis, Paris, 1970), pp. 90-96.
8 ADSM 6P6/16, 29-9-1787.
9 ADSM 6P6/6, 22-9-1764.
10 I am grateful to Herbert S. Klein for unpublished information on the Portuguese trade; see also his article with Stanley L. Engerman, "La mortalité des esclaves dans la traite française au XVIIIe siècle," *Annales: E.S.C.* 31 (1976), 1213-24. Also, see Herbert S. Klein, *The Middle Passage* (Princeton, 1978), pp. 193-203.
11 ADLA B4594, 24-7-1767.
12 APL 1P256B; André Delcourt, *La France et les établissements françaises au Sénégal entre 1713 et 1763* (Dakar, 1952), pp. 398-99.
13 After 1783, the documents are not clear on this point.
14 This was noted by G. T. Raynal, *Histoire philosophique et politique des établissements et du commerce des Européens dans les deux indes,* 6 vols. (Geneva, 1775), vol. 2, p. 392.
15 The difference was less than 1 percent.
16 For an armateur's instructions, see Rinchon, *Alstein,* p. 83.
17 ADLA B4596, 28-8-1777.
18 This section is based on BMN, ms 878, "Observations touchant le soin des nègres dans un voyage de Guinée," quoted in Rinchon, *Alstein,* pp. 184-87, and the "Déscription d'un navire négrier," quoted in the same, pp. 272-73.
19 On diseases, see Chiche.
20 Rinchon, *Alstein,* pp.184-87, and 272-73.
21 The phrase used by Hubert Gerbeau, *Les esclaves noirs* (Paris, 1972).
22 For example, ADLA, B4592, 11-8-1753; B4596, 26-6-1777.
23 For example, ADLA B4589, 28-12-1743; B4595, 8-5-1772.
24 ADLA B4594, 7-7-1770.
25 ADLA B4595, 16-4-1775. The ambiguity in the pronouns is found in the original.
26 Quoted in Jehan Mousnier, *Journal de la traite des noirs* (Paris, 1957), pp. 36-44.
27 For discipline in general, see ADG C4392 no. 7.
28 ADLA B4596, 28-8-1777.

29 ADLA B4591, 12-8-1751.

30 ADLA B4592, 28-9-1755.

31 For example, ADI-V, 9B488, 5-5-1721.

32 ADLA B4594, 26-5-1769; 2-6-1769; 12-1-1770; 23-1-1770.

33 DeGuer was honest about the *Saint François;* ADLA B4595, 5-8-1771, says the ship went to Puerto Rico, "as planned."

34 Even after the Seven Years' War, trade between the French islands was difficult; see, for example, ADGuad, Minutes des notaires 2/1, *notaire* Debat, 25-11-1774.

35 This was a familiar complaint of the slavers; see, for example, ADG C4266, 28-5-1785.

36 This can be found in ADB-P,. B supp. (amirauté de Bayonne) no. 14, 25-7-1724, which cites the 3-4-1718 decree as well.

37 Rinchon, *Alstein,* p. 191.

38 ADLA B4577, 29-8-1715.

39 In J. Mousnier, p. 115.

40 For example, ADG C4383, 17-12-1743, complaints about the certificates received from the La Rochelle Chamber of Commerce.

41 Raynal, vol. 2, p. 395. Occasionally, large merchants bought from twenty to thirty slaves for resale, but never a full cargo; see ADSM 1Mi646, Ro 1.

42 Agents also had to lend money to the captains, Rinchon, *Alstein,* p. 192.

43 This is a recurring theme in the letters; for example, ADLA 1JJ2, 8-1-1785 and 29-4-1785.

44 ADLA 1JJ2, 20-7-1783. The Chaurands and the Gerbiers were related through marriage to the Deurbroucqs.

45 See ADSM, Fonds Begouen Demeaux; also Maurice Begouen Demeaux, *Mémorial d'une famille du Havre,* 2 vols. (Le Havre, 1948), vol. 1, and Moreau de Saint-Méry, *Déscription topographique, physique, civile, politique, et historique de la partie française de l'isle de Saint Domingue* (1797; Paris, 1958), p. 724.

46 ADLA *notaire* Lambert, 3-9-1791.

47 BMN ms 859.

48 ADLA 1JJ2, 22-11-1785.

49 ADG 7B1574, 1-10-1785.

50 ADLA 1JJ3, 23-2-1786.

51 For example, ADLA B4577, 7-9-1715.

52 ADG 7B3041, 27-3-1785. The italicized words were handwritten, while the rest was printed.

53 Rinchon, *Alstein,* p. 314.

54 Victor Advielle, *L'odyssée d'un Normand à Saint Domingue au XVIIIe siècle* (Paris, 1790), p. 44.

55 Robert Lacombe, *Histoire monétaire de Saint Domingue et de la République d'Haiti jusqu'en 1874* (Paris, 1958), pp. 28-33.

56 ADG 7B1582, 4-1-1786; Pierre Lalle to Broc (Saint Domingue).

57 Rinchon, *Alstein,* pp. 213-17. Alstein stayed behind, and after seven months, only 235,347 of 481,069 livres owing was paid.

58 Ibid., p. 214.
59 ADG 7B1582, 4-1-1786.
60 ADLA 1JJ5, 17-9-1788.
61 ADG C4381, 19-7-1764.
62 ADG C4381, 5-2-1765.
63 Ibid., 27-6-1765.
64 For political attitudes, see below, ch. 12.
65 ADLA C714-15, for the 1785 and 1789 returns (which were only 43 percent full); these documents list all cargoes on all returning ships.
66 For a description of life aboard a ship from France to the colonies, see Justin Girod-Chantrans, *Voyage d'un suisse dans différentes colonies de l'amérique* (Neuchatel, 1785), pp. 5 ff.
67 ADBR C200E, 29-3-1788.
68 See any account books; for example, ADLA 1JJ26-28.
69 AMBx Fonds Delpit, no. 156, "Etat. . . ."
70 See Robert Paul Thomas and Richard Nelson Bean, "The Fishers of Men: The Profits of the Slave Trade," *Journal of Economic History* 34 (1974), 885-914.
71 ADLA 1JJ39.
72 ADLA L366 for exports; C 715 for imports.
73 ADLA C396, 23-1-1789.
74 ADLA L366.

Chapter 9
The East African Trade

1 In the old regime, Reunion was known as Ile de Bourbon, and Mauritius as Ile de France.
2 For a summary of "older" works on this subject, see Edward A. Alpers, *The East African Slave Trade* (Nairobi, 1967) and "The French Slave Trade in East Africa," *Cahiers d'études africaines* 10 (1970), 80-124; J. M. Filliot, *La traite des esclaves vers les mascareignes au XVIIIe siècle* (thesis, Paris, 1970); and J. Verguin, "La politique de la Compagnie des Indes dans la traite des noirs à l'Ile Bourbon (1662-1762)," *Revue historique* 216 (1956), 45-58.
3 Description based on Auguste Toussaint, *Histoire de l'Ile Maurice* (Paris, 1971), pp. 9-12.
4 This section based on Filliot, *Traite des esclaves,* pp. 52-65.
5 Alpers, *East,* p. 6.
6 Filliot, pp. 139-296.
7 Alpers, *East,* p. 8.
8 ADI-V 9B513, 27-3-1786.
9 ADG 6B115, 29-11-1791 (the *Pauline* from France to Mauritius, India, and Mozambique); 2-1-1792 (the *Phénix* from France to India and the trade).
10 ADG 6B114, 9-9-1788; also Françoise Thésée, *Négociants bordelais et colons de Saint Domingue* (Paris, 1972), pp. 81, 139-45.

11 ADG 6B114, 7-9-1790.
12 Verguin, "Politique," p. 5.
13 ADG 7B1568, 18-3-1785, letter from Lalle to Pelgrom. It is possible that another double trade existed involving a second trip to Africa for a West Indies-bound ship. The *Bouteiller* may have sailed from Nantes to West Africa, Port-au-Prince, West Africa, Port-au-Prince, and Nantes. See ADSM, fonds Begouen Demeaux, liasse 50, 10-3-1785.

Chapter 10
The Slaving Business

1 Jean Meyer, *L'armement nantais dans la deuxième moitié du XVIIIe siècle* (Paris, 1969), p. 66, corrected figures.
2 ADLA 1M2132, 27-2-1828, letter from G. Ducoudray Bourgault to the Prefect of the Loire-Inférieure.
3 ADLA C713-715.
4 Meyer, *Armement,* pp. 83-84.
5 ADLA 1JJ26-28. On the Chaurands' twenty-eight ships *en droiture,* the average cargo was worth 22,713 livres, while the other expenses averaged 44,427 livres. For their ten slavers, the averages for 1783-91 were 178,252 livres and 63,441 livres, respectively (not including expenses—usually for cargo—at Lisbon).
6 ADLA 1JJ26-28.
7 BMN ms 846, 24-6-1790, letter from Musson (Saint Domingue) to Le Roux (Nantes).
8 ADLA 1JJ3, 3-4-1787, letter from the Chaurands to Guilbaud, Gerbier and Company.
9 ADLA 1JJ27, second voyage, 1784.
10 This conclusion is based on ADLA 1JJ26-28; compare ADG 7B2179.
11 T. J. A. LeGoff and Jean Meyer, "Les constructions navales en France pendant la seconde moitié du XVIIIe siècle," *Annales: E.S.C.* 26 (1971), 178.
12 APL 55^{1}3 and ADMorb 11B119.
13 See ADLA C740, "Memoire pour les fabricants d'indiennes. . . ."
14 Bernard Roy, *Une capitale d'indiennage: Nantes* (Nantes, 1948), p. 141.
15 Eric Williams, *Capitalism and Slavery* (North Carolina, 1944), pp. 68-71.
16 See also Pierre H. Boulle, "Slave Trade, Commercial Organization, and Industrial Growth in Eighteenth-Century Nantes," *Revue française d'histoire d'outre-mer* 59 (1972), 106, who claims that Nantes never recovered from the Seven Years' War.
17 *Capitalism and Slavery.*
18 Paul Butel, *Les négociants bordelais, l'Europe et les îles au XVIIIe siècle* (Paris, 1974), p. 16, and *La croissance commerciale bordelaise dans la seconde moitié du XVIIIe siècle* (thesis, Paris, 1973), pp. 83-85.
19 Butel, *Négociants,* p. 34.
20 Butel, *Croissance,* p. 660.

21 Butel, *Négociants,* p. 26 for 1750; ADG C4435 for the 1780s.
22 Théophile Malvezin, *Histoire du commerce de Bordeaux,* 4 vols. (Bordeaux, 1892), vol. 3, pp. 302-5; ADG C4435.
23 Jean Tarrade, *Le commerce colonial de la France à la fin de l'ancien régime* (Paris, 1972), p. 755. Direct evidence is lacking for the earlier period.
24 Butel, *Croissance,* p. 600.
25 On this company, see Françoise Thésée, *Négociants bordelais et colons de Saint Domingue* (Paris, 1972).
26 Ibid., pp. 26-27.
27 See, for example, the prospectus in Schweitzerischer Wirtschaftarchiv (Basel), Handschriften 420, N 1.
28 See, for example, Dieudonné Rinchon, *Les armements négriers au XVIIIe siècle* (Brussels, 1956), p. 127, columns II and VI, adjusted for colonial pounds.
29 ADLA 1JJ4, 29-2-1788, letter from the Chaurands to Bénie.
30 ADLA 1JJ5, 9-6-1788, letter from the Chaurands to Guilbaud, Gerbier and Company.
31 Gaston Martin, *Nantes au XVIIIe siècle: L'ère des négriers (1714-1774)* (Paris, 1931), p. 425.
32 Especially *Armements négriers.*
33 *Armements négriers,* pp. 204-48.
34 Ibid., p. 224. Tarrade, p. 777, says nonetheless that the trade was the only incontestably profitable commerce late in the old regime.
35 See Robert Lacombe, *Histoire monétaire de Saint Domingue et de la République d'Haiti jusqu'en 1874* (Paris, 1958), pp. 15-17.
36 To avoid confusion, all references to livres mean the French livre unless otherwise stated.
37 *Armement,* p. 144.
38 Meyer, *Armement,* p. 296; ADG 7B2773; 7B2129 f° 38; ADLA B4497, 11-1-1741; B4498, 20-2-1745.
39 APL 1P241 1.6J; André Delcourt, *La France et les établissements françaises au Sénégal entre 1713 et 1763* (Dakar, 1952), pp. 398-99.
40 Based on over seventy examples from various sources; over forty-five appear in Meyer, *Armement,* pp. 301-2.
41 For example, ADLA 1JJ27, "Alexandrine."
42 ADLA C741, "Observations . . ." (1752).
43 Tarrade, p. 140, note 66; see also Meyer, *Armement,* p. 226.
44 Meyer, *Armement,* p. 226. Either Meyer or the eighteenth-century author has increased all the profits by 100 percent, ignoring the colonial livre problem. Counting this, the profits were 150, 650, and 275 percent, respectively.
45 ADLA 1JJ26-27. Some deductions probably had to be made, thereby lowering profits somewhat.
46 See Robert Paul Thomas and Richard Nelson Bean, "The Fishers of Men: The Profits of the Slave Trade," *Journal of Economic History* 34 (1974), 885-914. On the slight differences in prices, see Thésée, pp. 77, 161-62, and 220-21; Tarrade, pp. 136-40; and Butel, *Croissance,* p. 178, who claims that armateurs made big profits from the differences.

47 ADLA 1JJ26-27, *Brune* (voyages one and two), *Jeanne Thérèse* (voyages one and two), *Aimable Aline*.

48 Some deductions were related to slaving (e.g., wages), but others to colonial merchandise.

49 See Robert Stein, "The Profitability of the Nantes Slave Trade, 1783-1792," *Journal of Economic History* 35 (1975), 779-93.

50 ADLA 1JJ26-28.

51 ADLA 6JJ30; values expressed in francs.

52 See Thésée; also Butel, *Croissance,* pp. 802ff.

53 ADLA 1JJ2, 27-2-1785, letter from Chaurands to Ramville.

54 ADLA 1JJ3, 13-4-1786, letter from Chaurands to LaFosse and Gauvin.

55 See also Butel, *Croissance* and *Négociants;* Meyer, *Armement,* etc.

56 Herbert Lüthy, *La banque protestante en France de la révocation de l'Edit de Nantes à la Révolution* (Paris, 1959-61), vol. 1, pp. 298ff; Guy Chaussignand-Nogaret, *Les financiers de Languedoc au XVIIIe siècle* (Paris, 1970), pp. 227ff.

57 Lüthy, *Banque protestante,* vol. 2, pp. 42-44, 168-71, 303-6.

58 Maurice Begouen Demeaux, *Mémorial d'une famille du Havre,* 2 vols. (Le Havre, 1948), vol. 1, p. 81.

59 Jean Mettas, "Honfleur et la traite des noirs au XVIIIe siècle," *Revue française d'histoire d'outre-mer* 60 (1973), 14; AMHonfleur, II 521, 29-11-1754, 12-1-1763, etc.

60 Thésée, p. 26.

61 This is true only for traders in the Atlantic ports; the Marseillais remained independent. This is one of the main theses of Charles Carrière, *Négociants marseillais au XVIIIe siècle* (Marseilles, 1973).

62 ADLA C608, 14-11-1789, letter from the Consulat to Guinebaud, Nantes' representative in Paris.

63 This of course, could be a two-way street, and the bankruptcy of a major banker or financier often ruined the merchants whose deposits the banker had lost. For example, Pierre Morin of Nantes went broke in 1786 because of the failure of Pelletier and Carrier, bankers in Paris (ADLA 1JJ3, 27-12-1782; ADLA E/XVI/55, 19-6-1790).

64 ADLA E/II/434, 2-6-1787. This was also true of traders who did not go bankrupt.

65 AMBx, Fonds Nairac.

66 ADLA *notaire* Lambert, 8-1-1789 (retroactive to 1-1-1788).

67 ADLA B4510, B4511.

68 Pierre Dardel, *Commerce, industrie et navigation à Rouen et au Havre au XVIIIe siècle* (Rouen, 1966), p. 182; Lüthy, vol. 2, p. 451.

Chapter 11
Armateurs and Investors

1 This is the implication of the balance sheets in the failures of Giraud and Raimbaud (ADLA *notaire* Briand, 5-9-1785) and Préau and Fleuriau (ADLA *notaire* Varsavaux, 10-12-1790).

2 ADLA C607, 18-12-1784, letter to the Orléans Chamber of Commerce.

3 On négociants, see Charles Carrière, *Négociants marseillais au XVIIIe siècle* (Marseilles, 1973), pp. 237-51. *Négociant* is here translated as "merchant."

4 Actually 2,902 expeditions, but the armateurs of 102 are not known.

5 Gaston Martin, *Nantes au XVIIIe siècle: L'ère des négriers (1714-1774)* (Paris, 1931), p. 423, claimed that there were no "pure" slave traders.

6 More properly, an individual and not a family. Only Antoine was active, and then for a ten-year period.

7 Schweitzerisher Wirtschaftarchiv, Handschriften 420; Herbert Lüthy, *La banque protestante en France de la révocation de l'Edit de Nantes à la Révolution* (Paris, 1959-61), vol. 2, p. 231.

8 On the origins of the slavers, see: for Nantes, ACN, état-civil, and René Kerviler, *Répértoire général de bio-bibliographie bretonne,* 17 vols. (Rennes, 1886-1908); on La Rochelle, Emile Garnault, *Familles rochelaises* (ms in ADCM); on Bordeaux, Pierre Meller, *Les familles protestantes de Bordeaux* (Bordeaux, 1902), etc.

9 Pierre H. Boulle, "Slave Trade, Commercial Organization and Industrial Growth in Eighteenth-Century Nantes," *Revue française d'histoire d'outre-mer* 59 (1972), 79, claims that as late as the mid-eigthteenth century, the Dutch formed a tightly knit community in Nantes, but this was not the case later in the century, at least as far as the slave traders were concerned.

10 Arthur Young, *Travels in France,* ed. Jeffrey Kaplow (New York: Anchor, 1965), pp. 96-98.

11 According to "local gossip"; see Jean Meyer, *L'armement nantais dans la deuxième moitié du XVIIIe siècle* (Paris, 1969), p. 183.

12 Jean Meyer, *La noblesse bretonne* (Paris, 1966), pp. 386-88, 406.

13 Meyer, *Armement,* p. 184.

14 For the meager assets of a typical clerk, see ADLA B9491, 1-12-1769.

15 Paul Butel, *La croissance commercial bordelaise dans la deuxième moitié du XVIIIe siècle* (thesis, Paris, 1973), pp. 664-9, mentions the importance of Jewish moneylenders in the first half of the eighteenth century, but not with respect to the trade in particular. Gradis sent fourteen ships to Africa, but nine of these went to Gorée, where he enjoyed a commercial monopoly.

16 Guy Richard, *La noblesse d'affaires au XVIIIe siècle* (Paris, 1974), p. 112.

17 Lüthy, *Banque protestante,* vol. 2, p. 306.

18 Henri Robert, *Les trafics coloniaux du port de la Rochelle au XVIIIe siècle* (Poitiers, 1960), p. 35; Perry Viles, "The Slaving Interest in the Atlantic Ports, 1763-1792," *French Historical Studies* 7 (1972), 535-37.

19 On the profits of the Chaurands' colonial company (Guilbaud, Gerbier and Company), see ADLA 1JJ4, 3-4-1787, and 1JJ5, 14-5-1788; even the Chaurands—chronic complainers—were satisfied.

Chapter 12
Slave Traders in Public

1 On this, see Herbert Lüthy, *La banque protestante en France de la révocation de l'Edit de Nantes à la Révolution* (Paris, 1959-61), 2 vols.; and Guy Chaussinand-Nogaret, *Les financiers de Languedoc au XVIIIe siècle* (Paris, 1970).

2 Jean Meyer, *L'armement nantais dans la deuxième moitié du XVIIIe siècle* (Paris, 1969), p. 213.

3 All Nantes group information is based on the *actes de propriété*, ADLA B4477-4511.

4 ADLA B4484, 6-2-1720, *Favory*.

5 ADLA B4485, 16-8-1721, *Intrepide*.

6 ADLA B4483, 5-7-1717.

7 ADLA B4486, 17-3-1722.

8 Jean Meyer, *La noblesse bretonne* (Paris, 1966), pp. 245, 258-59.

9 Nantes information from ACN, état-civil; La Rochelle information from ADCM IIJ5-9.

10 Dieudonné Rinchon, *Pierre-Ignace-Liévin van Alstein, capitain négrier* (Dakar, 1965), pp. 295-96.

11 Georges Collas, *René Auguste de Chateaubriand (1718-1786)* (Paris, 1949), pp. 94ff.

12 ADI-V 9B174, 18-6-1763, *Phoenix*.

13 ADI-V 9B176, 3-8-1785 and 4-4-1791.

14 For disputes between the different ports and the general weakness of the ports in politics, see Jean Tarrade, *Le commerce colonial de la France à la fin de l'ancien régime* (Paris, 1972).

15 See Marcel Quénet, *Le Général du Commerce de Nantes* (Nantes, 1973), for the institutions established by the Nantes merchants in the eighteenth century.

16 For the office-holders in these institutions, see Pierre Alexandre Perthius and Stephane Praud, *Le livre doré de l'hôtel de ville de Nantes* (Nantes, 1873-92), 2 vols.

17 *Archives parlementaires de 1787 à 1860, première série (1787 à 1799)* (Liechtenstein, 1969; Paris, 1966-71), vol. 4, pp. 94-101.

18 ADLA C607, 26-4-1788.

19 ADLA 1JJ4, 13-5-1787, letter from Chaurands to Daugagne Trigant and Company.

20 ADLA C607, 26-4-1788, letter from the Consulat to the Marquis du Chillon.

21 ADLA C608, 22-8-1789, letter from the Consulat.

22 According to the *Feuille maritime de Nantes* (BMN 60580, 5-7-1788), 106 foreign and 114 French ships arrived in Saint Domingue during the same period (first quarter of 1788?).

23 ADLA C607, letter from the Consulat to Drouet, 3-2-1784.

24 For a detailed analysis of the *exclusif* from the government point of veiw, see Tarrade.

25 ADLA C607, 12-7-1783, letter from the consulat to the Maréchal de Castries.

26 For example, see the correspondence relating to Madagascar and the Compagnie des Indes, ADLA C607 (20-5-1786) and C608 (5-9-1789).

27 ADLA C607, 30-1-1785, letter from the Consulat to the Maréchal de Castries.

28 Not too pressing, though. On 23-5-1789 (ADLA C608), the Nantes Consulat listed its main concerns in a letter to its representative in the capital, and abolition was not included.

29 ADLA C608, 12-5-1789, letter from the Consulat to Guinebaud.

30 ADLA C608, 3-9-1789, letter from the Consulat to the Comte de la Luzerne.

31 ADLA C608, 22-8-1789, letter from the Consulat to Mosneron.

32 For example, see the letter to the Consulat from a Parisian merchant, ADLA C626, 16-1-1783, which justifies war but does not recommend it.

33 ADLA C607, 20-12-1783, letter from the Consulat to the Maréchal de Castries. Such problems had existed in the 1760s and 1770s as well; see the various mémoires on the subject in ADLA C738.

34 ADLA C607, 17-1-1784.

35 ADLA C607, 14-2-1784.

36 ADLA C607, 8-5-1784.

37 ADLA C607, 24-2-1785. Tarrade, p. 781, says that the Maréchal de Castries liked to work in strict secrecy.

38 *Archives parlementaires,* vol. 4, pp. 94-101.

39 Ibid., articles 85, 105, 83, 86, and 87.

40 Ibid., articles 84, 88, and 95.

41 Ibid., article 61.

42 Ibid., articles 3, 4, and 7.

43 Ibid., article 80.

44 Ibid., articles 10, 11, and 13.

45 Ibid., articles 42, 63-79, 110-25, and 130.

46 Ibid., article 137.

47 Typical of this was the Nantes *fête patriotique* of 1788. Camille Mellinet, *La commune et la milice de Nantes* (Nantes, 1841-43), vol. 5, pp. 339-44, says that "almost all of the old Nantes families" participated in thanking their king for thinking only of his subjects. It was hardly a revolutionary act.

Chapter 13
The Slave Traders at Work

1 ADLA C608, 24-3-1789, letter from the Consulat to the Comte de la Luzerne.

2 ADLA C607, 26-7-1783, letter from the Consulat to Drouet.

3 Quoted in Jean Meyer, *La noblesse bretonne* (Paris, 1966), p. 630. Meyer concluded that Bouteiller's mother was the only person besides Bouteiller himself to be up to date on all of his commercial activities.

4 This section is based on Paul Butel, *La croissance commerciale bordelaise dans la seconde moitié du XVIIIe siècle* (thesis, Paris, 1973), pp. 557ff; the same author's *Les négociants bordelais, l'Europe et les îles au XVIIIe siècle* (Paris, 1974), pp. 163-72; and Charles Carrière, *Négociants marseillais au XVIIIe siècle* (Marseilles, 1973), pp. 717-79.

5 Butel, *Négociants,* p. 165.

6 Ibid.

7 For example, ADLA *notaire* Lambert, 8-1-1789 (Riedy and Thurninger); see also ADLA B5581, 14-12-1785 (Millet and Caillaud), free rent; and Carrière, p. 722.

8 ADG 3E13250, 28-2-1765, inventory.

9 Butel, *Négociants,* p. 164.

10 Ibid.; also Carrière, pp. 779-92.
11 ADLA 1JJ1-25.
12 Jean Meyer, *L'armement nantais dans la deuxième moitié du XVIIIe siècle* (Paris, 1969), pp. 119-42.
13 Also Butel, *Négociants,* p. 170.
14 ADG 7B1008, 21-4-1791.
15 ADLA 1JJ71, the Chaurands' *grand-livre* of the 1780s.
16 *Négociants,* p. 172.
17 For the *capitation,* see Jean Villain, *Le recouvrement des impôts directs sous l'ancien régime* (Paris, 1952), especially p. 207.
18 Butel, *Croissance,* p. 969.
19 ADI-V C4097.
20 AMHonfleur, CC1226.
21 ADLA B3496 (1788 and 1789), B3530 (1789), and C554 (1789); also ADLA B3499 (1710), B3520 (1750), ACN CC459 (1754), CC460 (1762), and CC462 (1764).
22 Three traders did not appear on the lists at all.
23 Meyer, *Armement,* pp. 183 and 186.
24 ADLA *notaire* Bertrand, 19-6-1790.
25 ADLA *notaire* Chesnard, 12 Thermidor II and 9 Prairial III. This is a particularly confusing case, not only because of the length of time between the tax assessment and Aubry's death but also because of the inflation.
26 ADLA 6JJ30. The manuscript is undated but probably comes from the mid-1790s. In any event, it seems oblivious to the inflation.
27 Meyer, *Armement,* pp. 184-85. Meyer says that their plantations were worth 1,800,000 and 3,000,000 livres respectively. Debts could easily account for the remainder. Also, the document (ADLA 6JJ30) says that Michel was owed 1,600,000 livres, the same figure the Chaurands mentioned in 1785 (ADLA 1JJ2, 27-2-1785).
28 Also useful in determining the values of landed assets in the colonies is Ministère des Finances, *Etat détaillé des liquidations* (Paris, 1829-34), 6 vols., which lists all the indemnities paid by the new Haitian government to former property owners. Supposedly, the expropriated owners were reimbursed for 10 percent of their losses. For example (vol. 3, pp. 364-65, 378-79, and 440-41) the Bouteillers' heirs received 489,610 francs on property losses evaluated at 4,896,100 francs.
29 *Armement,* p. 185.
30 According to the *Etat détaillé des liquidations,* vol. 2, pp. 110-11, 262-63, and 336-37, and vol. 4, pp. 188-89, the Chaurands' heirs were indemnified 190,894 francs on property losses of 1,908,940 francs.
31 The *vingtième* lists only one house; the *contrôle des actes* nothing between 1783 and 1792; Meyer, *Noblesse,* nothing. The 500,000 livres represented 200,000 livres (one slaver per year), 200,000 livres (two direct ships per year), and 100,000 livres (annual investments). Meyer, *Armement,* p. 193, citing Rinchon, says that the company was worth 200,000 livres in 1778 and 2,000,000 livres in 1785. This latter figure obviously considers colonial assets.

32 A condition valid not just for Nantes but for Bordeaux (Butel, *Croissance*, pp. 1036-37) and Le Havre (Guy Richard, *La noblesse d'affaires au XVIIIe siècle* [Paris, 1974], p. 101).

33 See Meyer, *Noblesse*, pp. 386-88, 406.

34 ADLA E/IIbis/10-11, *répertoire* of *notaire* Boufflet; the notarial fees were 187 livres.

35 Jeanne received 20,000 livres, her husband 11,000 livres; the fees were 145 livres; 16-11-1739, ADLA E/IIbis/10-11. The fees for the other wedding were also 145 livres, 27-3-1740, ibid.

36 He "mobilized" 4,000 livres, while his wife received 13,000 livres and "mobilized" 4,000 more; the notarial fees were 200 livres; ADLA 2C2910, 1-9-1763.

37 This was divided as follows: house in Nantes, 40,000 livres; wife's goods, 180,000; furniture, 20,000; plantations, 200,000; and ships, 140,000; Meyer, *Noblesse*, pp. 406ff.

38 Meyer, *Armement*, p. 184.

39 Figuring the direct expeditions to require .5 million livres and the slaving ones .4 million livres, Drouin's one-third share in the company made up of himself, Charles Drouin, and Thomas Pesneau would be .3m livres. Also note that Bouteiller Father and Son, reputedly the largest firm in Nantes, had a capital of 800,000 livres (Meyer, *Armement*, p. 267).

40 There was only one listing for Drouin in the *vingtième* and nothing else in the *contrôle des actes* (after 1783) or in Meyer, *Noblesse*.

41 According to the *Etat détaillé des liquidations*, vol. 1, pp. 202-3 and 218-19, and vol. 6, pp. 774-75, Drouin's heirs received 216,019 francs in indemnities for property losses of 2,160,190 francs in Saint Domingue.

42 According to ADLA E/IIbis/10-11 (*répertoire* of *notaire* Fouqueraux), 8-9-1753, Arnous put 9,000 livres and Millet 6,000 livres into the marriage community, but the entire dowries are not listed, and the complete document is missing. The registration fees were 70 livres, which would usually imply a value of 35,000 livres. It is possible that Nicolas (II) was taken into his father's business after the wedding, since the son first appears on the tax rolls the following year.

43 By the end of the old regime, the company of Nicolas Arnous Father and Son included Nicolas (II), his son Nicolas Pierre and his cousin's son Jean Joseph for one-fifth (ADLA *notaire* Girard, 14-12-1787); it probably included Pierre, Nicolas (II)'s brother as well. Pierre was definitely an associate in the 1760s (ADLA B4504, 18-7-1767).

44 Marie Suzanne, 7-12-1778, *notaire* Girard, ADLA; Felicité married Christophe François Pion, *chevalier*, ADLA 2C3393, 10-8-1792; Sophie married Jean Merot, *écuyer*, ADLA *notaire* Girard, 2-7-1784.

45 Meyer, *Noblesse*, p. 259.

46 For Jean Joseph's holdings, see ADLA *notaire* Varsavaux 31-6-1791 and 15-12-1791; for Nicolas' assets see the inventory after death, 24-4-1807, *notaire* Guillet. The inventory mentions one and one-half plantations, but 27 Floréal VIII, ADLA *notaire* Guillet, mentions two and one-half.

47 ADLA *notaire* Guillet, 24-4-1788. According to the *Etat détaillé des liquida-tions,* vol. 1, pp. 244-45, the heirs of Nicolas Arnous received 99,324 francs in indemnities for property lost in Saint Domingue estimated at 993,240 francs.

48 ADLA *notaire* Guillet, 18-12-1788. There is no evidence to suggest that Arnous had bought, sold, or given away other property.

49 The company was worth about .7 million livres, of which Arnous himself held four-fifths, or .56 million.

50 See the inventory, ADLA *notaire* Guillet, 24-4-1807.

51 Butel, *Croissance,* p. 1158; *Négociants,* pp. 317-19. The Gradis' were not only slavers, by any means.

52 Richard, pp. 99-103; Begouen Demeaux, *Mémorial d'une famille du Havre,* 2 vol. (Le Havre, 1948), vol. 1; ADSM 1Mi638-76.

53 There are several instances of this, for example ADLA B5582, 22-1-1789, *traité entre Jean Charles Gerbier et Jean Baptiste de Lanallet.*

54 This agrees with Butel, *Croissance,* pp. 1157-58, but goes against Meyer, *Armement,* pp. 248-50.

Chapter 14
A Slaving Civilization

1 Quoted in Paul Butel, *Les négociants bordelais, l'Europe et les îles au XVIIIe siècle* (Paris, 1974), p. 378.

2 Ibid.

3 See Gaston Martin, *Carrier et sa mission à Nantes* (Paris, 1924), pp. 7-8.

4 For the noble merchants in various ports, see Guy Richard, *La noblesse d'af-faires au XVIIIe siècle* (Paris, 1974), pp. 71-119.

5 Jean Meyer, *La noblesse bretonne* (Paris, 1966), p. 362; and for 1771 and 1772 at least, see Pierre Alexandre Perthius and Stephane Praud, *Le livre doré de l'hôtel de ville de Nantes* (Nantes, 1873-92).

6 Arthur Young, *Travels in France,* ed. Jeffrey Kaplow (New York, 1965), pp. 132-34.

7 In fact, they made only two known investments between 1783 and 1792; ADLA B4507-11.

8 The Espivents made one detailed declaration, on 1-6-1769 (ADLA B4504). They said that Vve. Ducoudray Bourgault had one-sixteenth of their *Duc du Duras,* while they retained the other fifteen-sixteenths. It is possible that the Espivents may have received money from other nobles too shy to have it an-nounced.

9 See their demands for the end of venal ennoblement. *Archives parlementaires de 1787 à 1860, première série (1787 à 1799)* (Liechtenstein, 1969; Paris, 1966-71), vol. 4, p. 98, article 139.

10 Richard, *Noblesse d'affaires,* pp. 21-52.

11 Ibid., p. 50.

12 Jean Cavignac, *Jean Pellet, Commerçant de gros (1694-1772)* (Paris, 1967), p. 326.

13 Occasionally, an anobli refused to participate in local government (Meyer, *Noblesse*, p. 362); but these isolated incidents were not necessarily socially motivated. Commoners, too, occasionally turned down positions; for example, P. J. Lincoln of Nantes: "At this moment, I cannot accept a place on the committee of commerce" (ADLA C626, 26-11-1789).

14 ADLA C624, 23-7-1783, letter from Joubert to the Consulat.

15 ADG 7B1008, 21-4-1791.

16 ADLA C552, complaint about the capitation by Ozenne.

17 See Cavignac, *Jean Pellet*, p. 155. But, Robert Forster, *The House of Saulx-Tavanes* (Baltimore, 1971), tells of avaricious nobles, too.

18 Guillet de la Brosse complained to the Etats de Bretagne over the 4-livre 17-sou tax on his holdings in Le Cellier. He felt that a 1-livre tax was fair, and finally paid 3 livres. There were several other complaints over taxes (ADLA C552-56; this case, C555).

19 ADLA *notaire* Lambert, 8-1-1789.

20 For example, Hervé Halgouet, *Nantes: Ses relations commerciales avec les Iles d'Amérique au XVIIIe siècle: Ses armateurs* (Rennes, 1939), pp. 242ff.

21 Butel, *Négociants,* pp. 331, 371.

22 Paul Butel, *La croissance commerciale bordelaise dans la seconde moitié du XVIIIe siècle* (thesis, Paris, 1973), pp. 1083-84.

23 Ibid., p. 1110.

24 Dieudonné Rinchon, *Pierre-Ignace-Liévin van Alstein, capitaine négrier* (Dakar, 1964), pp. 409-10. See also ADG 3E13250, 28-2-1765, inventory of Pierre Feydieu, and ADG 3E15433, 17-12-1789, inventory of Raphael Mendez.

25 See Butel, *Croissance,* pp. 1083ff. On daily expenses, see Rinchon, *Alstein,* pp. 382-84.

26 For lists of books owned by slave traders, see (all ADLA): 14 Germinal IV, *notaire* Guillet (for J. Berthault); 4 Frimaire XII, *notaire* Jalaber (for N. Dupoirier); 30 Floréal XIII, *notaire* Guillet (for S. U. Deurbroucq); 18-7-1806, *notaire* Bertrand (for A. A. Espivent); and 17-3-1806, *notaire* Bertrand (for M. P. Rousseau). According to Meyer, *Noblesse,* pp. 1156-57, the nobility preferred religious books.

27 For example, ADLA 1JJ1-6; and 1JJ65, 13-4-1782, relating to the Chaurands' subscriptions to foreign papers.

28 P. 98.

29 Slaves were mentioned as commodities even in marriage contracts between nobles (ADLA 26-4-1790, *notaire* Jalaber): ". . . Negroes, beasts, and utensils. . . ."

30 Jacques Savary, *Le parfait négociant,* 4th ed. (Lyon, 1697), p. 206.

31 See, for example, Hubert Deschamps, *Histoire de la traite des noirs de l'antiquité à nos jours* (Paris, 1971), pp. 133-34. Justin Girod-Chantrans, *Voyage d'un suisse dans différentes colonies de l'amérique* (Neuchatel, 1785), pp. 175-76, was surprised that slaves were not killed off like old horses.

32 ADLA 1JJ5, 25-8-1788, letter to Hamon.

33 Ibid., 3-8-1788, letter to Hamon.

34 ADLA 1JJ6, 26-1-1790, letter to Dutrejet.

35 AMBx XII^c X^{b}25 no. 3190, 27-1-1790.
36 ADLA 1JJ2, 23-9-1785, letter to Hamon from the Chaurands.
37 Gabriel Debien, quoted in Richard Sheridan, *The Development of the Plantations* (Barbados, 1970), p. 54. See also Philip Curtin, *The Atlantic Slave Trade: A Census* (Wisconsin, 1969), for estimates of mortality rates.
38 Quoted in Dieudonné Rinchon, *Le trafic négrier* (Brussels, 1938), p. 11.
39 ADG 6B14, 9-8-1777, *Déclaration du Roi*. Legislation on this was subject to frequent change, but always with the same goal: to limit the number of blacks in France.
40 Often their existence was so "normal" that they almost went unnoticed. For example, Rinchon, *Alstein,* p. 384.
41 ACN *état-civil,* Parish Saint Nicolas, 30-7-1787.
42 For example, ADLA *notaire* Lambert, 8-10-1784, 8-11-1784, and 12-1-1791 (a significantly late date).
43 They even thought that commerce could overcome much of the difference between black and white, ADLA C608, 13-11-1790.

Conclusion

1 *Archives parlementaires,* vol. 12, p. 76.
2 Maurice Begouen Demeaux, *Memorial d'une famille du Havre,* 2 vols. (Le Havre, 1948), vol. 1, pp. 84ff. For Demeaux' own view of slavery, see ADSM 1Mi676, "Discours de Jacques François à la constituante sur la traite des noirs."
3 *Archives parlementaires,* vol. 12, p. 77.
4 Eric Williams, *Capitalism and Slavery* (North Carolina, 1944).
5 Felix Libaudière, *Histoire de Nantes sous le règne de Louis Philippe (1830-1848)* (Nantes, 1900), p. 9.
6 ADLA 1M2132 and 1M2260. See also F. S. Verger, *Archives curieuses de la ville de Nantes et des départements de l'ouest* (Nantes, 1837-41), vol. 1, p. 148.
7 The nineteenth-century euphemism for slaves.
8 Guy Richard, *La noblesse d'affaires au XVIIIe siècle* (Paris, 1974), pp. 102-3.
9 ADLA B4528.
10 ADLA fonds marine, "Tableau général des prises amenées à Nantes." The armateur was Felix Cossin, in Years V, VI, and VII.
11 On the significance of family relationships in business, see Burton Benedict, "Family Firms and Economic Development," *Southwestern Journal of Anthropology* 24 (1968), 1-19.

Index

Abbreviations Used in the Index

A	Africa
capt	captain
co	company
F	France
f	family
st	slave trader
WI	West Indies

Abolition, xvi, 43–47, 171–72, 197–99, 200

Accounting. *See* Bookkeeping

Accra (A), 79, 86, 92

Acquits de Guinée, 14, 33, 40–41

Alsace (F), 62

Alstein, Pierre van (capt), xvii, 113, 167

American Revolution. *See* War of American Independence

Amerindians, xiv, 9

Amsterdam, 66, 72, 136, 148, 178. *See also* Holland

Amyrault (f) (st), 167, 168. *See also* Philippe and Amyrault

Anamabou (A), 91–92

Angola (A): popularity of, xv, 20, 124; sites in, 76, 79; status of slaves sold in, 83; barter system used in, 84–85; mentioned, 65, 74, 77, 195

Antoine (st), 63

Antoine and Boittard (co), 63, 182

Aquitaine, 158

Arabs, 10, 123, 124

Archer, Patric (st), 20

Arnoult, Jean (capt), 81, 96

Arnous (f) (st): company organization, 63; shipbuilding activity, 134, 159; wealth, 181, 182, 184–85, 187; investment group, 190; mentioned, 143, 144

Ascension Islands, 96

Asiento, 11, 13

Aubry de la Fosse, René (st), 158, 166, 181, 190. *See also* Doré and Aubry

Auger, Jean (st), 91–92

Austria, 43

Badagri (A), 79, 92

Baignoux (st), 178, 191

Banana Islands (A), 86–87

Barbados (WI), 42, 88

Bartering for slaves, xv, 52, 53, 67, 82–86, 112–13, 123

Barthelemi (st), 200. *See also* Delaville and Barthelemi

Basel, 156, 163

Baudard de Saint-James, Claude, xiii, 40, 149

Baudouin (st), 65

Bayonne (F), 15, 58

Beaufils (st), 153. *See also* Mouchel and Beaufils

Beaumarchais, xiii

Begouen Demeaux and Company (f)(st): company organization, 61, 148; colonial affairs of, 111; slaving activity, 153; moved to Le Havre, 158; wealth of, 186, 196, 199; ennobled, 190

Belgium, xvii, 118, 158. *See also* Brussels

Belin (f) (st), 167

Belloc, Hilaire (st), 159

Benin (A), 79

Benin River (A), 40, 76

Bernard (f) (st), 182. *See also* Canel, Meslé, and Bernard

Bertrand (f) (st), 153, 155

Bight of Benin (A), xv, 79

Bight of Biafra (A), 79

COMPOSED BY CREATIVE COMPOSITION CO., ALBUQUERQUE, NEW MEXICO
MANUFACTURED BY CUSHING-MALLOY, INC., ANN ARBOR, MICHIGAN
TEXT IS SET IN TIMES ROMAN, DISPLAY LINES IN BASKERVILLE

Library of Congress Cataloging in Publication Data
Stein, Robert Louis.
The French slave trade in the eighteenth century.
Bibliography: p.
Includes index.
1. Slave-trade—France—History.   I. Title
HT985.S73   382′.44′0944   3970
ISBN 0-299-07910-4